NO FEAR
SHAKESPEARE™

NO FEAR SHAKESPEARE

Antony and Cleopatra

As You Like It

The Comedy of Errors

Coriolanus

Hamlet

Henry IV, Parts One and Two

Henry V

Julius Caesar

King Lear

Macbeth

Measure for Measure

The Merchant of Venice

A Midsummer Night's Dream

Much Ado About Nothing

Othello

Richard III

Romeo and Juliet

Sonnets

The Taming of the Shrew

The Tempest

Twelfth Night

The Two Gentlemen of Verona

The Winter's Tale

NO FEAR SHAKESPEARE™

Romeo and Juliet

DELUXE STUDENT EDITION

*sparknotes

There's matter in these sighs, these
profound heaves. You must translate.
'Tis fit we understand them.

(Hamlet, IV.i.)

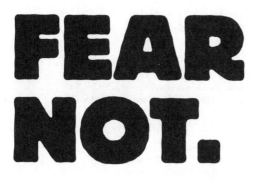

Have you ever found yourself looking at a Shakespeare
play, then down at the footnotes, then back up at the play,
and still not understanding? You know what the individual
words mean, but they don't add up. SparkNotes' *No Fear
Shakespeare* will help you break through all that. Put the
pieces together with our easy-to-read translations. Soon
you'll be reading Shakespeare's own words fearlessly—
and actually enjoying it.

No Fear Shakespeare puts Shakespeare's language side-by-
side with a facing-page translation into modern English—
the kind of English people actually speak today. When
Shakespeare's words make your head spin, our translation
will help you sort out what's happening, who's saying
what, and why.

*sparknotes

ISBN 978-1-4114-7971-5

Distributed in Canada by Sterling Publishing Co., Inc.
c/o Canadian Manda Group, 664 Annette Street
Toronto, Ontario M6S 2C8, Canada
Distributed in the United Kingdom by GMC Distribution Services
Castle Place, 166 High Street, Lewes, East Sussex BN7 1XU, England
Distributed in Australia by NewSouth Books
University of New South Wales, Sydney, NSW 2052, Australia

For information about custom editions, special sales, and premium
and corporate purchases, please contact Sterling Special Sales at
800-805-5489 or specialsales@sterlingpublishing.com.

Manufactured in Canada

Lot #:
4   6   8   10 9   7   5   3
03/22

sterlingpublishing.com
sparknotes.com

Cover design by Elizabeth Mihaltse Lindy
Interior design by Sharon Jacobs

CONTENTS

PART I

LITERATURE GUIDE

PART II

THE PLAY

PART III

STUDY GUIDE

PART I

LITERATURE GUIDE

NOTES

1

CONTEXT

THE MOST INFLUENTIAL WRITER in all of English literature, William Shakespeare was born in 1564 to a successful middle-class glove-maker in Stratford-upon-Avon, England. Shakespeare attended grammar school, but his formal education proceeded no further. In 1582 he married an older woman, Anne Hathaway, and had three children with her. Around 1590 he left his family behind and traveled to London to work as an actor and playwright. Public and critical success quickly followed, and Shakespeare eventually became the most popular playwright in England and part-owner of the Globe Theater. His career bridged the reigns of Elizabeth I (ruled 1558–1603) and James I (ruled 1603–1625), and he was a favorite of both monarchs. Indeed, James granted Shakespeare's company the greatest possible compliment by bestowing upon its members the title of King's Men. Wealthy and renowned, Shakespeare retired to Stratford and died in 1616 at the age of fifty-two. At the time of Shakespeare's death, literary luminaries such as Ben Jonson hailed his works as timeless.

Shakespeare's works were collected and printed in various editions in the century following his death, and by the early eighteenth century his reputation as the greatest poet ever to write in English was well established. The unprecedented admiration garnered by his works led to a fierce curiosity about Shakespeare's life, but the dearth of biographical information has left many details of Shakespeare's personal history shrouded in mystery. Some people have concluded from this fact that Shakespeare's plays were really written by someone else—Francis Bacon and the Earl of Oxford are the two most popular candidates—but the support for this claim is overwhelmingly circumstantial, and the theory is not taken seriously by many scholars.

In the absence of credible evidence to the contrary, Shakespeare must be viewed as the author of the thirty-seven plays and 154 sonnets that bear his name. The legacy of this body of work is immense. A number of Shakespeare's plays seem to have transcended even the category of brilliance, becoming so influential as to profoundly affect the course of Western literature and culture ever after. Shakespeare did not invent the story of *Romeo and Juliet*. He did not, in fact, even introduce the story into the English language. A poet named Arthur Brooks first brought the story of *Romeus and Juliet* to an English-speaking audience in a long and plodding poem that was itself not original, but rather an adaptation of adaptations that stretched across nearly a hundred years and two languages. Many of the details of Shakespeare's plot are lifted directly from Brooks' poem, including the meeting of Romeo and Juliet at the ball, their secret marriage, Romeo's fight with Tybalt, the sleeping potion, and the timing of the lovers' eventual suicides. Such appropriation of other stories is characteristic of Shakespeare, who often wrote plays based on earlier works. Shakespeare's use of existing material as fodder for his plays should not, however, be taken as a lack of originality. Instead, readers should note how Shakespeare crafts his sources in new ways while displaying a remarkable understanding of the literary tradition in which he is working. Shakespeare's version of *Romeo and Juliet* is no exception. The play distinguishes itself from its predecessors in several important aspects: the subtlety and originality of its characterization (Shakespeare almost wholly created Mercutio); the intense pace of its action, which is compressed from nine months into four frenetic days; a powerful enrichment of the story's thematic aspects; and, above all, an extraordinary use of language.

Shakespeare's play not only bears a resemblance to the works on which it is based, it is also quite similar in plot, theme, and dramatic ending to the story of Pyramus and Thisbe, told by the great Roman poet Ovid in his *Metamorphoses*. Shakespeare was well aware of this similarity; he includes a reference to Thisbe in *Romeo and Juliet*. Shakespeare also includes scenes from the story of Pyramus and Thisbe in the comically awful play-within-a-play put on by Bottom and his friends in *A Midsummer Night's Dream*—a play Shakespeare wrote around the same time he was composing *Romeo and Juliet*. Indeed, one can look at the play-within-a-play in *A Midsummer Night's Dream* as parodying the very story that Shakespeare seeks to tell in *Romeo and Juliet*. Shakespeare wrote *Romeo and Juliet* in full knowledge that the story he was telling was old, clichéd, and an easy target for parody. In writing *Romeo and Juliet*, Shakespeare, then, implicitly set himself the task of telling a love story despite the considerable forces he knew were stacked against its success. Through the incomparable intensity of his language Shakespeare succeeded in this effort, writing a play that is universally accepted in Western culture as the preeminent, archetypal love story.

NOTES

2

PLOT OVERVIEW

IN THE STREETS OF VERONA another brawl breaks out between the servants of the feuding noble families of Capulet and Montague. Benvolio, a Montague, tries to stop the fighting, but is himself embroiled when the rash Capulet, Tybalt, arrives on the scene. After citizens outraged by the constant violence beat back the warring factions, Prince Escalus, the ruler of Verona, attempts to prevent any further conflicts between the families by decreeing death for any individual who disturbs the peace in the future.

Romeo, the son of Montague, runs into his cousin Benvolio, who had earlier seen Romeo moping in a grove of sycamores. After some prodding by Benvolio, Romeo confides that he is in love with Rosaline, a woman who does not return his affections. Benvolio counsels him to forget this woman and find another, more beautiful one but Romeo remains despondent.

Meanwhile, Paris, a kinsman of the Prince, seeks Juliet's hand in marriage. Her father Capulet, though happy at the match, asks Paris to wait two years, since Juliet is not even fourteen yet. Capulet dispatches a servant with a list of people to invite to a masquerade and feast he traditionally holds. He invites Paris to the feast, hoping that Paris will begin to win Juliet's heart.

Romeo and Benvolio, still discussing Rosaline, encounter the Capulet servant bearing the list of invitations. Benvolio suggests they attend, since that will allow Romeo to compare his beloved to other beautiful women in Verona. Romeo agrees to go with Benvolio to the feast, but only because Rosaline, whose name he reads on the list, will be there.

In Capulet's household, young Juliet talks with her mother, Lady Capulet, and her nurse about the possibility of marrying

Paris. Juliet has not yet considered marriage, but agrees to look at Paris during the feast to see if she thinks she *could* fall in love with him.

The feast begins. A melancholy Romeo follows Benvolio and their witty friend Mercutio to Capulet's house. Once inside, Romeo sees Juliet from a distance and instantly falls in love with her; he forgets about Rosaline completely. As Romeo watches Juliet, entranced, a young Capulet, Tybalt, recognizes him, and is enraged that a Montague would sneak into a Capulet feast. He prepares to attack, but Capulet holds him back. Soon, Romeo speaks to Juliet, and the two experience a profound attraction. They share a kiss without even knowing each other's names. When he finds out from Juliet's nurse that she is the daughter of Capulet—his family's enemy—he becomes distraught. When Juliet learns that the young man she has just kissed is the son of Montague, she grows equally upset.

As Mercutio and Benvolio leave the Capulet estate, Romeo leaps over the orchard wall into the garden, unable to leave Juliet behind. From his hiding place, he sees Juliet in a window above the orchard and hears her speak his name. He calls out to her, and they exchange vows of love.

Romeo hurries to see his friend and confessor Friar Lawrence, who, though shocked at the sudden turn of Romeo's heart, agrees to marry the young lovers in secret since he sees in their love the possibility of ending the age-old feud between Capulet and Montague. The following day, Romeo and Juliet meet at Friar Lawrence's cell and are married. The Nurse, who is privy to the secret, procures a ladder, which Romeo will use to climb into Juliet's window for their wedding night.

The next day, Benvolio and Mercutio encounter Tybalt— Juliet's cousin—who, still enraged that Romeo attended Capulet's feast, has challenged Romeo to a duel. Romeo appears. Now Tybalt's kinsman by marriage, Romeo begs the Capulet to hold off the duel until he understands why Romeo does not want to fight. Disgusted with this plea for peace, Mercutio says that he will fight Tybalt himself. The two begin to duel. Romeo tries to stop them by leaping between the combatants. Tybalt stabs Mercutio under

Romeo's arm, and Mercutio dies. Romeo, in a rage, kills Tybalt. He then flees from the scene. Soon after, the Prince declares him forever banished from Verona for his crime. Friar Lawrence arranges for Romeo to spend his wedding night with Juliet before he has to leave for Mantua the following morning.

In her room, Juliet awaits the arrival of her new husband. The Nurse enters, and, after some confusion, tells Juliet that Romeo has killed Tybalt. Distraught, Juliet suddenly finds herself married to a man who has killed her kinsman. But she resettles herself, and realizes that her duty belongs with her love: to Romeo.

Romeo sneaks into Juliet's room that night, and at last they consummate their marriage and their love. Morning comes, and the lovers bid farewell, unsure when they will see each other again. Juliet learns that her father, affected by the recent events, now intends for her to marry Paris in just three days. Unsure of how to proceed—unable to reveal to her parents that she is married to Romeo, but unwilling to marry Paris now that she is Romeo's wife—Juliet asks her Nurse for advice. She counsels Juliet to proceed as if Romeo were dead and to marry Paris, who is a better match anyway. Disgusted with the Nurse's disloyalty, Juliet disregards her advice and hurries to Friar Lawrence. He concocts a plan to reunite Juliet with Romeo in Mantua. The night before her wedding to Paris, Juliet must drink a potion that will make her appear to be dead. After she is laid to rest in the family's crypt, the Friar and Romeo will secretly retrieve her, and she will be free to live with Romeo, away from their parents' feuding.

Juliet returns home to discover the wedding has been moved ahead one day, and she is to be married tomorrow. That night, Juliet drinks the potion, and the Nurse discovers her, apparently dead, the next morning. The Capulets grieve, and Juliet is entombed according to plan. But Friar Lawrence's message explaining the plan to Romeo never reaches Mantua. Its bearer, Friar John, gets confined to a quarantined house. Romeo hears only that Juliet is dead.

Romeo learns only of Juliet's death and decides to kill himself rather than live without her. He buys a vial of poison from a reluctant Apothecary, then speeds back to Verona to take his own life at Juliet's tomb. Outside the Capulet crypt, Romeo comes upon Paris, who is scattering flowers on Juliet's grave. They fight, and Romeo kills Paris. He enters the tomb, sees Juliet's inanimate body, drinks the poison, and dies by her side. Just then, Friar Lawrence enters and realizes that Romeo has killed Paris and himself. At the same time, Juliet awakes. Friar Lawrence hears the coming of the watch. When Juliet refuses to leave with him, he flees alone. Juliet sees her beloved Romeo and realizes he has killed himself with poison. She kisses his poisoned lips, and when that does not kill her, buries his dagger in her chest, falling dead upon his body.

The watch arrives, followed closely by the Prince, the Capulets, and Montague. Montague declares that Lady Montague has died of grief over Romeo's exile. Seeing their children's bodies, Capulet and Montague agree to end their long-standing feud and to raise gold statues of their children side-by-side in a newly peaceful Verona.

3

IN-DEPTH REVIEW OF CHARACTERS

ROMEO

The son and heir of Montague and Lady Montague. A young man of about sixteen, Romeo is handsome, intelligent, and sensitive. Though impulsive and immature, his idealism and passion make him an extremely likable character. He lives in the middle of a violent feud between his family and the Capulets, but he is not at all interested in violence. His only interest is love. At the beginning of the play he is madly in love with a woman named Rosaline, but the instant he lays eyes on Juliet, he falls in love with her and forgets Rosaline. Thus, Shakespeare gives us every reason to question how real Romeo's new love is, but Romeo goes to extremes to prove the seriousness of his feelings. He secretly marries Juliet, the daughter of his father's worst enemy; he happily takes abuse from Tybalt; and he would rather die than live without his beloved. Romeo is also an affectionate and devoted friend to his cousin Benvolio, Mercutio, and Friar Lawrence.

JULIET

The daughter of Capulet and Lady Capulet. A beautiful thirteen-year-old girl, Juliet begins the play as a naïve child who has thought little about love and marriage, but she grows up quickly upon falling in love with Romeo, the son of her family's great enemy. Because she is a girl in an aristocratic family, she has none of the freedom Romeo has to roam around the city, climb over walls in the middle of the night, or get into swordfights. Nevertheless, she shows amazing courage in trusting her entire life and future to Romeo, even refusing to believe the worst reports about him after he gets involved in a fight with her cousin. Juliet's closest friend and confidant is her Nurse, though she's willing to shut the Nurse out of her life the moment the Nurse turns against Romeo.

FRIAR LAWRENCE

A Franciscan friar, friend to both Romeo and Juliet. Kind, civic-minded, a proponent of moderation, and always ready with a plan, Friar Lawrence secretly marries the impassioned lovers in hopes that the union might eventually bring peace to Verona. As well as being a Catholic holy man, Friar Lawrence is also an expert in the use of seemingly mystical potions and herbs.

MERCUTIO

A kinsman to the Prince, and Romeo's close friend. One of the most extraordinary characters in all of Shakespeare's plays, Mercutio overflows with imagination, wit, and, at times, a strange, biting satire and brooding fervor. Mercutio loves wordplay, especially sexual double entendres. He can be quite hotheaded, and hates people who are affected, pretentious, or obsessed with the latest fashions. He finds Romeo's romanticized ideas about love tiresome, and tries to convince Romeo to view love as a simple matter of sexual appetite.

THE NURSE

Juliet's nurse, the woman who breast-fed Juliet when she was a baby and has cared for Juliet her entire life. A vulgar, long-winded, and sentimental character, the Nurse provides comic relief with her frequently inappropriate remarks and speeches. But, until a disagreement near the play's end, the Nurse is Juliet's faithful confidante and loyal intermediary in Juliet's affair with Romeo. She provides a contrast with Juliet, given that her view of love is earthy and sexual, whereas Juliet's is idealistic and intense. The Nurse believes in love and wants Juliet to have a good-looking husband, but the idea that Juliet would want to sacrifice herself for love is incomprehensible to her.

TYBALT

A Capulet, Juliet's cousin on her mother's side. Vain, fashionable, supremely aware of courtesy and the lack of it, he becomes aggressive, violent, and quick to draw his sword when he feels his pride has been injured. Once drawn, his sword is something to be feared. He loathes Montagues.

CAPULET

The patriarch of the Capulet family, father of Juliet, husband of Lady Capulet, and enemy, for unexplained reasons, of Montague. He truly loves his daughter, though he is not well acquainted with Juliet's thoughts or feelings, and seems to think that what is best for her is a "good" match with Paris. Often prudent, he commands respect and propriety, but he is liable to fly into a rage when either is lacking.

LADY CAPULET

Juliet's mother, Capulet's wife. A woman who herself married young (by her own estimation she gave birth to Juliet at close to the age of fourteen), she is eager to see her daughter marry Paris. She is an ineffectual mother, relying on the Nurse for moral and pragmatic support.

MONTAGUE

Romeo's father, the patriarch of the Montague clan and bitter enemy of Capulet. At the beginning of the play, he is chiefly concerned about Romeo's melancholy.

LADY MONTAGUE

Romeo's mother, Montague's wife. She dies of grief after Romeo is exiled from Verona.

PARIS

A kinsman of the Prince, and the suitor of Juliet most preferred by Capulet. Once Capulet has promised him he can marry Juliet, he behaves very presumptuously toward her, acting as if they are already married.

BENVOLIO

Montague's nephew, Romeo's cousin and thoughtful friend, he makes a genuine effort to defuse violent scenes in public places, though Mercutio accuses him of having a nasty temper in private. He spends most of the play trying to help Romeo get his mind off Rosaline, even after Romeo has fallen in love with Juliet.

PRINCE ESCALUS

The Prince of Verona. A kinsman of Mercutio and Paris. As the seat of political power in Verona, he is concerned about maintaining the public peace at all costs.

FRIAR JOHN

A Franciscan friar charged by Friar Lawrence with taking the news of Juliet's false death to Romeo in Mantua. Friar John is held up in a quarantined house, and the message never reaches Romeo.

BALTHASAR

Romeo's dedicated servant, who brings Romeo the news of Juliet's death, unaware that her death is a ruse.

SAMPSON & GREGORY,

Two servants of the house of Capulet, who, like their master, hate the Montagues. At the outset of the play, they successfully provoke some Montague men into a fight.

ABRAM

Montague's servant, who fights with Sampson and Gregory in the first scene of the play.

THE APOTHECARY

An apothecary in Mantua. Had he been wealthier, he might have been able to afford to value his morals more than money, and refused to sell poison to Romeo.

PETER

A Capulet servant who invites guests to Capulet's feast and escorts the Nurse to meet with Romeo. He is illiterate, and a bad singer.

ROSALINE

The woman with whom Romeo is infatuated at the beginning of the play. Rosaline never appears onstage, but it is said by other characters that she is very beautiful and has sworn to live a life of chastity.

THE CHORUS

The Chorus is a single character who, as developed in Greek drama, functions as a narrator offering commentary on the play's plot and themes.

CHAPTER

4

ANALYSIS OF MAJOR CHARACTERS

ROMEO

The name Romeo, in popular culture, has become nearly synonymous with "lover." Romeo, in *Romeo and Juliet*, does indeed experience a love of such purity and passion that he kills himself when he believes that the object of his love, Juliet, has died. The power of Romeo's love, however, often obscures a clear vision of Romeo's character, which is far more complex.

Even Romeo's relation to love is not so simple. At the beginning of the play, Romeo pines for Rosaline, proclaiming her the paragon of women and despairing at her indifference toward him. Taken together, Romeo's Rosaline-induced histrionics seem rather juvenile. Romeo is a great reader of love poetry, and the portrayal of his love for Rosaline suggests he is trying to re-create the feelings that he has read about. After their first kiss, Juliet tells him "You kiss by th' book," meaning that he kisses according to the rules, and implying that while proficient, his kissing lacks originality (I.v.). In reference to Rosaline, it seems, Romeo loves by the book. Rosaline, of course, slips from Romeo's mind at first sight of Juliet. But Juliet is no mere replacement. The love she shares with Romeo is far deeper, more authentic and unique than the clichéd puppy love Romeo felt for Rosaline. Romeo's love matures over the course of the play from the shallow desire to be in love to a profound and intense passion. One must ascribe Romeo's development at least in part to Juliet. Her level-headed observations, such as the one about Romeo's kissing, seem just the thing to snap Romeo from his superficial idea of love and to inspire him to begin to speak some of the most beautiful and intense love poetry ever written.

Yet Romeo's deep capacity for love is merely a part of his larger capacity for intense feeling of all kinds. Put another way, it is possible to describe Romeo as lacking the capacity for moderation. Love compels him to sneak into the garden of his enemy's daughter, risking death simply to catch a glimpse of her. Anger compels him to kill his wife's cousin in a reckless duel to avenge the death of his friend.

Despair compels him to suicide upon hearing of Juliet's death. Such extreme behavior dominates Romeo's character throughout the play and contributes to the ultimate tragedy that befalls the lovers. Had Romeo restrained himself from killing Tybalt, or waited even one day before killing himself after hearing the news of Juliet's death, matters might have ended happily. Of course, though, had Romeo not had such depths of feeling, the love he shared with Juliet would never have existed in the first place.

Among his friends, especially while bantering with Mercutio, Romeo shows glimpses of his social persona. He is intelligent, quick-witted, fond of verbal jousting (particularly about sex), loyal, and unafraid of danger.

JULIET

Having not quite reached her fourteenth birthday, Juliet is of an age that stands on the border between immaturity and maturity. At the play's beginning, however, she seems merely an obedient, sheltered, naïve child. Though many girls her age—including her mother—get married, Juliet has not given the subject any thought. When Lady Capulet mentions Paris's interest in marrying Juliet, Juliet dutifully responds that she will try to see if she can love him, a response that seems childish in its obedience and in its immature conception of love. Juliet seems to have no friends her own age, and she is not comfortable talking about sex (as seen in her discomfort when the Nurse goes on and on about a sexual joke at Juliet's expense in Act I, scene iii).

Juliet gives glimpses of her determination, strength, and sober-mindedness in her earliest scenes, and offers a preview of the woman she will become during the four-day span of *Romeo and*

Juliet. While Lady Capulet proves unable to quiet the Nurse, Juliet succeeds with one word (also in Act I, scene iii). In addition, even in Juliet's dutiful acquiescence to try to love Paris, there is some seed of steely determination. Juliet promises to consider Paris as a possible husband to the precise degree her mother desires. While an outward show of obedience, such a statement can also be read as a refusal through passivity. Juliet will accede to her mother's wishes, but she will not go out of her way to fall in love with Paris.

Juliet's first meeting with Romeo propels her full-force toward adulthood. Though profoundly in love with him, Juliet is able to see and criticize Romeo's rash decisions and his tendency to romanticize things. After Romeo kills Tybalt and is banished, Juliet does not follow him blindly. She makes a logical and heartfelt decision that her loyalty and love for Romeo must be her guiding priorities. Essentially, Juliet cuts herself loose from her prior social moorings—her nurse, her parents, and her social position in Verona—in order to try to reunite with Romeo. When she wakes in the tomb to find Romeo dead, she does not kill herself out of feminine weakness, but rather out of an intensity of love, just as Romeo did. Juliet's suicide actually requires more nerve than Romeo's: while he swallows poison, she stabs herself through the heart with a dagger.

Juliet's development from a wide-eyed girl into a self-assured, loyal, and capable woman is one of Shakespeare's early triumphs of characterization. It also marks one of his most confident and rounded treatments of a female character.

FRIAR LAWRENCE

Friar Lawrence occupies a strange position in *Romeo and Juliet*. He is a kindhearted cleric who helps Romeo and Juliet throughout the play. He performs their marriage and gives generally good advice, especially in regard to the need for moderation. He is the sole figure of religion in the play. But Friar Lawrence is also the most scheming and political character in the play: he marries Romeo and Juliet as part of a plan to end the civil strife in Verona; he spirits Romeo into Juliet's room and then out of Verona; he devises the plan to reunite Romeo and Juliet through the deceptive ruse of a sleeping potion that seems to arise from almost mystic knowledge. This mystical knowledge seems out of place for a Catholic friar; why does he have such knowledge, and what could such knowledge mean? The answers are not clear. In addition, though Friar Lawrence's plans all seem well conceived and well intentioned, they serve as the main mechanisms through which the fated tragedy of the play occurs. Readers should recognize that the Friar is not only subject to the fate that dominates the play—in many ways he brings that fate about.

MERCUTIO

With lightning-quick wit and a clever mind, Mercutio is a scene stealer and one of the most memorable characters in all of Shakespeare's works. Though he constantly puns, jokes, and teases—sometimes in fun, sometimes with bitterness—Mercutio is not a mere jester or prankster. With his wild words, Mercutio punctures the romantic sentiments and blind self-love that exist within the play. He mocks Romeo's self-indulgence just as he ridicules Tybalt's hauteur and adherence to fashion. The critic Stephen Greenblatt describes Mercutio as a force within the play that functions to deflate the possibility of romantic love and the power of tragic fate. Unlike the other characters who blame their deaths on fate, Mercutio dies cursing all Montagues and Capulets. Mercutio believes that specific people are responsible for his death rather than some external impersonal force.

PART II

THE PLAY

NOTES

Romeo and Juliet

THE ORIGINAL PLAY
WITH A MODERN TRANSLATION

William Shakespeare

NO FEAR SHAKESPEARE

CHARACTER LIST*

Romeo

Juliet

Friar Lawrence

Mercutio

The Nurse

Tybalt

Capulet

Lady Capulet

Montague

Lady Montague

Paris

Benvolio

Prince Escalus

Friar John

Balthasar

Sampson and Gregory

Abraham

The Apothecary

Peter

Rosaline

The Chorus

*See page 11 for an in-depth review of the characters.

THE PROLOGUE

Enter CHORUS

CHORUS
    Two households, both alike in dignity
    (In fair Verona, where we lay our scene),
    From ancient grudge break to new mutiny,
    Where civil blood makes civil hands unclean.
    From forth the fatal loins of these two foes
5   A pair of star-crossed lovers take their life,
    Whose misadventured piteous overthrows
    Doth with their death bury their parents' strife.
    The fearful passage of their death-marked love
    And the continuance of their parents' rage,
10   Which, but their children's end, naught could remove,
    Is now the two hours' traffic of our stage—
    The which, if you with patient ears attend,
    What here shall miss, our toil shall strive to mend.
                                     Exit

THE PROLOGUE

The CHORUS *enters.*

CHORUS

In the beautiful city of Verona, where our story takes place, a long-standing hatred between two families erupts into new violence, and citizens stain their hands with the blood of their fellow citizens. Two unlucky children of these enemy families become lovers and commit suicide. Their unfortunate deaths put an end to their parents' feud. For the next two hours, we will watch the story of their doomed love and their parents' anger, which nothing but the children's deaths could stop. If you listen to us patiently, we'll make up for everything we've left out in this prologue onstage.

The CHORUS *exits.*

ACT ONE

Scene 1

Enter SAMPSON *and* GREGORY *of the house of Capulet,
with swords and bucklers*

SAMPSON
  Gregory, on my word, we'll not carry coals.

GREGORY
  No, for then we should be colliers.

SAMPSON
  I mean, an we be in choler, we'll draw.

GREGORY
  Ay, while you live, draw your neck out of collar.

5

SAMPSON
  I strike quickly, being moved.

GREGORY
  But thou art not quickly moved to strike.

SAMPSON
  A dog of the house of Montague moves me.

GREGORY
  To move is to stir, and to be valiant is to stand.
10 Therefore if thou art moved thou runn'st away.

SAMPSON
  A dog of that house shall move me to stand. I will
  take the wall of any man or maid of Montague's.

ACT ONE

Scene 1

SAMPSON and GREGORY, servants of the Capulet family, enter carrying swords and small shields.

SAMPSON

Gregory, I swear, we can't let them humiliate us. We won't take their garbage.

GREGORY

(teasing SAMPSON) No, because then we'd be garbagemen.

SAMPSON

What I mean is, if they make us angry we'll pull out our swords.

GREGORY

Maybe you should focus on pulling yourself out of trouble, Sampson.

SAMPSON

I hit hard when I'm angry.

GREGORY

But it's hard to make you angry.

Gregory continually implies that Sampson isn't as tough as he's acting.

SAMPSON

One of those dogs from the Montague house can make me angry.

GREGORY

Angry enough to run away. You won't stand and fight.

SAMPSON

A dog from that house will make me angry enough to take a stand. If I pass one of them on the street, I'll take the side closer to the wall and let him walk in the gutter.

GREGORY

That shows thee a weak slave, for the weakest goes to the wall.

SAMPSON

'Tis true, and therefore women, being the weaker ves-
sels, are ever thrust to the wall. Therefore I will push
Montague's men from the wall, and thrust his maids to
the wall.

GREGORY

The quarrel is between our masters and us their men.

SAMPSON

'Tis all one. I will show myself a tyrant. When I have fought
with the men, I will be civil with the maids. I will cut off
their heads.

GREGORY

The heads of the maids?

SAMPSON

Ay, the heads of the maids, or their maidenheads. Take it in
what sense thou wilt.

GREGORY

They must take it in sense that feel it.

SAMPSON

Me they shall feel while I am able to stand, and 'tis known
I am a pretty piece of flesh.

GREGORY

'Tis well thou art not fish. If thou hadst, thou hadst been
poor-john.

Enter ABRAM *and another* SERVINGMAN

Draw thy tool! Here comes of the house of Montagues.

SAMPSON

My naked weapon is out. Quarrel! I will back thee.

GREGORY

That means you're the weak one, because weaklings get pushed up against the wall.

SAMPSON

You're right. That's why girls get pushed up against walls—they're weak. So what I'll do is push the Montague men into the street and the Montague women up against the wall.

GREGORY

The fight is between our masters, and we men who work for them.

SAMPSON

It's all the same. I'll be a harsh master to them. After I fight the men, I'll be nice to the women—I'll cut off their heads.

GREGORY

"Maidenhead" = virginity.

Cut off their heads? You mean their maidenheads?

SAMPSON

Cut off their heads, take their maidenheads—whatever. Take my remark in whichever sense you like.

GREGORY

The women you rape are the ones who'll have to "sense" it.

SAMPSON

They'll feel me as long as I can keep an erection. Everybody knows I'm a nice piece of flesh.

GREGORY

They're joking about Sampson's private parts.

It's a good thing you're not a piece of fish. You're dried and shriveled like salted fish.

ABRAM *and another servant of the Montagues enter.*

Pull out your tool now. These guys are from the house of Montague.

SAMPSON

I have my naked sword out. Fight, I'll back you up.

GREGORY
How? Turn thy back and run?

SAMPSON
Fear me not.

GREGORY
No, marry. I fear thee.

SAMPSON
35   Let us take the law of our sides. Let them begin.

GREGORY
I will frown as I pass by, and let them take it as they list.

SAMPSON
Nay, as they dare. I will bite my thumb at them, which is a disgrace to them, if they bear it. *(bites his thumb)*

ABRAM
Do you bite your thumb at us, sir?

SAMPSON
40   I do bite my thumb, sir.

ABRAM
Do you bite your thumb at us, sir?

SAMPSON
(aside to GREGORY*)* Is the law of our side if I say "ay"?

GREGORY
(aside to SAMPSON*)* No.

SAMPSON
No, sir. I do not bite my thumb at you, sir, but I bite my
45   thumb, sir.

GREGORY
Do you quarrel, sir?

ABRAM
Quarrel, sir? No, sir.

GREGORY

How will you back me up—by turning your back and running away?

SAMPSON

Don't worry about me.

GREGORY

No, really. I *am* worried about you!

SAMPSON

Let's not break the law by starting a fight. Let them start something.

GREGORY

I'll frown at them as they pass by, and they can react however they want.

SAMPSON

Biting the thumb is a gesture of disrespect.

You mean however they dare. I'll bite my thumb at them. That's an insult, and if they let me get away with it they'll be dishonored. (**SAMPSON** *bites his thumb*)

ABRAM

Hey, are you biting your thumb at us?

SAMPSON

I'm biting my thumb.

ABRAM

Are you biting your thumb at us?

SAMPSON

(*aside to* **GREGORY**) Is the law on our side if I say yes?

GREGORY

(*aside to* **SAMPSON**) No.

SAMPSON

(*to* **ABRAM**) No, sir, I'm not biting my thumb at you, but I am biting my thumb.

GREGORY

Are you trying to start a fight?

ABRAM

Start a fight? No, sir.

ACT ONE

SAMPSON
But if you do, sir, I am for you. I serve as good a man as you.

ABRAM
No better.

SAMPSON
50   Well, sir.

Enter **BENVOLIO**

GREGORY
(aside to **SAMPSON***)* Say "better." Here comes one of my master's kinsmen.

SAMPSON
(to **ABRAM***)* Yes, better, sir.

ABRAM
You lie.

SAMPSON
55   Draw, if you be men.—Gregory, remember thy washing blow.

They fight

BENVOLIO
(draws his sword) Part, fools!
Put up your swords. You know not what you do.

Enter **TYBALT**

TYBALT
What, art thou drawn among these heartless hinds?
60   Turn thee, Benvolio. Look upon thy death.

SAMPSON

If you want to fight, I'm your man. My employer is as good as yours.

ABRAM

But he's not better than mine.

SAMPSON

Well then.

BENVOLIO enters.

GREGORY

(speaking so that only SAMPSON can hear) Say "better." Here comes one of my employer's relatives.

SAMPSON

(to ABRAM) Yes, "better," sir.

ABRAM

You lie.

SAMPSON

Pull out your swords, if you're men. Gregory, remember how to slash.

They fight.

BENVOLIO

(pulling out his sword) Break it up, you fools. Put your swords away. You don't know what you're doing.

TYBALT enters.

TYBALT

What? You've pulled out your sword to fight with these worthless servants? Turn around, Benvolio, and look at the man who's going to kill you.

BENVOLIO
I do but keep the peace. Put up thy sword,
Or manage it to part these men with me.

TYBALT
What, drawn, and talk of peace? I hate the word,
As I hate hell, all Montagues, and thee.
65   Have at thee, coward!

They fight
Enter three or four CITIZENS, *with clubs or partisans*

CITIZENS
Clubs, bills, and partisans! Strike! Beat them down!
Down with the Capulets! Down with the Montagues!

Enter old CAPULET *in his gown, and his wife,* LADY CAPULET

CAPULET
What noise is this? Give me my long sword, ho!

LADY CAPULET
A crutch, a crutch! Why call you for a sword?

Enter old MONTAGUE *and his wife,* LADY MONTAGUE

CAPULET
70   My sword, I say! Old Montague is come,
And flourishes his blade in spite of me.

MONTAGUE
Thou villain Capulet! Hold me not. Let me go.

LADY MONTAGUE
Thou shalt not stir one foot to seek a foe.

BENVOLIO

I'm only trying to keep the peace. Either put away your sword or use it to help me stop this fight.

TYBALT

What? You take out your sword and then talk about peace? I hate the word peace like I hate hell, all Montagues, and you. Let's go at it, coward!

BENVOLIO and TYBALT fight. Three or four CITIZENS of the watch enter with clubs and spears.

CITIZENS

Use your clubs and spears! Hit them! Beat them down! Down with the Capulets! Down with the Montagues!

CAPULET enters in his gown, together with his wife, LADY CAPULET.

CAPULET

What's this noise? Give me my long sword! Come on!

LADY CAPULET

A crutch, you need a crutch—why are you asking for a sword?

MONTAGUE enters with his sword drawn, together with his wife, LADY MONTAGUE.

CAPULET

I want my sword. Old Montague is here, and he's waving his sword around just to make me mad.

MONTAGUE

Capulet, you villain! *(his wife holds him back)* Don't stop me. Let me go.

LADY MONTAGUE

You're not taking one step toward an enemy.

Enter PRINCE ESCALUS, *with his train*

PRINCE
　　　　Rebellious subjects, enemies to peace,
75　　　Profaners of this neighbor-stainèd steel!—
　　　　Will they not hear?—What, ho! You men, you beasts,
　　　　That quench the fire of your pernicious rage
　　　　With purple fountains issuing from your veins,
　　　　On pain of torture, from those bloody hands
80　　　Throw your mistempered weapons to the ground,
　　　　And hear the sentence of your movèd prince.
　　　　Three civil brawls, bred of an airy word,
　　　　By thee, old Capulet, and Montague,
　　　　Have thrice disturbed the quiet of our streets
85　　　And made Verona's ancient citizens
　　　　Cast by their grave-beseeming ornaments,
　　　　To wield old partisans in hands as old,
　　　　Cankered with peace, to part your cankered hate.
　　　　If ever you disturb our streets again,
90　　　Your lives shall pay the forfeit of the peace.
　　　　For this time, all the rest depart away.
　　　　You, Capulet, shall go along with me,
　　　　And, Montague, come you this afternoon
　　　　To know our farther pleasure in this case,
95　　　To old Free-town, our common judgment-place.
　　　　Once more, on pain of death, all men depart.

Exeunt all but MONTAGUE, LADY MONTAGUE, *and* BENVOLIO

MONTAGUE
　　　　Who set this ancient quarrel new abroach?
　　　　Speak, nephew. Were you by when it began?

PRINCE ESCALUS *enters with his escort.*

PRINCE

(shouting at the rioters) You rebels! Enemies of the peace! Men who turn their weapons against their own neighbors—They won't listen to me?—You there! You men, you beasts, who satisfy your anger with fountains of each others' blood! I'll have you tortured if you don't put down your swords and listen to your angry prince. *(MONTAGUE, CAPULET, and their followers throw down their weapons)* Three times now riots have broken out in this city, all because of a casual word from you, old Capulet and Montague. Three times the peace has been disturbed in our streets, and Verona's old citizens have had to take off their dress clothes and pick up rusty old spears to part you. If you ever cause a disturbance on our streets again, you'll pay for it with your lives. Everyone else, go away for now. *(to CAPULET)* You, Capulet, come with me. *(to MONTAGUE)* Montague, this afternoon come to old Free-town, the court where I deliver judgments, and I'll tell you what else I want from you. As for the rest of you, I'll say this once more: go away or be put to death.

Everyone exits except MONTAGUE,
LADY MONTAGUE, *and* BENVOLIO.

MONTAGUE

Who started this old fight up again? Speak, nephew. Were you here when it started?

BENVOLIO

Here were the servants of your adversary,
100   And yours, close fighting ere I did approach.
I drew to part them. In the instant came
The fiery Tybalt, with his sword prepared,
Which, as he breathed defiance to my ears,
He swung about his head and cut the winds,
105   Who, nothing hurt withal, hissed him in scorn.
While we were interchanging thrusts and blows,
Came more and more and fought on part and part,
Till the Prince came, who parted either part.

LADY MONTAGUE

Oh, where is Romeo? Saw you him today?
110   Right glad I am he was not at this fray.

BENVOLIO

Madam, an hour before the worshipped sun
Peered forth the golden window of the east,
A troubled mind drove me to walk abroad,
Where, underneath the grove of sycamore
115   That westward rooteth from this city side,
So early walking did I see your son.
Towards him I made, but he was 'ware of me
And stole into the covert of the wood.
I, measuring his affections by my own,
120   Which then most sought where most might not be found,
Being one too many by my weary self,
Pursued my humor not pursuing his,
And gladly shunned who gladly fled from me.

MONTAGUE

Many a morning hath he there been seen,
125   With tears augmenting the fresh morning's dew,
Adding to clouds more clouds with his deep sighs.
But all so soon as the all-cheering sun
Should in the farthest east begin to draw
The shady curtains from Aurora's bed,
130   Away from light steals home my heavy son,

BENVOLIO

Your servants were fighting your enemy's servants before I got here. I drew my sword to part them. Right then, that hothead Tybalt showed up with his sword ready. He taunted me and waved his sword around, making the air hiss. As we were trading blows, more and more people showed up to join the fight, until the Prince came and broke everyone up.

LADY MONTAGUE

Oh, where's Romeo? Have you seen him today? I'm glad he wasn't here for this fight.

BENVOLIO

Madam, I had a lot on my mind an hour before dawn this morning, so I went for a walk. Underneath the Sycamore grove that grows on the west side of the city, I saw your son taking an early-morning walk. I headed toward him, but he saw me coming and hid in the woods. I thought he must be feeling the same way I was—wanting to be alone and tired of his own company. I figured he was avoiding me, and I was perfectly happy to leave him alone and keep to myself.

MONTAGUE

He's been seen there many mornings, crying tears that add drops to the morning dew and making a cloudy day cloudier with his sighs. But as soon as the sun rises in the east, my sad son comes home to escape the light.

And private in his chamber pens himself,
Shuts up his windows, locks fair daylight out,
And makes himself an artificial night.
Black and portentous must this humor prove
135   Unless good counsel may the cause remove.

BENVOLIO
My noble uncle, do you know the cause?

MONTAGUE
I neither know it nor can learn of him.

BENVOLIO
Have you importuned him by any means?

MONTAGUE
Both by myself and many other friends.
140   But he, his own affections' counselor,
Is to himself—I will not say how true,
But to himself so secret and so close,
So far from sounding and discovery,
As is the bud bit with an envious worm,
145   Ere he can spread his sweet leaves to the air,
Or dedicate his beauty to the same.
Could we but learn from whence his sorrows grow.
We would as willingly give cure as know.

Enter ROMEO

BENVOLIO
See, where he comes. So please you, step aside.
150   I'll know his grievance or be much denied.

MONTAGUE
I would thou wert so happy by thy stay
To hear true shrift.—Come, madam, let's away.

Exeunt MONTAGUE *and* LADY MONTAGUE

He locks himself up alone in his bedroom, shuts his windows to keep out the beautiful daylight, and makes himself an artificial night. This mood of his is going to bring bad news, unless someone smart can fix what's bothering him.

BENVOLIO

My noble uncle, do you know why he acts this way?

MONTAGUE

I don't know, and he won't tell me.

BENVOLIO

Have you done everything you could to make him tell you the reason?

MONTAGUE

I've tried, and many of our friends have tried to make him talk, but he keeps his thoughts to himself. He doesn't want any friend but himself, and though I don't know whether he's a *good* friend to himself, he certainly keeps his own secrets. He's like a flower bud that won't open itself up to the world because it's been poisoned from within by parasites. If we could only find out why he's sad, we'd be as eager to help him as we were to learn the reason for his sadness.

ROMEO *enters.*

BENVOLIO

Look—here he comes. If you don't mind, please step aside. He'll either have to tell me what's wrong or else tell me no over and over.

MONTAGUE

I hope you're lucky enough to hear the true story by sticking around. *(to his wife)* Come, madam, let's go.

MONTAGUE *and* **LADY MONTAGUE** *exit.*

BENVOLIO
Good morrow, cousin.

ROMEO
                              Is the day so young?

BENVOLIO
But new struck nine.

ROMEO
                              Ay me! Sad hours seem long.
155   Was that my father that went hence so fast?

BENVOLIO
It was. What sadness lengthens Romeo's hours?

ROMEO
Not having that which, having, makes them short.

BENVOLIO
In love?

ROMEO
Out.

BENVOLIO
160   Of love?

ROMEO
Out of her favor, where I am in love.

BENVOLIO
Alas, that love, so gentle in his view,
Should be so tyrannous and rough in proof!

ROMEO
Alas, that love, whose view is muffled still,
165   Should, without eyes, see pathways to his will!
Where shall we dine?—O me! What fray was here?
Yet tell me not, for I have heard it all.
Here's much to do with hate but more with love.
Why then, O brawling love, O loving hate,
170   O anything of nothing first created!
O heavy lightness, serious vanity,
Misshapen chaos of well-seeming forms!
Feather of lead, bright smoke, cold fire, sick health,

BENVOLIO

Good morning, cousin.

ROMEO

Is it that early in the day?

BENVOLIO

It's only just now nine o'clock.

ROMEO

Oh my, time goes by slowly when you're sad. Was that my father who left here in such a hurry?

BENVOLIO

It was. What's making you so sad and your hours so long?

ROMEO

I don't have the thing that makes time fly.

BENVOLIO

You're in love?

ROMEO

Out.

BENVOLIO

Out of love?

ROMEO

I love someone. She doesn't love me.

BENVOLIO

It's sad. Love looks like a nice thing, but it's actually very rough when you experience it.

ROMEO

What's sad is that love is supposed to be blind, but it can still make you do whatever it wants. So, where should we eat? *(seeing blood)* Oh my! What fight happened here? No, don't tell me—I know all about it. This fight has a lot to do with hatred, but it has more to do with love. O brawling love! O loving hate! Love that comes from nothing! Sad happiness! Serious foolishness! Beautiful things muddled together into an ugly mess! Love is heavy and light, bright and dark, hot and cold, sick and healthy, asleep and awake—it's

Still-waking sleep, that is not what it is!
175   This love feel I, that feel no love in this.
Dost thou not laugh?

BENVOLIO
                No, coz, I rather weep.

ROMEO
Good heart, at what?

BENVOLIO
At thy good heart's oppression.

ROMEO
Why, such is love's transgression.
180   Griefs of mine own lie heavy in my breast,
Which thou wilt propagate, to have it pressed
With more of thine. This love that thou hast shown
Doth add more grief to too much of mine own.
Love is a smoke raised with the fume of sighs;
185   Being purged, a fire sparkling in lovers' eyes;
Being vexed, a sea nourished with loving tears.
What is it else? A madness most discreet,
A choking gall, and a preserving sweet.
Farewell, my coz.

BENVOLIO
             Soft! I will go along.
190   And if you leave me so, you do me wrong.

ROMEO
Tut, I have lost myself. I am not here.
This is not Romeo. He's some other where.

BENVOLIO
Tell me in sadness, who is that you love.

ROMEO
What, shall I groan and tell thee?

BENVOLIO
195   Groan! Why, no. But sadly, tell me who.

everything except what it is! This is the love I feel, though no one loves me back. Are you laughing?

BENVOLIO

No, cousin, I'm crying.

ROMEO

Good man, why are you crying?

BENVOLIO

I'm crying because of how sad you are.

ROMEO

Yes, this is what love does. My sadness sits heavy in my chest, and you want to add your own sadness to mine so there's even more. I have too much sadness already, and now you're going to make me sadder by feeling sorry for you. Here's what love is: a smoke made out of lovers' sighs. When the smoke clears, love is a fire burning in your lover's eyes. If you frustrate love, you get an ocean made out of lovers' tears. What else is love? It's a wise form of madness. It's a sweet lozenge that you choke on. Goodbye, cousin.

BENVOLIO

Wait. I'll come with you. If you leave me like this, you're doing me wrong.

ROMEO

I'm not myself. I'm not here. This isn't Romeo—he's somewhere else.

BENVOLIO

Tell me seriously, who is the one you love?

ROMEO

Seriously? You mean I should groan and tell you?

BENVOLIO

Groan? No. But tell me seriously who it is.

ROMEO
A sick man in sadness makes his will,
A word ill urged to one that is so ill.
In sadness, cousin, I do love a woman.

BENVOLIO
I aimed so near when I supposed you loved.

ROMEO
200   A right good markman! And she's fair I love.

BENVOLIO
A right fair mark, fair coz, is soonest hit.

ROMEO
Well, in that hit you miss. She'll not be hit
With Cupid's arrow. She hath Dian's wit.
And, in strong proof of chastity well armed
205   From love's weak childish bow, she lives uncharmed.
She will not stay the siege of loving terms,
Nor bide th' encounter of assailing eyes,
Nor ope her lap to saint-seducing gold.
Oh, she is rich in beauty, only poor
210   That when she dies, with beauty dies her store.

BENVOLIO
Then she hath sworn that she will still live chaste?

ROMEO
She hath, and in that sparing makes huge waste,
For beauty, starved with her severity,
Cuts beauty off from all posterity.
215   She is too fair, too wise, wisely too fair,
To merit bliss by making me despair.
She hath forsworn to love, and in that vow
Do I live dead that live to tell it now.

BENVOLIO
Be ruled by me. Forget to think of her.

ROMEO
220   O, teach me how I should forget to think!

ROMEO

You wouldn't tell a sick man he "seriously" has to make his will—it would just make him worse. Seriously, cousin, I love a woman.

BENVOLIO

I guessed that already when I guessed you were in love.

ROMEO

Then you were right on target. The woman I love is beautiful.

BENVOLIO

A beautiful target is the one that gets hit the fastest.

ROMEO

Well, you're not on target there. She refuses to be hit by Cupid's arrow. She's as clever as Diana, and shielded by the armor of chastity. She can't be touched by the weak and childish arrows of love. She won't listen to words of love, or let you look at her with loving eyes, or open her lap to receive gifts of gold. She's rich in beauty, but she's also poor, because when she dies her beauty will be destroyed with her.

Cupid, the Roman god of love, shoots arrows at humans that make them fall in love. Diana is the Roman goddess of virginity and hunting.

BENVOLIO

So she's made a vow to be a virgin forever?

ROMEO

Yes she has, and by keeping celibate, she wastes her beauty. If you starve yourself of sex you can't ever have children, and so your beauty is lost to future generations. She's too beautiful and too wise to deserve heaven's blessing by making me despair. She's sworn off love, and that promise has left me alive but dead, living only to talk about it now.

BENVOLIO

Take my advice. Don't think about her.

ROMEO

Teach me to forget to think!

BENVOLIO

By giving liberty unto thine eyes.
Examine other beauties.

ROMEO

'Tis the way
To call hers exquisite, in question more.
These happy masks that kiss fair ladies' brows,
225   Being black, puts us in mind they hide the fair.
He that is strucken blind cannot forget
The precious treasure of his eyesight lost.
Show me a mistress that is passing fair;
What doth her beauty serve but as a note
230   Where I may read who passed that passing fair?
Farewell. Thou canst not teach me to forget.

BENVOLIO

I'll pay that doctrine or else die in debt.

Exeunt

BENVOLIO

Do it by letting your eyes wander freely. Look at other beautiful girls.

ROMEO

That will only make me think more about how beautiful *she* is. Beautiful women like to wear black masks over their faces—those black masks only make us think about how beautiful they are underneath. A man who goes blind can't forget the precious eyesight he lost. Show me a really beautiful girl. Her beauty is like a note telling me where I can see someone even more beautiful. Goodbye. You can't teach me to forget.

BENVOLIO

I'll show you how to forget, or else I'll die owing you that lesson.

They exit.

ACT ONE, Scene 2

Enter CAPULET, *County* PARIS, *and* PETER, *a servant*

CAPULET

But Montague is bound as well as I,
In penalty alike. And 'tis not hard, I think,
For men so old as we to keep the peace.

PARIS

Of honorable reckoning are you both.
5   And pity 'tis you lived at odds so long.
But now, my lord, what say you to my suit?

CAPULET

But saying o'er what I have said before.
My child is yet a stranger in the world.
She hath not seen the change of fourteen years.
10   Let two more summers wither in their pride
Ere we may think her ripe to be a bride.

PARIS

Younger than she are happy mothers made.

CAPULET

And too soon marred are those so early made.
Earth hath swallowed all my hopes but she.
15   She's the hopeful lady of my earth.
But woo her, gentle Paris, get her heart.
My will to her consent is but a part.
An she agreed within her scope of choice,
Lies my consent and fair according voice.
20   This night I hold an old accustomed feast,
Whereto I have invited many a guest
Such as I love. And you among the store,
One more, most welcome, makes my number more.
At my poor house look to behold this night
25   Earth-treading stars that make dark heaven light.

ACT ONE, Scene 2

County = Count, a title of nobility.

CAPULET *enters with County* PARIS, *followed by* PETER, *a servant.*

CAPULET

(continuing a conversation) But Montague has sworn an oath just like I have, and he's under the same penalty. I don't think it will be hard for men as old as we are to keep the peace.

PARIS

You both have honorable reputations, and it's too bad you've been enemies for so long. But what do you say to my request?

CAPULET

I can only repeat what I've said before. My daughter is still very young. She's not even fourteen years old. Let's wait two more summers before we start thinking she's ready to get married.

PARIS

Girls younger than she often marry and become happy mothers.

CAPULET

Girls who marry so young grow up too soon. But go ahead and charm her, gentle Paris; make her love you. My permission is only part of her decision. If she agrees to marry you, my blessing and fair words will confirm her choice. Tonight I'm having a feast that we've celebrated for many years. I've invited many of my closest friends, and I'd like to welcome you and add you to the guest list. At my humble house tonight, you can expect to see dazzling stars that walk on the ground and light the sky from below.

Such comfort as do lusty young men feel
When well-appareled April on the heel
Of limping winter treads. Even such delight
Among fresh fennel buds shall you this night
30   Inherit at my house. Hear all, all see,
And like her most whose merit most shall be—
Which on more view of many, mine, being one,
May stand in number, though in reckoning none,
Come, go with me.
(to PETER, *giving him a paper)*
                    Go, sirrah, trudge about
35   Through fair Verona. Find those persons out
Whose names are written there, and to them say
My house and welcome on their pleasure stay.
                    Exeunt CAPULET *and* PARIS

PETER
Find them out whose names are written here? It is written,
that the shoemaker should meddle with his yard and the
40   tailor with his last, the fisher with his pencil and the painter
with his nets. But I am sent to find those persons whose
names are here writ, and can never find what names the
writing person hath here writ. I must to the learned in
good time!

Enter BENVOLIO *and* ROMEO

BENVOLIO
45   Tut man, one fire burns out another's burning.
One pain is lessened by another's anguish.
Turn giddy, and be helped by backward turning.
One desperate grief cures with another's languish.
Take thou some new infection to thy eye,
50   And the rank poison of the old will die.

You'll be delighted by young women as fresh as spring flowers. Look at anyone you like, and choose whatever woman seems best to you. Once you see a lot of girls, you might not think my daughter's the best anymore. Come along with me.

(to PETER, *handing him a paper)* Go, little fellow, walk all around Verona. Find the people on this list and tell them they're welcome at my house tonight.

CAPULET *and* PARIS *exit.*

PETER

Find the people whose names are on this list? It is written that shoemakers and tailors should play with each others' tools, that fisherman should play with paints, and painters should play with with fishing nets. But I've been sent to find the people whose names are written on this list, and I can't read! I'll never find them on my own. I've got to find somebody who knows how to read to help me. But here come some people, right in the nick of time.

BENVOLIO *and* ROMEO *enter.*

BENVOLIO

(to ROMEO*)* Come on, man. You can put out one fire by starting another. A new pain will make the one you already have seem less. If you make yourself dizzy, you can cure yourself by spinning back around in the opposite direction. A new grief will put the old one out of your mind. Make yourself lovesick by gazing at some new girl, and your old lovesickness will be cured.

ROMEO
Your plantain leaf is excellent for that.

BENVOLIO
For what, I pray thee?

ROMEO
For your broken shin.

BENVOLIO
Why Romeo, art thou mad?

ROMEO
55 Not mad, but bound more than a madman is,
Shut up in prison, kept without my food,
Whipped and tormented and—Good e'en, good fellow.

PETER
God 'i' good e'en. I pray, sir, can you read?

ROMEO
Ay, mine own fortune in my misery.

PETER
60 Perhaps you have learned it without book. But I
pray, can you read anything you see?

ROMEO
Ay, if I know the letters and the language.

PETER
Ye say honestly. Rest you merry.

ROMEO
Stay, fellow. I can read. *(he reads the letter)*
65 "Seigneur Martino and his wife and daughters;
County Anselme and his beauteous sisters;
The lady widow of Vitruvio;
Seigneur Placentio and his lovely nieces;
Mercutio and his brother Valentine;
70 Mine uncle Capulet, his wife and daughters;
My fair niece Rosaline and Livia;

ROMEO

The plantain leaf is excellent for that.

The plantain leaf was thought to have healing powers.

BENVOLIO

For what, Romeo?

ROMEO

For when you cut your shin.

BENVOLIO

What? Romeo, are you crazy?

ROMEO

I'm not crazy, but I'm tied up tighter than a mental patient in a straitjacket. I'm locked up in a prison and deprived of food. I'm whipped and tortured—*(to* PETER*)* Good evening, good fellow.

PETER

May God give you a good evening. Excuse me, sir, do you know how to read?

ROMEO

I can read my own fortune in my misery.

PETER

Perhaps you've learned from life and not from books. But please tell me, can you read anything you see?

ROMEO

Yes, if I know the language and the letters.

PETER

Peter assumes Romeo means he doesn't know his letters.

I see. Well, that's an honest answer. Have a nice day.

ROMEO

Stay, fellow. I can read. *(he reads the letter)*
"Signor Martino and his wife and daughters,
Count Anselme and his beautiful sisters,
Vitruvio's widow,
Signor Placentio and his lovely nieces,
Mercutio and his brother Valentine,
My uncle Capulet and his wife and daughters,
My fair niece Rosaline and Livia,

Seigneur Valentio and his cousin Tybalt;
Lucio and the lively Helena."
A fair assembly. Whither should they come?

PETER
75   Up.

ROMEO
Whither? To supper?

PETER
To our house.

ROMEO
Whose house?

PETER
My master's.

ROMEO
80   Indeed, I should have asked thee that before.

PETER
Now I'll tell you without asking. My master is the great rich
Capulet, and if you be not of the house of Montagues, I pray
come and crush a cup of wine. Rest you merry!

Exit PETER

BENVOLIO
At this same ancient feast of Capulet's
85   Sups the fair Rosaline whom thou so loves
With all the admired beauties of Verona.
Go thither, and with unattainted eye
Compare her face with some that I shall show,
And I will make thee think thy swan a crow.

ROMEO
90   When the devout religion of mine eye
Maintains such falsehood, then turn tears to fires,
And these, who, often drowned, could never die,
Transparent heretics, be burnt for liars!
One fairer than my love? The all-seeing sun
95   Ne'er saw her match since first the world begun.

Signor Valentio and his cousin Tybalt,
Lucio and the lively Helena."
That's a nice group of people. Where are they sup-
posed to come?

PETER

Up.

ROMEO

Where? To supper?

PETER

To our house.

ROMEO

Whose house?

PETER

My master's house.

ROMEO

Indeed, I should have asked you before who he was.

PETER

Now I'll tell you so you don't have to ask. My master
is the great and rich Capulet, and if you don't belong
to the house of Montague, please come and drink a
cup of wine. Have a nice day!

> **PETER** *exits.*

BENVOLIO

The beautiful Rosaline whom you love so much will
be at Capulet's traditional feast, along with every
beautiful woman in Verona. Go there and compare her
objectively to some other girls I'll show you. The
woman who you think is as beautiful as a swan is going
to look as ugly as a crow to you.

ROMEO

If my eyes ever lie to me like that, let my tears turn into
flames and burn them for being such obvious liars! A
woman more beautiful than the one I love? The sun
itself has never seen anyone as beautiful since the
world began.

BENVOLIO
> Tut, you saw her fair, none else being by,
> Herself poised with herself in either eye.
> But in that crystal scales let there be weighed
> Your lady's love against some other maid
100 > That I will show you shining at the feast,
> And she shall scant show well that now shows best.

ROMEO
> I'll go along, no such sight to be shown,
> But to rejoice in splendor of mine own.

> *Exeunt*

BENVOLIO

Come on, you first decided she was beautiful when no one else was around. There was no one to compare her to except herself. But let your eyes compare her to another beautiful woman who I'll show you at this feast, and you won't think she's the best anymore.

ROMEO

I'll go with you. Not because I think you'll show me anything better, but so I can see the woman I love.

They exit.

ACT ONE, Scene 3

Enter LADY CAPULET *and* NURSE

LADY CAPULET
Nurse, where's my daughter? Call her forth to me.

NURSE
Now, by my maidenhead at twelve year old
I bade her come. What, lamb! What, ladybird!
God forbid! Where's this girl? What, Juliet!

Enter JULIET

JULIET
5   How now, who calls?

NURSE
Your mother.

JULIET
Madam, I am here. What is your will?

LADY CAPULET
This is the matter.—Nurse, give leave awhile,
We must talk in secret.—Nurse, come back again.
10   I have remembered me. Thou's hear our counsel.
Thou know'st my daughter's of a pretty age.

NURSE
Faith, I can tell her age unto an hour.

LADY CAPULET
She's not fourteen.

NURSE
I'll lay fourteen of my teeth—and yet, to my teen be it
15   spoken, I have but four—she is not fourteen. How long is it
now to Lammastide?

LADY CAPULET
A fortnight and odd days.

ACT ONE, Scene 3

LADY CAPULET *and the* NURSE *enter.*

LADY CAPULET
>Nurse, where's my daughter? Tell her to come to me.

NURSE
>I swear to you by my virginity at age twelve, I already told her to come. Come on! Where is she? What is she doing? What, Juliet!

JULIET *enters.*

JULIET
>What is it? Who's calling me?

NURSE
>Your mother.

JULIET
>Madam, I'm here. What do you want?

LADY CAPULET
>I'll tell you what's the matter—Nurse, leave us alone for a little while. We must talk privately—Nurse, come back here. I just remembered, you can listen to our secrets. You know how young my daughter is.

NURSE
>Yes, I know her age down to the hour.

LADY CAPULET
>She's not even fourteen.

NURSE
>I'd bet fourteen of my own teeth—but, I'm sorry to say, I only have four teeth—she's not fourteen. How long is it until Lammastide?

Lammastide = August 1.

LADY CAPULET
>Two weeks and a few odd days.

NURSE
Even or odd, of all days in the year,
Come Lammas Eve at night shall she be fourteen.

20 Susan and she—God rest all Christian souls!—
Were of an age. Well, Susan is with God.
She was too good for me. But, as I said,
On Lammas Eve at night shall she be fourteen.
That shall she. Marry, I remember it well.

25 'Tis since the earthquake now eleven years,
And she was weaned—I never shall forget it—
Of all the days of the year, upon that day.
For I had then laid wormwood to my dug,
Sitting in the sun under the dovehouse wall.

30 My lord and you were then at Mantua.—
Nay, I do bear a brain.—But, as I said,
When it did taste the wormwood on the nipple
Of my dug and felt it bitter, pretty fool,
To see it tetchy and fall out with the dug!

35 "Shake!" quoth the dovehouse. 'Twas no need, I trow,
To bid me trudge.
And since that time it is eleven years,
For then she could stand alone. Nay, by the rood,
She could have run and waddled all about,

40 For even the day before, she broke her brow.
And then my husband—God be with his soul!
He was a merry man—took up the child.
"Yea," quoth he, "Dost thou fall upon thy face?
Thou wilt fall backward when thou hast more wit,

45 Wilt thou not, Jule?" and, by my holy dame,
The pretty wretch left crying and said "ay."
To see now, how a jest shall come about!
I warrant, an I should live a thousand years,
I never should forget it. "Wilt thou not, Jule?" quoth he.

50 And, pretty fool, it stinted and said "ay."

LADY CAPULET
Enough of this. I pray thee, hold thy peace.

NURSE
Whether it's even or odd, of all the days in the year, on the night of Lammas Eve, she'll be fourteen. She and Susan—God rest her and all Christian souls—were born on the same day. Well, Susan died and is with God. She was too good for me. But like I said, on the night of Lammas Eve, she will be fourteen. Yes, she will. Indeed, I remember it well. It's been eleven years since the earthquake. She stopped nursing from my breast on that very day. I'll never forget it. I had put bitter wormwood on my breast as I was sitting in the sun, under the wall of the dovehouse. You and your husband were in Mantua. Boy, do I have some memory! But like I said, when she tasted the bitter wormwood on my nipple, the pretty little babe got irritated and started to quarrel with my breast. Then the dovehouse shook with the earthquake. There was no need to tell me to get out of there. That was eleven years ago. By then she could stand up all by herself. No, I swear, by that time she could run and waddle all around. I remember because she had cut her forehead just the day before. My husband—God rest his soul, he was a happy man—picked up the child. "Oh," he said, "Did you fall on your face? You'll fall backward when you grow smarter. Won't you, Jule." And I swear, the poor pretty thing stopped crying and said, "Yes." Oh, to watch a joke come true! I bet if I live a thousand years, I'll never forget it. "Won't you, Jule," he said. And the pretty fool stopped crying and said, "Yes."

"Fall backward" = have sex.

LADY CAPULET
Enough of this. Please be quiet.

NURSE
Yes, madam. Yet I cannot choose but laugh
To think it should leave crying and say "ay."
And yet, I warrant, it had upon its brow
A bump as big as a young cockerel's stone,
A perilous knock, and it cried bitterly.
"Yea," quoth my husband, "Fall'st upon thy face?
Thou wilt fall backward when thou comest to age.
Wilt thou not, Jule?" It stinted and said "ay."

JULIET
And stint thou too, I pray thee, Nurse, say I.

NURSE
Peace, I have done. God mark thee to his grace!
Thou wast the prettiest babe that e'er I nursed.
An I might live to see thee married once,
I have my wish.

LADY CAPULET
Marry, that "marry" is the very theme
I came to talk of. Tell me, daughter Juliet,
How stands your disposition to be married?

JULIET
It is an honor that I dream not of.

NURSE
An honor! Were not I thine only nurse,
I would say thou hadst sucked wisdom from thy teat.

LADY CAPULET
Well, think of marriage now. Younger than you
Here in Verona, ladies of esteem
Are made already mothers. By my count,
I was your mother much upon these years
That you are now a maid. Thus then in brief:
The valiant Paris seeks you for his love.

NURSE
A man, young lady! Lady, such a man
As all the world. Why, he's a man of wax.

NURSE

Yes, madam. But I can't help laughing to think that the baby stopped crying and said, "Yes." I swear, she had a bump on her forehead as big as a rooster's testicle. It was a painful bruise, and she was crying bitterly. "Yes," said my husband, "Did you fall on your face? You'll fall backward when you grow up, won't you, Jule?" And she stopped crying and said, "Yes."

JULIET

Now you stop too, Nurse, please.

NURSE

Peace. I'm done talking. May God choose you to receive his grace. You were the prettiest baby I ever nursed. If I live to see you get married someday, all my wishes will come true.

LADY CAPULET

Well, marriage is exactly what we have to discuss. Tell me, my daughter Juliet, what is your attitude about getting married?

JULIET

It is an honor that I do not dream of.

NURSE

"An honor?" If I weren't your only nurse, I'd say you had sucked wisdom from the breast that fed you.

LADY CAPULET

Well, start thinking about marriage now. Here in Verona there are girls younger than you—girls from noble families—who have already become mothers. By my count, I was already your mother at just about your age, while you remain a virgin. Well then, I'll say this quickly: the valiant Paris wants you as his bride.

NURSE

What a man, young lady. He's as great a man as any in the whole world. He's as perfect as if he were sculpted from wax.

LADY CAPULET
Verona's summer hath not such a flower.

NURSE
80   Nay, he's a flower. In faith, a very flower.

LADY CAPULET
What say you? Can you love the gentleman?
This night you shall behold him at our feast.
Read o'er the volume of young Paris' face
And find delight writ there with beauty's pen.
85   Examine every married lineament
And see how one another lends content,
And what obscured in this fair volume lies
Find written in the margin of his eyes.
This precious book of love, this unbound lover,
90   To beautify him only lacks a cover.
The fish lives in the sea, and 'tis much pride
For fair without the fair within to hide.
That book in many's eyes doth share the glory
That in gold clasps locks in the golden story.
95   So shall you share all that he doth possess
By having him, making yourself no less.

NURSE
No less? Nay, bigger. Women grow by men.

LADY CAPULET
Speak briefly. Can you like of Paris, love?

JULIET
I'll look to like if looking liking move.
100   But no more deep will I endart mine eye
Than your consent gives strength to make it fly.

Enter PETER

LADY CAPULET

Summertime in Verona has no flower as fine as him.

NURSE

No, he's a fine flower, truly, a flower.

LADY CAPULET

(to JULIET) What do you say? Can you love this gentleman? Tonight you'll see him at our feast. Study Paris's face and find pleasure in his beauty. Examine every line of his features and see how they work together to make him handsome. If you are confused, just look into his eyes. This man is single, and he lacks only a bride to make him perfect and complete. As is right, fish live in the sea, and it's wrong for a beauty like you to hide from a handsome man like him. Many people think he's handsome, and whoever becomes his bride will be just as admired. You would share all that he possesses, and by having him, you would lose nothing.

NURSE

Lose nothing? In fact, you'd get bigger. Men make women bigger by getting them pregnant.

LADY CAPULET

(to JULIET) Give us a quick answer. Can you accept Paris's love?

JULIET

I'll look at him and try to like him, at least if what I see is likable. But I won't let myself fall for him any more than your permission allows.

PETER *enters.*

PETER
Madam, the guests are come, supper served up, you called,
my young lady asked for, the Nurse cursed in the pantry,
and every thing in extremity. I must hence to wait. I beseech
105   you, follow straight.

LADY CAPULET
We follow thee.—Juliet, the county stays.

NURSE
Go, girl, seek happy nights to happy days.

Exeunt

PETER
Madam, the guests are here, dinner is served, people are calling for you, people have asked for Juliet, and in the pantry, people are cursing the Nurse. Everything's out of control. I must go and serve the guests. Please, follow straight after me.

LADY CAPULET
We'll follow you. Juliet, the count is waiting for you.

NURSE
Go, girl, look for a man who'll give you happy nights at the end of happy days.

They all exit.

ACT ONE, Scene 4

Enter ROMEO, MERCUTIO, BENVOLIO, *with five or six other*
MASKERS *and* TORCHBEARERS

ROMEO
What, shall this speech be spoke for our excuse?
Or shall we on without apology?

BENVOLIO
The date is out of such prolixity.
5   We'll have no Cupid hoodwinked with a scarf,
Bearing a Tartar's painted bow of lath,
Scaring the ladies like a crowkeeper,
Nor no without-book prologue, faintly spoke
After the prompter for our entrance.
10   But let them measure us by what they will.
We'll measure them a measure and be gone.

ROMEO
Give me a torch. I am not for this ambling.
Being but heavy, I will bear the light.

MERCUTIO
Nay, gentle Romeo, we must have you dance.

ROMEO
15   Not I, believe me. You have dancing shoes
With nimble soles. I have a soul of lead
So stakes me to the ground I cannot move.

MERCUTIO
You are a lover. Borrow Cupid's wings
And soar with them above a common bound.

ROMEO
20   I am too sore enpiercèd with his shaft
To soar with his light feathers, and so bound,
I cannot bound a pitch above dull woe.
Under love's heavy burden do I sink.

ACT ONE, Scene 4

ROMEO, MERCUTIO, and BENVOLIO enter dressed as maskers, along with five or six other MASKERS, carrying a drum and torches.

Maskers are masked party-goers who perform a dance they've invented at a party.

ROMEO

What will we say is our excuse for being here? Or should we enter without apologizing?

BENVOLIO

It's out of fashion to give lengthy explanations like that. We're not going to introduce our dance by having someone dress up as Cupid, blindfolded and carrying a toy bow to frighten the ladies like a scarecrow. Nor are we going to recite a memorized speech to introduce ourselves. Let them judge us however they please. We'll give them a dance and then hit the road.

ROMEO

Give me a torch. I don't want to dance. I feel sad, so let me be the one who carries the light.

MERCUTIO

No, noble Romeo, you've got to dance.

ROMEO

Not me, believe me. You're wearing dancing shoes with nimble soles. My soul is made out of lead, and it's so heavy it keeps me stuck on the ground so I can't move.

MERCUTIO

You're a lover. Take Cupid's wings and fly higher than the average man.

ROMEO

His arrow has pierced me too deeply, so I can't fly high with his cheerful feathers. Because this wound keeps me down, I can't leap any higher than my dull sadness. I sink under the heavy weight of love.

MERCUTIO
And to sink in it, should you burthen love—
25   Too great oppression for a tender thing.

ROMEO
Is love a tender thing? It is too rough,
Too rude, too boisterous, and it pricks like thorn.

MERCUTIO
If love be rough with you, be rough with love.
Prick love for pricking, and you beat love down.—
30   Give me a case to put my visage in!
A visor for a visor.—What care I
What curious eye doth cote deformities?
Here are the beetle brows shall blush for me.

BENVOLIO
Come, knock and enter. And no sooner in
35   But every man betake him to his legs.

ROMEO
A torch for me. Let wantons light of heart
Tickle the senseless rushes with their heels.
For I am proverbed with a grandsire phrase,
I'll be a candle holder, and look on.
40   The game was ne'er so fair, and I am done.

MERCUTIO
Tut, dun's the mouse, the constable's own word.
If thou art dun, we'll draw thee from the mire,
Or—save your reverence—love, wherein thou stick'st
Up to the ears. Come, we burn daylight, ho!

ROMEO
45   Nay, that's not so.

MERCUTIO
                I mean, sir, in delay.
We waste our lights in vain, like lights by day.
Take our good meaning, for our judgment sits
Five times in that ere once in our fine wits.

MERCUTIO

If you sink, you're dragging love down. It's not right to drag down something as tender as love.

ROMEO

Is love really tender? I think it's too rough, too rude, too rowdy, and it pricks like a thorn.

MERCUTIO

Mercutio suggests that Romeo cure himself of love by having sex.

If love plays rough with you, play rough with love. If you prick love when it pricks you, you'll beat love down. Give me a mask to put my face in. A mask to put over my other mask. What do I care if some curious person sees my flaws? Let this mask, with its black eyebrows, blush for me. *(they put on masks)*

BENVOLIO

Come on, let's knock and go in. The minute we get in let's all start dancing.

ROMEO

I'll take a torch. Let playful people with light hearts dance. There's an old saying that applies to me: you can't lose if you don't play the game. I'll just hold a torch and watch you guys. It looks like a lot of fun, but I'll sit this one out.

MERCUTIO

Hey, you're being a stick in the mud, as cautious as a policemen on night patrol. If you're a stick in the mud, we'll pull you out of the mud—I mean out of love, if you'll excuse me for being so rude—where you're stuck up to your ears. Come on, we're wasting precious daylight. Let's go!

ROMEO

No we're not—it's night.

MERCUTIO

I mean, we're wasting the light of our torches by delaying, which is like wasting the sunshine during the day. Use your common sense to figure out what I mean, instead of trying to be clever or trusting your five senses.

ROMEO
And we mean well in going to this mask,
50   But 'tis no wit to go.

MERCUTIO
                Why, may one ask?

ROMEO
I dreamt a dream tonight.

MERCUTIO
                    And so did I.

ROMEO
Well, what was yours?

MERCUTIO
                    That dreamers often lie.

ROMEO
In bed asleep while they do dream things true.

MERCUTIO
Oh, then, I see Queen Mab hath been with you.

BENVOLIO
55   Queen Mab, what's she

MERCUTIO
She is the fairies' midwife, and she comes
In shape no bigger than an agate stone
On the forefinger of an alderman,
Drawn with a team of little atomi
60   Over men's noses as they lie asleep.
Her wagon spokes made of long spinners' legs,
The cover of the wings of grasshoppers,
Her traces of the smallest spider's web,
Her collars of the moonshine's watery beams,
65   Her whip of cricket's bone, the lash of film,
Her wagoner a small gray-coated gnat,
Not half so big as a round little worm
Pricked from the lazy finger of a maid.

ROMEO

We mean well by going to this masquerade ball, but it's not smart of us to go.

MERCUTIO

Why, may I ask?

ROMEO

I had a dream last night.

MERCUTIO

So did I.

ROMEO

Well, what was your dream?

MERCUTIO

My dream told me that dreamers often lie.

ROMEO

They lie in bed while they dream about the truth.

MERCUTIO

"Quean" is slang for whore, and Mab is a stereotypical prostitute's name.

Oh, then I see you've been with Queen Mab.

BENVOLIO

Who's Queen Mab?

MERCUTIO

She's the fairies' midwife. She's no bigger than the stone on a city councilman's ring. She rides around in a wagon drawn by tiny little atoms, and she rides over men's noses as they lie sleeping. The spokes of her wagon are made of spiders' legs. The cover of her wagon is made of grasshoppers' wings. The harnesses are made of the smallest spiderwebs. The collars are made out of moonbeams. Her whip is a thread attached to a cricket's bone. Her wagon driver is a tiny bug in a gray coat; he's not half the size of a little round worm that comes from the finger of a lazy young girl.

It was believed that worms sprung from the fingers of young girls who sat about doing nothing.

Her chariot is an empty hazelnut
70 Made by the joiner squirrel or old grub,
Time out o' mind the fairies' coachmakers.
And in this state she gallops night by night
Through lovers' brains, and then they dream of love;
On courtiers' knees, that dream on curtsies straight;
75 O'er lawyers' fingers, who straight dream on fees;
O'er ladies' lips, who straight on kisses dream,
Which oft the angry Mab with blisters plagues,
Because their breaths with sweetmeats tainted are.
Sometime she gallops o'er a courtier's nose,
80 And then dreams he of smelling out a suit.
And sometime comes she with a tithe-pig's tail
Tickling a parson's nose as he lies asleep,
Then he dreams of another benefice.
Sometime she driveth o'er a soldier's neck,
85 And then dreams he of cutting foreign throats,
Of breaches, ambuscadoes, Spanish blades,
Of healths five fathom deep, and then anon
Drums in his ear, at which he starts and wakes,
And being thus frighted swears a prayer or two
90 And sleeps again. This is that very Mab
That plaits the manes of horses in the night
And bakes the elflocks in foul sluttish hairs,
Which once untangled, much misfortune bodes.
This is the hag, when maids lie on their backs,
95 That presses them and learns them first to bear,
Making them women of good carriage.
This is she—

ROMEO
                    Peace, peace, Mercutio, peace!
Thou talk'st of nothing.

MERCUTIO
                              True, I talk of dreams,
Which are the children of an idle brain,
100 Begot of nothing but vain fantasy,

Her chariot is a hazelnut shell. It was made by a carpenter squirrel or an old grubworm; they've made wagons for the fairies as long as anyone can remember. In this royal wagon, she rides every night through the brains of lovers and makes them dream about love. She rides over courtiers' knees, and they dream about curtsying. She rides over lawyers' fingers, and right away, they dream about their fees. She rides over ladies' lips, and they immediately dream of kisses. Queen Mab often puts blisters on their lips because their breath smells like candy, which makes her mad. Sometimes she rides over a courtier's lips, and he dreams of making money off of someone. Sometimes she tickles a priest's nose with a tithe-pigs tail, and he dreams of a large donation. Sometimes she rides over a soldier's neck, and he dreams of cutting the throats of foreign enemies, of breaking down walls, of ambushes, of Spanish swords, and of enormous cups of liquor. And then, drums beat in his ear and he wakes up. He's frightened, so he says a couple of prayers and goes back to sleep. She is the same Mab who tangles the hair in horses' manes at night and makes the tangles hard in the dirty hairs, which bring bad luck if they're untangled. Mab is the old hag who gives false sex dreams to virgins and teaches them how to hold a lover and bear a child. She's the one—

A tithe-pig was a pig given to the church to support a priest.

ROMEO

Enough, enough! Mercutio, be quiet. You're talking nonsense.

MERCUTIO

True. I'm talking about dreams, which are the products of a brain that's doing nothing. Dreams are nothing but silly imagination, as thin as air, and less

Which is as thin of substance as the air
And more inconstant than the wind, who woos
Even now the frozen bosom of the north,
And, being angered, puffs away from thence,
105   Turning his face to the dew-dropping south.

BENVOLIO
This wind you talk of, blows us from ourselves.
Supper is done, and we shall come too late.

ROMEO
I fear too early, for my mind misgives
Some consequence yet hanging in the stars
110   Shall bitterly begin his fearful date
With this night's revels, and expire the term
Of a despisèd life closed in my breast
By some vile forfeit of untimely death.
But he that hath the steerage of my course,
115   Direct my sail. On, lusty gentlemen.

BENVOLIO
Strike, drum.

March about the stage and exeunt

predictable than the wind, which sometimes blows on the frozen north and then gets angry and blows south.

BENVOLIO

The wind you're talking about is blowing us off our course. Dinner is over, and we're going to get there too late.

ROMEO

I'm worried we'll get there too early. I have a feeling this party tonight will be the start of something bad, something that will end with my own death. But whoever's in charge of where my life's going can steer me wherever they want. Onward, lover boys!

BENVOLIO

Beat the drum.

They march about the stage and exit.

ACT ONE, Scene 5

PETER and other SERVINGMEN *come forth with napkins*

PETER
Where's Potpan, that he helps not to take away? He shift a
trencher? He scrape a trencher!

FIRST SERVINGMAN
When good manners shall lie all in one or two men's hands,
and they unwashed too, 'tis a foul thing.

PETER
5   Away with the joint-stools, remove the court-cupboard,
look to the plate. Good thou, save me a piece of marchpane,
and, as thou loves me, let the porter let in Susan Grindstone
and Nell.—Antony and Potpan!

SECOND SERVINGMAN
Ay, boy, ready.

PETER
10   You are looked for and called for, asked for and sought for,
in the great chamber.

FIRST SERVINGMAN
We cannot be here and there too. Cheerly, boys. Be brisk
awhile, and the longer liver take all.

Exeunt PETER *and* SERVINGMEN

Enter CAPULET *with* CAPULET'S COUSIN, TYBALT, LADY
CAPULET, JULIET, *and others of the house, meeting* ROMEO,
BENVOLIO, MERCUTIO, *and other* GUESTS *and* MASKERS

CAPULET
Welcome, gentlemen! Ladies that have their toes
15   Ah, my mistresses! Which of you all
Unplagued with corns will walk a bout with you.—
Will now deny to dance? She that makes dainty,
She, I'll swear, hath corns. Am I come near ye now?—
Welcome, gentlemen! I have seen the day

ACT ONE, Scene 5

PETER *and other* SERVINGMEN *come forward with napkins.*

PETER

Where's Potpan? Why isn't he helping us clear the table? He should be moving and scraping plates!

FIRST SERVINGMAN

When only one or two men have all the good manners, and even they are dirty, things are bad.

PETER

Take away the stools, the sideboards, and the plates. You, good friend, save me a piece of marzipan, and if you love me, have the porter let in Susan Grindstone and Nell. Antony and Potpan!

SECOND SERVINGMAN

Yes, boy, I'm ready.

PETER

They're looking for you in the great chamber.

FIRST SERVINGMAN

We can't be in two places at once, both here and there! Cheers, boys. Be quick for a while and let the one who lives the longest take everything.

PETER *and the* SERVINGMEN *exit.*

CAPULET *enters with his* COUSIN, TYBALT, LADY CAPULET, JULIET, *and other members of the house. They meet* ROMEO, BENVOLIO, MERCUTIO, *and other guests and* MASKERS.

CAPULET

Welcome, gentlemen. The ladies who don't have corns on their toes will dance with you. Ha, my ladies, which of you will refuse to dance now? Whichever of you acts shy, I'll swear she has corns. Does that hit close to home? Welcome, gentlemen. There was a time when I could wear a mask over my eyes and charm a

20 That I have worn a visor and could tell
A whispering tale in a fair lady's ear
Such as would please. 'Tis gone, 'tis gone, 'tis gone.—
You are welcome, gentlemen.—Come, musicians, play.
   (music plays and they dance)
A hall, a hall, give room!—And foot it, girls.—
25 More light, you knaves! And turn the tables up,
And quench the fire. The room is grown too hot.—
Ah, sirrah, this unlooked-for sport comes well.—
Nay, sit, nay, sit, good cousin Capulet,
For you and I are past our dancing days.
30 How long is 't now since last yourself and I
Were in a mask?

CAPULETS' COUSIN
     By'r Lady, thirty years.

CAPULET
What, man, 'tis not so much, 'tis not so much.
'Tis since the nuptials of Lucentio,
Come Pentecost as quickly as it will,
35 Some five and twenty years, and then we masked.

CAPULET'S COUSIN
'Tis more, 'tis more. His son is elder, sir.
His son is thirty.

CAPULET
     Will you tell me that?
His son was but a ward two years ago.

ROMEO
(to a **SERVINGMAN***)* What lady is that which doth enrich the
    hand
40 Of yonder knight?

SERVINGMAN
     I know not, sir.

ROMEO
Oh, she doth teach the torches to burn bright!
It seems she hangs upon the cheek of night
Like a rich jewel in an Ethiope's ear,

lady by whispering a story in her ear. That time is gone, gone, gone. You are welcome gentlemen. Come on, musicians, play music. *(music plays and they dance,* ROMEO *stands apart)* Make room in the hall. Make room in the hall. Shake a leg, girls. *(to* SERVING-MEN*)* More light, you rascals. Flip over the tables and get them out of the way. And put the fire out—it's getting too hot in here. *(to his* COUSIN*)* Ah, my man, this unexpected fun feels good. No, sit down, sit down, my good Capulet cousin. You and I are too old to dance. *(*CAPULET *and his* COUSIN *sit down)* How long is it now since you and I last wore masks at a party like this?

CAPULET'S COUSIN

I swear, it must be thirty years.

CAPULET

What, man? It's not that long, it's not that long. It's been since Lucentio's wedding. Let the years fly by as fast as they like, it's only been twenty-five years since we wore masks.

CAPULET'S COUSIN

It's been longer, it's been longer. Lucentio's son is older than that, sir. He's thirty years old.

CAPULET

Are you really going to tell me that? His son was a minor only two years ago.

ROMEO

(to a SERVINGMAN*)* Who is the girl on the arm of that lucky knight over there?

SERVINGMAN

I don't know, sir.

ROMEO

Oh, she shows the torches how to burn bright! She stands out against the darkness like a jeweled earring hanging against the cheek of an African. Her beauty is too good for this world; she's too beautiful to die and

Beauty too rich for use, for earth too dear.
45 So shows a snowy dove trooping with crows
As yonder lady o'er her fellows shows.
The measure done, I'll watch her place of stand,
And, touching hers, make blessèd my rude hand.
Did my heart love till now? Forswear it, sight!
50 For I ne'er saw true beauty till this night.

TYBALT
This, by his voice, should be a Montague.—
(to his PAGE*)* Fetch me my rapier, boy.—
What, dares the slave
Come hither, covered with an antic face,
55 To fleer and scorn at our solemnity?
Now, by the stock and honor of my kin,
To strike him dead I hold it not a sin.

CAPULET
Why, how now, kinsman? Wherefore storm you so?

TYBALT
Uncle, this is a Montague, our foe,
60 A villain that is hither come in spite
To scorn at our solemnity this night.

CAPULET
Young Romeo is it?

TYBALT
                'Tis he, that villain Romeo.

CAPULET
Content thee, gentle coz. Let him alone.
He bears him like a portly gentleman,
65 And, to say truth, Verona brags of him
To be a virtuous and well-governed youth.
I would not for the wealth of all the town
Here in my house do him disparagement.
Therefore be patient. Take no note of him.
70 It is my will, the which if thou respect,
Show a fair presence and put off these frowns,
An ill-beseeming semblance for a feast.

be buried. She outshines the other women like a white dove in the middle of a flock of crows. When this dance is over, I'll see where she stands, and then I'll touch her hand with my rough and ugly one. Did my heart ever love anyone before this moment? My eyes were liars, then, because I never saw true beauty before tonight.

TYBALT

I can tell by his voice that this man is a Montague. *(to his* PAGE*)* Get me my sword, boy.—What, does this peasant dare to come here with his face covered by a mask to sneer at and scorn our celebration? Now, by the honor of our family, I do not consider it a crime to kill him.

CAPULET

Why, what's going on here, nephew? Why are you acting so angry?

TYBALT

Uncle, this man is a Montague—our enemy. He's a scoundrel who's come here out of spite to mock our party.

CAPULET

Is it young Romeo?

TYBALT

That's him, that villain Romeo.

CAPULET

Calm down, gentle cousin. Leave him alone. He carries himself like a dignified gentleman, and, to tell you the truth, he has a reputation throughout Verona as a virtuous and well-behaved young man. I wouldn't insult him in my own house for all the wealth in this town. So calm down. Just ignore him. That's what I want, and if you respect my wishes, you'll look nice and stop frowning because that's not the way you should behave at a feast.

ACT ONE

TYBALT
    It fits when such a villain is a guest.
    I'll not endure him.

CAPULET
                 He shall be endured.
75   What, goodman boy! I say, he shall. Go to.
    Am I the master here, or you? Go to.
    You'll not endure him! God shall mend my soul,
    You'll make a mutiny among my guests.
    You will set cock-a-hoop. You'll be the man!

TYBALT
80   Why, uncle, 'tis a shame.

CAPULET
                 Go to, go to.
    You are a saucy boy. Is 't so, indeed?
    This trick may chance to scathe you, I know what.
    You must contrary me. Marry, 'tis time.—
    Well said, my hearts!—You are a princox, go.
85   Be quiet, or—More light, more light!—For shame!
    I'll make you quiet.—What, cheerly, my hearts!

Music plays again, and the guests dance

TYBALT
    Patience perforce with willful choler meeting
    Makes my flesh tremble in their different greeting.
    I will withdraw, but this intrusion shall
90   Now seeming sweet, convert to bitterest gall.

                       Exit **TYBALT**

TYBALT

It's the right way to act when a villain like him shows up. I won't tolerate him.

CAPULET

You *will* tolerate him. What, little man? I say you will. What the—Am I the boss here or you? What the— You won't tolerate him! God help me! You'll start a riot among my guests! There will be chaos! It will be your fault, you'll be the rabble-rouser!

TYBALT

But, uncle, we're being disrespected.

CAPULET

Go on, go on. You're an insolent little boy. Is that how it is, really? This stupidity will come back to bite you. I know what I'll do. You have to contradict me, do you? I'll teach you a lesson. *(to the* GUESTS*)* Well done, my dear guests! *(to* TYBALT*)* You're a punk, get away. Keep your mouth shut, or else— *(to* SERVINGMEN*)* more light, more light! *(to* TYBALT*)* You should be ashamed. I'll shut you up. *(to the guests)* Keep having fun, my dear friends!

The music plays again, and the guests dance.

TYBALT

The combination of forced patience and pure rage is making my body tremble. I'll leave here now, but Romeo's prank, which seems so sweet to him now, will turn bitter to him later.

TYBALT *exits.*

ACT ONE

ROMEO
> *(taking JULIET's hand)* If I profane with my unworthiest hand
> This holy shrine, the gentle sin is this:
> My lips, two blushing pilgrims, ready stand
> To smooth that rough touch with a tender kiss.

JULIET
95
> Good pilgrim, you do wrong your hand too much,
> Which mannerly devotion shows in this,
> For saints have hands that pilgrims' hands do touch,
> And palm to palm is holy palmers' kiss.

ROMEO
> Have not saints lips, and holy palmers too?

JULIET
100
> Ay, pilgrim, lips that they must use in prayer.

ROMEO
> O, then, dear saint, let lips do what hands do.
> They pray; grant thou, lest faith turn to despair.

JULIET
> Saints do not move, though grant for prayers' sake.

ROMEO
> Then move not, while my prayer's effect I take.

> *Kisses her*

105
> Thus from my lips, by thine, my sin is purged.

JULIET
> Then have my lips the sin that they have took.

ROMEO
> Sin from thy lips? O trespass sweetly urged!
> Give me my sin again.

> *They kiss again*

ROMEO

The first fourteen lines Romeo and Juliet speak together form a sonnet.

(taking JULIET*'s hand)* Your hand is like a holy place that my hand is unworthy to visit. If you're offended by the touch of my hand, my two lips are standing here like blushing pilgrims, ready to make things better with a kiss.

JULIET

Good pilgrim, you don't give your hand enough credit. By holding my hand you show polite devotion. After all, pilgrims touch the hands of statues of saints. Holding one palm against another is like a kiss.

ROMEO

Don't saints and pilgrims have lips too?

JULIET

Yes, pilgrim—they have lips that they're supposed to pray with.

ROMEO

Well then, saint, let lips do what hands do. I'm praying for you to kiss me. Please grant my prayer so my faith doesn't turn to despair.

JULIET

Saints don't move, even when they grant prayers.

ROMEO

Then don't move while I act out my prayer.

He kisses her.

Now my sin has been taken from my lips by yours.

JULIET

Then do my lips now have the sin they took from yours?

ROMEO

Sin from my lips? You encourage crime with your sweetness. Give me my sin back.

They kiss again.

JULIET
You kiss by th' book.

NURSE
Madam, your mother craves a word with you.

JULIET moves away

ROMEO
110 What is her mother?

NURSE
Marry, bachelor,
Her mother is the lady of the house,
And a good lady, and a wise and virtuous.
I nursed her daughter that you talked withal.
I tell you, he that can lay hold of her
115 Shall have the chinks.

ROMEO
(aside) Is she a Capulet?
O dear account! My life is my foe's debt.

BENVOLIO
(to ROMEO) Away, begone. The sport is at the best.

ROMEO
Ay, so I fear. The more is my unrest.

CAPULET
Nay, gentlemen, prepare not to be gone.
120 We have a trifling foolish banquet towards.—
Is it e'en so? Why, then, I thank you all.
I thank you, honest gentlemen. Good night.—
More torches here!—Come on then, let's to bed.
Ah, sirrah, by my fay, it waxes late.
125 I'll to my rest.

All but JULIET and NURSE move to exit

ACT ONE

JULIET

You kiss like you've studied how.

NURSE

Madam, your mother wants to talk to you.

JULIET moves away.

ROMEO

Who is her mother?

NURSE

Indeed, young man, her mother is the lady of the house. She is a good, wise, and virtuous lady. I nursed her daughter, whom you were just talking to. Let me tell you, the man who marries her will become very wealthy.

ROMEO

(to himself) Is she a Capulet? Oh, this is a heavy price to pay! My life is in the hands of my enemy.

BENVOLIO

(to ROMEO) Come on, let's go. Right when things are the most fun is the best time to leave.

ROMEO

Yes, but I'm afraid I'm in more trouble than ever.

CAPULET

No gentlemen, don't get ready to go now. We have a little dessert coming up. *(they whisper in his ear)* Is that really true? Well, then, I thank you both. I thank you, honest gentlemen. Good night. Bring more torches over here! Come on, let's all get to bed. *(to his cousin)* Ah, my man, I swear, it's getting late. I'm going to get some rest.

Everyone except JULIET and NURSE begins to exit.

JULIET
Come hither, Nurse. What is yond gentleman?

NURSE
The son and heir of old Tiberio.

JULIET
What's he that now is going out of door?

NURSE
Marry, that, I think, be young Petruchio.

JULIET
130　What's he that follows here, that would not dance?

NURSE
I know not.

JULIET
Go ask his name.—If he be married.
My grave is like to be my wedding bed.

NURSE
His name is Romeo, and a Montague,
135　The only son of your great enemy.

JULIET
(aside) My only love sprung from my only hate!
Too early seen unknown, and known too late!
Prodigious birth of love it is to me,
That I must love a loathèd enemy.

NURSE
140　What's this? What's this?

JULIET
　　　　　　　　　　　A rhyme I learned even now
Of one I danced withal.

One calls within "Juliet!"

NURSE
　　　　　　　Anon, anon!
Come, let's away. The strangers all are gone.
　　　　　　　　　　　　　　　Exeunt

JULIET

Come over here, nurse. Who is that gentleman?

NURSE

He is the son and heir of old Tiberio.

JULIET

Who's the one who's going out the door right now?

NURSE

Well, that one, I think, is young Petruchio.

JULIET

Who's the one following over there, the one who wouldn't dance?

NURSE

I don't know his name.

JULIET

Go ask. *(the nurse leaves)* If he's married, I think I'll die rather than marry anyone else.

NURSE

(returning) His name is Romeo. He's a Montague. He's the only son of your worst enemy.

JULIET

(to herself) The only man I love is the son of the only man I hate! I saw him too early without knowing who he was, and I found out who he was too late! Love is a monster for making me fall in love with my worst enemy.

NURSE

What's this? What's this?

JULIET

Just a rhyme I learned from somebody I danced with at the party.

Somebody calls, "Juliet!" from offstage.

NURSE

Right away, right away. Come, let's go. The strangers are all gone.

They exit.

ACT TWO

Prologue

Enter CHORUS

CHORUS
Now old desire doth in his deathbed lie,
And young affection gapes to be his heir.
That fair for which love groaned for and would die
With tender Juliet matched, is now not fair.
5   Now Romeo is beloved and loves again,
Alike bewitchèd by the charm of looks,
But to his foe supposed he must complain,
And she steal love's sweet bait from fearful hooks.
Being held a foe, he may not have access
10 To breathe such vows as lovers use to swear.
And she as much in love, her means much less
To meet her new beloved anywhere.
But passion lends them power, time means, to meet,
Tempering extremities with extreme sweet.

Exit

ACT TWO

Prologue

The CHORUS *enters.*

CHORUS

Now Romeo's old feelings of desire are dying, and a new desire is eager to take their place. Romeo groaned for the beautiful Rosaline and said he would die for her, but compared with tender Juliet, Rosaline doesn't seem beautiful now. Now someone loves Romeo, and he's in love again—both of them falling for each others' good looks. But he has to make his speeches of love to a woman who's supposed to be his enemy. And she's been hooked by someone she should fear. Because he's an enemy, Romeo has no chance to see Juliet and say the things a lover normally says. And Juliet's just as much in love as he, but she has even less opportunity to meet her lover. But love gives them power, and time gives them the chance to meet, sweetening the extreme danger with intense pleasure.

The CHORUS *exits.*

ACT TWO

Scene 1

Enter ROMEO *alone*

ROMEO
Can I go forward when my heart is here?
Turn back, dull earth, and find thy center out.

Moves away
Enter BENVOLIO *with* MERCUTIO

BENVOLIO
Romeo, my cousin Romeo! Romeo!

MERCUTIO
⠀⠀⠀⠀⠀⠀⠀⠀⠀⠀⠀⠀⠀⠀⠀⠀He is wise,
And, on my life, hath stol'n him home to bed.

BENVOLIO
5⠀⠀He ran this way and leapt this orchard wall.
Call, good Mercutio.

MERCUTIO
⠀⠀⠀⠀⠀⠀⠀⠀⠀⠀⠀Nay, I'll conjure too!
Romeo! Humours, madman, passion, lover!
Appear thou in the likeness of a sigh!
Speak but one rhyme, and I am satisfied.
10⠀⠀Cry but "Ay me!" Pronounce but "love" and "dove."
Speak to my gossip Venus one fair word,
One nickname for her purblind son and heir,
Young Abraham Cupid, he that shot so true
When King Cophetua loved the beggar maid.—
15⠀⠀He heareth not, he stirreth not, he moveth not.
The ape is dead, and I must conjure him.—
I conjure thee by Rosaline's bright eyes,
By her high forehead and her scarlet lip,
By her fine foot, straight leg, and quivering thigh,
20⠀⠀And the demesnes that there adjacent lie,
That in thy likeness thou appear to us.

ACT TWO

Scene 1

ROMEO *enters alone.*

ROMEO

Can I go away while my heart stays here? I have to go back to where my heart is.

ROMEO *moves away.* BENVOLIO *and* MERCUTIO *enter.*

BENVOLIO

(calling) Romeo, my cousin, Romeo, Romeo!

MERCUTIO

He's a smart boy. I bet he slipped away and went home to bed.

BENVOLIO

He ran this way and jumped over this orchard wall. Call to him, Mercutio.

MERCUTIO

I'll conjure him as if I were summoning a spirit. Romeo! Madman! Passion! Lover! Show yourself in the form of a sigh. Speak one rhyme, and I'll be satisfied. Just cry out, "Ah me!" Just say "love" and "dove." Say just one lovely word to my good friend Venus. Just say the nickname of her blind son Cupid, the one who shot arrows so well in the old story.— Romeo doesn't hear me. He doesn't stir. He doesn't move. The silly ape is dead, but I must make him appear.—I summon you by Rosaline's bright eyes, by her high forehead and her red lips, by her fine feet, by her straight legs, by her trembling thighs, and by the regions right next to her thighs. In the name of all of these things, I command you to appear before us in your true form.

Venus is the Roman goddess of love.

BENVOLIO
    An if he hear thee, thou wilt anger him.

MERCUTIO
    This cannot anger him. 'Twould anger him
    To raise a spirit in his mistress' circle
25   Of some strange nature, letting it there stand
    Till she had laid it and conjured it down.
    That were some spite. My invocation
    Is fair and honest. In his mistress' name
    I conjure only but to raise up him.

BENVOLIO
30   Come, he hath hid himself among these trees,
    To be consorted with the humorous night.
    Blind is his love and best befits the dark.

MERCUTIO
    If love be blind, love cannot hit the mark.
    Now will he sit under a medlar tree
35   And wish his mistress were that kind of fruit
    As maids call medlars when they laugh alone.—
    O Romeo, that she were! Oh, that she were
    An open arse, and thou a poperin pear.
    Romeo, good night. I'll to my truckle bed.
40   This field-bed is too cold for me to sleep.—
    Come, shall we go?

BENVOLIO
                 Go, then, for 'tis in vain
    To seek him here that means not to be found.

                                       Exeunt

BENVOLIO

If he hears you, you'll make him angry.

MERCUTIO

What I'm saying can't anger him. He would be angry if I summoned a strange spirit for her to have sex with—that's what would make him angry. The things I'm saying are fair and honest. All I'm doing is saying the name of the woman he loves to lure him out of the darkness.

BENVOLIO

Come on. He's hidden behind these trees to keep the night company. His love is blind, so it belongs in the dark.

MERCUTIO

The medlar is a tree whose fruit was considered to look like a vulva or an anus. The fruits were often called "open-arses." Popperins are Belgian pears; Mercutio uses the name in an obscene double entrendre.

If love is blind, it can't hit the target. Now he'll sit under a medlar tree and wish his mistress were one of those fruits that look like female genitalia. Oh Romeo, I wish she *were* an open-arse, and you a Popperin pear to "pop her in." Good night, Romeo. I'll go to my little trundle bed. This open field is too cold a place for me to sleep. *(to* **BENVOLIO***)* Come on, should we go?

BENVOLIO

Let's go. There's no point in looking for him if he doesn't want to be found.

BENVOLIO *and* **MERCUTIO** *exit.*

ACT TWO, Scene 2

ROMEO *returns*

ROMEO
He jests at scars that never felt a wound.

JULIET *appears in a window above*

But soft! What light through yonder window breaks?
It is the east, and Juliet is the sun.
Arise, fair sun, and kill the envious moon,
5   Who is already sick and pale with grief,
That thou, her maid, art far more fair than she.
Be not her maid since she is envious.
Her vestal livery is but sick and green,
And none but fools do wear it. Cast it off!
10   It is my lady. Oh, it is my love.
Oh, that she knew she were!
She speaks, yet she says nothing. What of that?
Her eye discourses. I will answer it.—
I am too bold. 'Tis not to me she speaks.
15   Two of the fairest stars in all the heaven,
Having some business, do entreat her eyes
To twinkle in their spheres till they return.
What if her eyes were there, they in her head?
The brightness of her cheek would shame those stars
20   As daylight doth a lamp. Her eye in heaven
Would through the airy region stream so bright
That birds would sing and think it were not night.
See how she leans her cheek upon her hand.
Oh, that I were a glove upon that hand
25   That I might touch that cheek!

JULIET
                Ay me!

ACT TWO, Scene 2

ROMEO *returns.*

ROMEO

It's easy for someone to joke about scars if they've never been cut.

JULIET *enters on the balcony.*

But wait, what's that light in the window over there? It is the east, and Juliet is the sun. Rise up, beautiful sun, and kill the jealous moon. The moon is already sick and pale with grief because you, Juliet, her maid, are more beautiful than she. Don't be her maid, because she is jealous. Virginity makes her look sick and green. Only fools hold on to their virginity. Let it go. Oh, there's my lady! Oh, it is my love. Oh, I wish she knew how much I love her. She's talking, but she's not saying anything. So what? Her eyes are saying something. I will answer them. I am too bold. She's not talking to me. Two of the brightest stars in the whole sky had to go away on business, and they're asking her eyes to twinkle in their places until they return. What if her eyes were in the sky and the stars were in her head?—The brightness of her cheeks would outshine the stars the way the sun outshines a lamp. If her eyes were in the night sky, they would shine so brightly through space that birds would start singing, thinking her light was the light of day. Look how she leans her hand on her cheek. Oh, I wish I was the glove on that hand so that I could touch that cheek.

Diana is the goddess of the moon and of virginity. Romeo implies that Juliet is a servant of the moon as long as she's a virgin.

JULIET

Oh, my!

ROMEO

                                 (aside) She speaks.
O, speak again, bright angel! For thou art
As glorious to this night, being o'er my head,
As is a wingèd messenger of heaven
Unto the white, upturnèd, wondering eyes

30 Of mortals that fall back to gaze on him
When he bestrides the lazy-puffing clouds
And sails upon the bosom of the air.

JULIET

O Romeo, Romeo! Wherefore art thou Romeo?
Deny thy father and refuse thy name.

35 Or, if thou wilt not, be but sworn my love,
And I'll no longer be a Capulet.

ROMEO

(aside) Shall I hear more, or shall I speak at this?

JULIET

'Tis but thy name that is my enemy.
Thou art thyself, though not a Montague.

40 What's Montague? It is nor hand, nor foot,
Nor arm, nor face, nor any other part
Belonging to a man. O, be some other name!
What's in a name? That which we call a rose
By any other word would smell as sweet.

45 So Romeo would, were he not Romeo called,
Retain that dear perfection which he owes
Without that title. Romeo, doff thy name,
And for that name, which is no part of thee
Take all myself.

ROMEO

                    I take thee at thy word.
50 Call me but love, and I'll be new baptized.
Henceforth I never will be Romeo.

JULIET

What man art thou that, thus bescreened in night,
So stumblest on my counsel?

ROMEO

(to himself) She speaks. Oh, speak again, bright angel. You are as glorious as an angel tonight. You shine above me, like a winged messenger from heaven who makes mortal men fall on their backs to look up at the sky, watching the angel walking on the clouds and sailing on the air.

JULIET

(not knowing ROMEO *hears her)* Oh, Romeo, Romeo, why do you have to be Romeo? Forget about your father and change your name. Or else, if you won't change your name, just swear you love me and I'll stop being a Capulet.

ROMEO

(to himself) Should I listen for more, or should I speak now?

JULIET

(still not knowing ROMEO *hears her)* It's only your name that's my enemy. You'd still be yourself even if you stopped being a Montague. What's a Montague anyway? It isn't a hand, a foot, an arm, a face, or any other part of a man. Oh, be some other name! What does a name mean? The thing we call a rose would smell just as sweet if we called it by any other name. Romeo would be just as perfect even if he wasn't called Romeo. Romeo, lose your name. Trade in your name—which really has nothing to do with you—and take all of me in exchange.

ROMEO

(to JULIET*)* I trust your words. Just call me your love, and I will take a new name. From now on I will never be Romeo again.

JULIET

Who are you? Why do you hide in the darkness and listen to my private thoughts?

ROMEO
                                        By a name
I know not how to tell thee who I am.
55   My name, dear saint, is hateful to myself
Because it is an enemy to thee.
Had I it written, I would tear the word.

JULIET
My ears have not yet drunk a hundred words
Of that tongue's uttering, yet I know the sound.
60   Art thou not Romeo, and a Montague?

ROMEO
Neither, fair maid, if either thee dislike.

JULIET
How camest thou hither, tell me, and wherefore?
The orchard walls are high and hard to climb,
And the place death, considering who thou art,
65   If any of my kinsmen find thee here.

ROMEO
With love's light wings did I o'erperch these walls,
For stony limits cannot hold love out,
And what love can do, that dares love attempt.
Therefore thy kinsmen are no stop to me.

JULIET
70   If they do see thee they will murder thee.

ROMEO
Alack, there lies more peril in thine eye
Than twenty of their swords. Look thou but sweet,
And I am proof against their enmity.

JULIET
I would not for the world they saw thee here.

ROMEO
75   I have night's cloak to hide me from their eyes,
And but thou love me, let them find me here.
My life were better ended by their hate
Than death proroguèd, wanting of thy love.

ROMEO

I don't know how to tell you who I am by telling you a name. I hate my name, dear saint, because my name is your enemy. If I had it written down, I would tear up the paper.

JULIET

I haven't heard you say a hundred words yet, but I recognize the sound of your voice. Aren't you Romeo? And aren't you a Montague?

ROMEO

I am neither of those things if you dislike them.

JULIET

Tell me, how did you get in here? And why did you come? The orchard walls are high, and it's hard to climb over them. If any of my relatives find you here they'll kill you because of who you are.

ROMEO

I flew over these walls with the light wings of love. Stone walls can't keep love out. Whatever a man in love can possibly do, his love will make him try to do it. Therefore your relatives are no obstacle.

JULIET

If they see you, they'll murder you.

ROMEO

Alas, one angry look from you would be worse than twenty of your relatives with swords. Just look at me kindly, and I'm invincible against their hatred.

JULIET

I'd give anything to keep them from seeing you here.

ROMEO

The darkness will hide me from them. And if you don't love me, let them find me here. I'd rather they killed me than have to live without your love.

JULIET

Who told you how to get here below my bedroom?

JULIET
By whose direction found'st thou out this place?

ROMEO
80
By love, that first did prompt me to inquire.
He lent me counsel and I lent him eyes.
I am no pilot. Yet, wert thou as far
As that vast shore washed with the farthest sea,
I would adventure for such merchandise.

JULIET
85
Thou know'st the mask of night is on my face,
Else would a maiden blush bepaint my cheek
For that which thou hast heard me speak tonight.
Fain would I dwell on form. Fain, fain deny
What I have spoke. But farewell compliment!
90
Dost thou love me? I know thou wilt say "ay,"
And I will take thy word. Yet if thou swear'st
Thou mayst prove false. At lovers' perjuries,
They say, Jove laughs. O gentle Romeo,
If thou dost love, pronounce it faithfully.
95
Or if thou think'st I am too quickly won,
I'll frown and be perverse and say thee nay,
So thou wilt woo. But else, not for the world.
In truth, fair Montague, I am too fond,
And therefore thou mayst think my 'havior light.
100
But trust me, gentleman, I'll prove more true
Than those that have more coying to be strange.
I should have been more strange, I must confess,
But that thou overheard'st, ere I was 'ware,
My true love's passion. Therefore pardon me,
105
And not impute this yielding to light love,
Which the dark night hath so discovered.

ROMEO
Lady, by yonder blessèd moon I vow,
That tips with silver all these fruit-tree tops—

ROMEO

Love showed me the way—the same thing that made me look for you in the first place. Love told me what to do, and I let love borrow my eyes. I'm not a sailor, but if you were across the farthest sea, I would risk everything to gain you.

JULIET

You can't see my face because it's dark out. Otherwise, you'd see me blushing about the things you've heard me say tonight. I would be happy to keep up good manners and deny the things I said. But forget about good manners. Do you love me? I know you'll say "yes," and I'll believe you. But if you swear you love me, you might turn out to be lying. They say Jove laughs when lovers lie to each other. Oh Romeo, if you really love me, say it truly. Or if you think it's too easy and quick to win my heart, I'll frown and play hard-to-get, as long as that will make you try to win me, but otherwise I wouldn't act that way for anything. In truth, handsome Montague, I like you too much, so you may think my behavior is loose. But trust me, gentleman, I'll prove myself more faithful than girls who act coy and play hard-to-get. I should have been more standoffish, I confess, but you overheard me talking about the love in my heart when I didn't know you were there. So excuse me, and do not assume that because you made me love you so easily my love isn't serious.

Jove, also called Jupiter, was the king of the Roman gods.

ROMEO

Lady, I swear by the sacred moon above, the moon that paints the tops of fruit trees with silver—

JULIET
O, swear not by the moon, th' inconstant moon,
110 That monthly changes in her circle orb,
Lest that thy love prove likewise variable.

ROMEO
What shall I swear by?

JULIET
       Do not swear at all.
Or, if thou wilt, swear by thy gracious self,
Which is the god of my idolatry,
115 And I'll believe thee.

ROMEO
        If my heart's dear love—

JULIET
Well, do not swear. Although I joy in thee,
I have no joy of this contract tonight.
It is too rash, too unadvised, too sudden,
Too like the lightning, which doth cease to be
120 Ere one can say "It lightens." Sweet, good night.
This bud of love, by summer's ripening breath,
May prove a beauteous flower when next we meet.
Good night, good night! As sweet repose and rest
Come to thy heart as that within my breast.

ROMEO
125 O, wilt thou leave me so unsatisfied?

JULIET
What satisfaction canst thou have tonight?

ROMEO
Th' exchange of thy love's faithful vow for mine.

JULIET
I gave thee mine before thou didst request it,
And yet I would it were to give again.

ROMEO
130 Wouldst thou withdraw it? For what purpose, love?

JULIET

Don't swear by the moon. The moon is always changing. Every month its position in the sky shifts. I don't want you to turn out to be that inconsistent too.

ROMEO

What should I swear by?

JULIET

Don't swear at all. But if you have to swear, swear by your wonderful self, which is the god I worship like an idol, and then I'll believe you.

ROMEO

If my heart's dear love—

JULIET

Well, don't swear. Although you bring me joy, I can't take joy in this exchange of promises tonight. It's too crazy. We haven't done enough thinking. It's too sudden. It's too much like lightning, which flashes and then disappears before you can say, "it's lightning." My sweet, good night. Our love, which right now is like a flower bud in the summer air, may turn out to be a beautiful flower by the next time we meet. I hope you enjoy the same sweet peace and rest I feel in my heart.

ROMEO

Oh, are you going to leave me so unsatisfied?

JULIET

What satisfaction could you possibly have tonight?

ROMEO

I would be satisfied if we made each other true promises of love.

JULIET

I pledged my love to you before you asked me to. Yet I wish I could take that promise back, so I had it to give again.

ROMEO

You would take it back? Why would you do that, my love?

JULIET
But to be frank, and give it thee again.
And yet I wish but for the thing I have.
My bounty is as boundless as the sea,
My love as deep. The more I give to thee,
135   The more I have, for both are infinite.

NURSE calls from within

I hear some noise within. Dear love, adieu.—
Anon, good Nurse!—Sweet Montague, be true.
Stay but a little. I will come again.

                                Exit JULIET, above

ROMEO
O blessèd, blessèd night! I am afeard,
140   Being in night, all this is but a dream,
Too flattering sweet to be substantial.

Enter JULIET, above

JULIET
Three words, dear Romeo, and good night indeed.
If that thy bent of love be honorable,
Thy purpose marriage, send me word tomorrow
145   By one that I'll procure to come to thee
Where and what time thou wilt perform the rite,
And all my fortunes at thy foot I'll lay
And follow thee my lord throughout the world.

NURSE
(from within) Madam!

JULIET
150   I come, anon.—But if thou mean'st not well,
I do beseech thee—

NURSE
(from within) Madam!

JULIET

Only to be generous and give it to you once more. But I'm wishing for something I already have. My generosity to you is as limitless as the sea, and my love is as deep. The more love I give you, the more I have. Both loves are infinite.

The NURSE *calls from offstage.*

I hear a noise inside. Dear love, goodbye—Just a minute, good Nurse. Sweet Montague, be true. Stay here for a moment. I'll come back.

JULIET *exits.*

ROMEO

Oh, blessed, blessed night! Because it's dark out, I'm afraid all this is just a dream, too sweet to be real.

JULIET *enters on her balcony.*

JULIET

Three words, dear Romeo, and then it's good night for real. If your intentions as a lover are truly honorable and you want to marry me, send me word tomorrow. I'll send a messenger to you, and you can pass on a message telling me where and when we'll be married. I'll lay all my fortunes at your feet and follow you, my lord, all over the world.

NURSE

(offstage) Madam!

JULIET

(to the NURSE*)* I'll be right there! *(to* ROMEO*)* But if you don't have honorable intentions, I beg you—

NURSE

(offstage) Madam!

JULIET
By and by, I come.—
To cease thy strife and leave me to my grief.
155   Tomorrow will I send.

ROMEO
So thrive my soul—

JULIET
A thousand times good night!

Exit **JULIET**, *above*

ROMEO
A thousand times the worse to want thy light.
Love goes toward love as schoolboys from their books,
160   But love from love, toward school with heavy looks.

Moves to exit
Reenter **JULIET**, *above*

JULIET
Hist! Romeo, hist!—Oh, for a falconer's voice,
To lure this tassel-gentle back again!
Bondage is hoarse, and may not speak aloud,
Else would I tear the cave where Echo lies,
165   And make her airy tongue more hoarse than mine,
With repetition of "My Romeo!"

ROMEO
It is my soul that calls upon my name.
How silver-sweet sound lovers' tongues by night,
Like softest music to attending ears!

JULIET

Alright, I'm coming!—I beg you to stop trying for me and leave me to my sadness. Tomorrow I'll send the messenger.

ROMEO

My soul depends on it—

JULIET

A thousand times good night.

JULIET *exits.*

ROMEO

Leaving you is a thousand times worse than being near you. A lover goes toward his beloved as enthusiastically as a schoolboy leaving his books, but when he leaves his girlfriend, he feels as miserable as the schoolboy on his way to school.

ROMEO *starts to leave.* JULIET *returns, on her balcony.*

JULIET

Juliet is trying to call to Romeo as if he was a falcon.

Echo, a mythical woman who was scorned by Narcissus, withered with sadness repeating his name, and after her death, her voice still reverberated in caves, which is why we have the word "echo."

Hist, Romeo! Hist! Oh, I wish I could make a falconer's call, so I could bring my little falcon back again. I'm trapped in my family's house, so I must be quiet. Otherwise I would rip open the cave where Echo sleeps. I would make her repeat his name until her voice grew more hoarse than mine by repeating, "My Romeo!"

ROMEO

My soul is calling out my name. The sound of lovers calling each others names through the night is silversweet. It's the sweetest sound a lover ever hears.

JULIET
170   Romeo!

ROMEO
                My nyas?

JULIET
                        What o'clock tomorrow
Shall I send to thee?

ROMEO
                        By the hour of nine.

JULIET
I will not fail. 'Tis twenty year till then.
I have forgot why I did call thee back.

ROMEO
Let me stand here till thou remember it.

JULIET
175   I shall forget, to have thee still stand there,
Remembering how I love thy company.

ROMEO
And I'll still stay, to have thee still forget,
Forgetting any other home but this.

JULIET
'Tis almost morning. I would have thee gone.
180   And yet no further than a wanton's bird,
That lets it hop a little from his hand
Like a poor prisoner in his twisted gyves,
And with a silken thread plucks it back again,
So loving-jealous of his liberty.

ROMEO
185   I would I were thy bird.

JULIET
                        Sweet, so would I.
Yet I should kill thee with much cherishing.
Good night, good night! Parting is such sweet sorrow
That I shall say good night till it be morrow.

                                Exit JULIET, *above*

JULIET

Romeo!

ROMEO

My baby hawk?

JULIET

What time tomorrow should I send a messenger to you?

ROMEO

By nine o'clock.

JULIET

I won't fail. From now until then seems like twenty years. I have forgotten why I called you back.

ROMEO

Let me stand here until you remember your reason.

JULIET

I'll forget it, and you'll have to stand there forever. I'll only remember how much I love your company.

ROMEO

I'll keep standing here, even if you keep forgetting. I'll forget that I have any home besides this spot right here.

JULIET

It's almost morning. I want to make you go, but I'd only let you go as far as a spoiled child lets his pet bird go. He lets the bird hop a little from his hand and then yanks him back by a string.

ROMEO

I wish I was your bird.

JULIET

My sweet, so do I. But I would kill you by petting you too much. Good night, good night. Parting is such sweet sorrow that I'll say good night until tonight becomes tomorrow.

JULIET exits.

ACT TWO

ROMEO
Sleep dwell upon thine eyes, peace in thy breast.
190   Would I were sleep and peace, so sweet to rest.
Hence will I to my ghostly friar's close cell,
His help to crave and my dear hap to tell.

Exit

ROMEO

I hope you sleep peacefully. I wish I were Sleep and Peace, so I could spend the night with you. Now I'll go see my priest, to ask for his help and tell him about my good luck.

He exits.

ACT TWO, Scene 3

Enter FRIAR LAWRENCE, *with a basket*

FRIAR LAWRENCE
    The gray-eyed morn smiles on the frowning night,
    Checkering the eastern clouds with streaks of light,
    And fleckled darkness like a drunkard reels
    From forth day's path and Titan's fiery wheels.
5   Now, ere the sun advance his burning eye,
    The day to cheer and night's dank dew to dry,
    I must upfill this osier cage of ours
    With baleful weeds and precious-juicèd flowers.
    The earth, that's nature's mother, is her tomb.
10   What is her burying, grave that is her womb.
    And from her womb children of divers kind
    We sucking on her natural bosom find,
    Many for many virtues excellent,
    None but for some and yet all different.
15   Oh, mickle is the powerful grace that lies
    In herbs, plants, stones, and their true qualities.
    For naught so vile that on the earth doth live
    But to the earth some special good doth give.
    Nor aught so good but, strained from that fair use
20   Revolts from true birth, stumbling on abuse.
    Virtue itself turns vice, being misapplied,
    And vice sometime by action dignified.

Enter ROMEO

    Within the infant rind of this small flower
    Poison hath residence and medicine power.
25   For this, being smelt, with that part cheers each part;
    Being tasted, stays all senses with the heart.
    Two such opposèd kings encamp them still,
    In man as well as herbs—grace and rude will.

ACT TWO, Scene 3

FRIAR LAWRENCE *enters by himself, carrying a basket.*

FRIAR LAWRENCE
The smiling morning is replacing the frowning night. Darkness is stumbling out of the sun's path like a drunk man. Now, before the sun comes up and burns away the dew, I have to fill this basket of mine with poisonous weeds and medicinal flowers. The Earth is nature's mother and also nature's tomb. Plants are born out of the Earth, and they are buried in the Earth when they die. From the Earth's womb, many different sorts of plants and animals come forth, and the Earth provides her children with many excellent forms of nourishment. Evertything nature creates has some special property, and each one is different. Herbs, plants, and stones possess great power. There is nothing on Earth that is so evil that it does not provide the earth with some special quality. And there is nothing that does not turn bad if it's put to the wrong use and abused. Virtue turns to vice if it's misused. Vice sometimes becomes virtue through the right activity.

ROMEO *enters.*

Inside the little rind of this weak flower, there is both poison and powerful medicine. If you smell it, you feel good all over your body. But if you taste it, you die. There are two opposite elements in everything, in men as well as in herbs—good and evil.

And where the worser is predominant,
30   Full soon the canker death eats up that plant.

ROMEO
Good morrow, Father.

FRIAR LAWRENCE
                        Benedicite.
What early tongue so sweet saluteth me?
Young son, it argues a distempered head
So soon to bid good morrow to thy bed.
35   Care keeps his watch in every old man's eye,
And where care lodges, sleep will never lie.
But where unbruisèd youth with unstuffed brain
Doth couch his limbs, there golden sleep doth reign.
Therefore thy earliness doth me assure
40   Thou art uproused by some distemperature.
Or if not so, then here I hit it right:
Our Romeo hath not been in bed tonight.

ROMEO
That last is true. The sweeter rest was mine.

FRIAR LAWRENCE
God pardon sin! Wast thou with Rosaline?

ROMEO
45   With Rosaline, my ghostly Father? No.
I have forgot that name and that name's woe.

FRIAR LAWRENCE
That's my good son. But where hast thou been, then?

ROMEO
I'll tell thee ere thou ask it me again.
I have been feasting with mine enemy,
50   Where on a sudden one hath wounded me,
That's by me wounded. Both our remedies
Within thy help and holy physic lies.
I bear no hatred, blessèd man, for, lo,
My intercession likewise steads my foe.

When evil is dominant, death soon kills the body like cancer.

ROMEO

Good morning, father.

FRIAR LAWRENCE

God bless you. Who greets me so early in the morning? Young man, something's wrong if you're getting out of bed this early. Every old man has worries, and worried men never get any sleep, but young men shouldn't have a care in the world. They should get to bed early and get plenty of sleep. Therefore, the fact that you're awake this early tells me you've been upset with some anxiety. If that's not the case, then this must be the answer: You, Romeo, have not been to bed tonight.

ROMEO

Your last guess is right. I enjoyed a sweeter rest than sleep.

FRIAR LAWRENCE

May God forgive you if you've sinned!—Were you with Rosaline?

ROMEO

With Rosaline, father? No, I have forgotten that girl and all the sadness she brought me.

FRIAR LAWRENCE

That's good, my boy. But where have you been?

ROMEO

I'll tell you before you have to ask me again. I have been feasting with my enemy. Suddenly someone wounded me with love and was wounded with love by me. You have the sacred power to cure both of us. I carry no hatred, holy man, because my request will benefit my enemy.

FRIAR LAWRENCE

55   Be plain, good son, and homely in thy drift.
      Riddling confession finds but riddling shrift.

ROMEO

      Then plainly know my heart's dear love is set
      On the fair daughter of rich Capulet.
      As mine on hers, so hers is set on mine,
60   And all combined, save what thou must combine
      By holy marriage. When and where and how
      We met, we wooed and made exchange of vow,
      I'll tell thee as we pass, but this I pray:
      That thou consent to marry us today.

FRIAR LAWRENCE

65   Holy Saint Francis, what a change is here!
      Is Rosaline, whom thou didst love so dear,
      So soon forsaken? Young men's love then lies
      Not truly in their hearts, but in their eyes.
      Jesu Maria, what a deal of brine
70   Hath washed thy sallow cheeks for Rosaline!
      How much salt water thrown away in waste
      To season love that of it doth not taste!
      The sun not yet thy sighs from heaven clears,
      Thy old groans ring yet in my ancient ears.
75   Lo, here upon thy cheek the stain doth sit
      Of an old tear that is not washed off yet.
      If e'er thou wast thyself and these woes thine,
      Thou and these woes were all for Rosaline.
      And art thou changed? Pronounce this sentence then:
80   Women may fall when there's no strength in men.

ROMEO

      Thou chid'st me oft for loving Rosaline.

FRIAR LAWRENCE

      For doting, not for loving, pupil mine.

ROMEO

      And badest me bury love.

FRIAR LAWRENCE

Speak plainly, make your meaning clear, my son. A jumbled confession can only receive a jumbled absolution.

ROMEO

I love rich Capulet's daughter. I love her, and she loves me. We're bound to each other in every possible way, except we need you to marry us. I'll tell you more later about when and where we met, how we fell in love, and how we exchanged promises, but now I'm begging you: please, agree to marry us today.

FRIAR LAWRENCE

Holy Saint Francis, this is a drastic change! Have you given up so quickly on Rosaline, whom you loved so much? Then young men love with their eyes, not with their hearts. Jesus and Mary, how many tears did you cry for Rosaline? How many salty tear-drops did you waste salting a love you never tasted? The sun hasn't yet melted away the fog you made with all your sighs. The groans you used to make are still ringing in my old ears. There's still a stain on your cheek from an old tear that hasn't been washed off yet. If you were ever yourself, and this sadness was yours, you and your sadness were all for Rosaline. And now you've changed? Then repeat this after me: you can't expect women to be faithful when men are so unreliable.

ROMEO

You scolded me often for loving Rosaline.

FRIAR LAWRENCE

I scolded you for obsessing about her, not for loving her, my student.

ROMEO

And you told me to bury my love.

FRIAR LAWRENCE
                          Not in a grave,
To lay one in, another out to have.

ROMEO
85   I pray thee, chide not. Her I love now
Doth grace for grace and love for love allow.
The other did not so.

FRIAR LAWRENCE
                   Oh, she knew well
Thy love did read by rote, that could not spell.
But come, young waverer, come, go with me,
90   In one respect I'll thy assistant be,
For this alliance may so happy prove
To turn your households' rancor to pure love.

ROMEO
Oh, let us hence. I stand on sudden haste.

FRIAR LAWRENCE
Wisely and slow. They stumble that run fast.

Exeunt

FRIAR LAWRENCE

> I didn't tell you to get rid of one love and replace her with another.

ROMEO

> Please, I beg you, don't scold me. The girl I love now returns my love. The other girl did not love me.

FRIAR LAWRENCE

> Oh, she knew very well that you were acting like you were in love without really knowing what love means. But come on, inconsistent young man, come with me. I'll help you with your secret wedding. This marriage may be lucky enough to turn the hatred between your families into pure love.

ROMEO

> Let's get out of here. I'm in a rush.

FRIAR LAWRENCE

> Go wisely and slowly. Those who rush stumble and fall.

> *They exit.*

ACT TWO, Scene 4

Enter BENVOLIO *and* MERCUTIO

MERCUTIO
Where the devil should this Romeo be?
Came he not home tonight?

BENVOLIO
Not to his father's. I spoke with his man.

MERCUTIO
Why, that same pale hard-hearted wench, that Rosaline,
5   Torments him so, that he will sure run mad.

BENVOLIO
Tybalt, the kinsman to old Capulet,
Hath sent a letter to his father's house.

MERCUTIO
A challenge, on my life.

BENVOLIO
Romeo will answer it.

MERCUTIO
10   Any man that can write may answer a letter.

BENVOLIO
Nay, he will answer the letter's master, how he dares, being
dared.

MERCUTIO
Alas, poor Romeo! He is already dead, stabbed with a white
wench's black eye, shot through the ear with a love song, the
15   very pin of his heart cleft with the blind bow-boy's butt
shaft. And is he a man to encounter Tybalt?

BENVOLIO
Why, what is Tybalt?

MERCUTIO
More than Prince of Cats. Oh, he's the courageous captain
of compliments. He fights as you sing prick-song, keeps
20   time, distance, and proportion. He rests his minim rests—

ACT TWO, Scene 4

BENVOLIO *and* MERCUTIO *enter.*

MERCUTIO

Where the devil can Romeo be? Didn't he come home last night?

BENVOLIO

Not to his father's house. I asked a servant.

MERCUTIO

That fair-skinned, hard-hearted hussy, Rosaline is going to torment him until he goes insane.

BENVOLIO

Tybalt, old Capulet's nephew, has sent a letter to Romeo's father's house.

MERCUTIO

I bet it's a challenge.

BENVOLIO

Romeo will answer the challenge.

MERCUTIO

Any man who knows how to write can answer a letter.

BENVOLIO

No, Romeo will respond to the letter's writer, telling him whether he accepts the challenge.

MERCUTIO

Oh, poor Romeo! He's already dead. He's been stabbed by a white girl's black eye. He's been cut through the ear with a love song. The center of his heart has been split by blind Cupid's arrow. Is he man enough at this point to face off with Tybalt?

BENVOLIO

Why, what's Tybalt's story?

MERCUTIO

The Prince of Cats is a figure from Medieval lore whose first name was also Tybalt.

He's tougher than the Prince of Cats. He does everything by the book. He fights like you sing at a recital, paying attention to time, distance, and proportion. He one, two, and the third in your bosom. The very butcher of a silk button, a duelist, a duelist, a gentleman of the very first house of the first and second cause. Ah, the immortal *passado*, the *punto reverso*, the *hai!*

BENVOLIO
25   The what?

MERCUTIO
The pox of such antic, lisping, affecting fantasmines, these new tuners of accents! "By Jesu, a very good blade! A very tall man! A very good whore!" Why, is not this a lamentable thing, grandsire, that we should be thus afflicted with these
30   strange flies, these fashion-mongers, these "pardon me's," who stand so much on the new form, that they cannot sit at ease on the old bench? Oh, their bones, their bones!

Enter ROMEO

BENVOLIO
Here comes Romeo, here comes Romeo.

MERCUTIO
Without his roe, like a dried herring. O flesh, flesh, how art
35   thou fishified! Now is he for the numbers that Petrarch flowed in. Laura to his lady was but a kitchen-wench— marry, she had a better love to berhyme her—Dido a dowdy, Cleopatra a gypsy, Helen and Hero hildings and harlots, Thisbe a grey eye or so, but not to the purpose.—
40   Signior Romeo, *bonjour!* There's a French salutation to your French slop. You gave us the counterfeit fairly last night.

takes the proper breaks: one, two, and the third in your heart. He's the butcher who can hit any silk button. A master of duels. He's a gentleman from the finest school of fencing. He knows how to turn any argument into a swordfight. He knows *passado*—the forward thrust—the *punto reverso*—the backhand thrust—and the *hai*—the thrust that goes straight through.

Mercutio lists Italian terms for fencing moves.

BENVOLIO

He knows what?

MERCUTIO

I hate these crazy, affected guys who use foreign phrases and newfangled expressions. I hate their strange manners and their weird accents! I hate it when they say, "By Jesus, this is a very good blade, a very brave man, a very good whore." Isn't this a sad thing, my good man? Why should we put up with these foreign buzzards, these fashionmongers, these guys who say "pardon me," these guys who care so much about manners that they can't kick back on a bench without whining? "Oh, my aching bones!"

ROMEO *enters.*

BENVOLIO

Here comes Romeo, here comes Romeo!

MERCUTIO

He looks skinny, like a dried herring without its eggs, and he hasn't got his girl. O flesh, flesh, you've turned pale and weak like a fish. Now he's ready for Petrarch's poetry. Compared to Romeo's girl, Laura was a kitchen slave. Surely she has a better love to make rhymes for her. Dido was shabbily dressed. Cleopatra was a gypsy girl. Helen and Hero were sluts and harlots. Thisbe might have had a blue eye or two, but that doesn't matter. Signor Romeo, *bonjour*. There's a French greeting that matches your drooping French-style pants. You faked us out pretty good last night.

Mercutio teases Romeo by alluding to the poet Petrarch and six mythical and historical women who inspired love poetry.

ROMEO
　　Good morrow to you both. What counterfeit did I give you?

MERCUTIO
　　The slip, sir, the slip. Can you not conceive?

ROMEO
45　　Pardon, good Mercutio, my business was great, and in such
　　a case as mine a man may strain courtesy.

MERCUTIO
　　That's as much as to say, such a case as yours constrains a
　　man to bow in the hams.

ROMEO
　　Meaning "to curtsy"?

MERCUTIO
　　Thou hast most kindly hit it.

ROMEO
50　　A most courteous exposition.

MERCUTIO
　　Nay, I am the very pink of courtesy.

ROMEO
　　Pink for flower.

MERCUTIO
　　Right.

ROMEO

Good morning to you both. What do you mean I faked you out?

MERCUTIO

You gave us the slip, sir, the slip. Can't you understand what I'm saying?

ROMEO

Excuse me, good Mercutio. I had very important business to take care of. It was so important that I had to forget about courtesy and good manners.

MERCUTIO

Mercutio implies Romeo's business was sexual.

In other words "important business" made you flex your buttocks.

ROMEO

You mean do a curtsy?

MERCUTIO

This is sexual double entedre.

You've hit the target, sir.

ROMEO

That's a very polite and courteous explanation.

MERCUTIO

Yes, I am the pink flower—the master, of courtesy and manners.

ROMEO

"Pink flower" suggests the female genitalia.

The pink flower.

MERCUTIO

Right.

ROMEO
Why, then is my pump well flowered.

MERCUTIO
55   Sure wit, follow me this jest now till thou hast worn out thy pump, that when the single sole of it is worn, the jest may remain, after the wearing solely singular.

ROMEO
O single-soled jest, solely singular for the singleness.

MERCUTIO
Come between us, good Benvolio. My wits faints.

ROMEO
60   Switch and spurs, switch and spurs, or I'll cry a match.

MERCUTIO
Nay, if our wits run the wild-goose chase, I am done, for thou hast more of the wild-goose in one of thy wits than, I am sure, I have in my whole five. Was I with you there for the goose?

ROMEO
65   Thou wast never with me for anything when thou wast not there for the goose.

MERCUTIO
I will bite thee by the ear for that jest.

ROMEO
Nay, good goose, bite not.

MERCUTIO
Thy wit is a very bitter sweeting. It is a most sharp sauce.

ROMEO
70   And is it not well served into a sweet goose?

MERCUTIO
Oh, here's a wit of cheveril, that stretches from an inch narrow to an ell broad!

ROMEO

Romeo plays along: pump= shoe and penis.

Well, then my pump is well decorated with flowers.

MERCUTIO

Alright my witty friend, this joke has worn out your pump. Its thin skin is all worn out. The joke is all you have left.

ROMEO

This is a bad joke. It's all silliness.

MERCUTIO

Come break this up, Benvolio. I'm losing this duel of wits.

ROMEO

Keep going, keep going, or I'll declare myself the winner.

MERCUTIO

Now, if our jokes go on a wild-goose chase, I'm finished. You have more wild goose in one of your jokes than I have in five of mine. Was I even close to you in the chase for the goose?

ROMEO

Romeo implies that Mercutio is only good for jokes.

You were never with me for anything if you weren't there for the goose.

MERCUTIO

I'll bite you on the ear for that joke.

ROMEO

No, good goose, don't bite me.

MERCUTIO

Your joke is a very bitter apple. Your humor is a spicy sauce.

ROMEO

Then isn't it just the right dish for a sweet goose?

MERCUTIO

Oh, that's a joke made out of leather that spreads itself thin, from the width of an inch to as fat as a yard.

ROMEO
I stretch it out for that word "broad," which, added to the goose, proves thee far and wide a broad goose.

MERCUTIO
75 Why, is not this better now than groaning for love? Now art thou sociable. Now art thou Romeo. Now art thou what thou art—by art as well as by nature, for this driveling love is like a great natural that runs lolling up and down to hide his bauble in a hole.

BENVOLIO
80 Stop there, stop there.

MERCUTIO
Thou desirest me to stop in my tale against the hair.

BENVOLIO
Thou wouldst else have made thy tale large.

MERCUTIO
Oh, thou art deceived. I would have made it short, for I was come to the whole depth of my tale, and meant, indeed, to
85 occupy the argument no longer.

Enter NURSE *and her man* PETER

ROMEO
Here's goodly gear.

BENVOLIO
A sail, a sail!

MERCUTIO
Two, two—a shirt and a smock.

NURSE
Peter!

ROMEO

I stretch my joke for that word "fat." If you add that word to the word "goose," it shows that you are a fat goose.

MERCUTIO

Why, isn't all this joking better than groaning about love? Now you're sociable. Now you're Romeo. Now you are what you've learned to be and what you are naturally. This love of yours was like a blithering idiot who runs up and down looking for a hole to hide his toy in.

Toy = a double entendre for penis

BENVOLIO

Stop there, stop there.

MERCUTIO

Tale = a double entendre for penis

You want me to stop my tale before I'm done.

BENVOLIO

Otherwise your tale would have gotten too long.

MERCUTIO

Oh, you're wrong. I would have made it short. I had come to the deepest part of my tale, and I planned to say nothing more on the topic.

The NURSE *enters with her servant,* PETER.

ROMEO

Here's something good.

BENVOLIO

Benvolio makes the cry of a sailor who spots another ship on the horizon because the nurse is fat and silly-looking.

A sail, a sail!

MERCUTIO

There's two—a man and a woman.

NURSE

Peter!

PETER

90   Anon!

NURSE

My fan, Peter.

MERCUTIO

Good, Peter, to hide her face, for her fan's the fairer face.

NURSE

God ye good morrow, gentlemen.

MERCUTIO

God ye good e'en, fair gentlewoman.

NURSE

95   Is it good e'en?

MERCUTIO

'Tis no less, I tell you, for the bawdy hand of the dial is now
upon the prick of noon.

NURSE

Out upon you! What a man are you?

MERCUTIO

One, gentlewoman, that God hath made, himself to mar.

NURSE

100   By my troth, it is well said. "For himself to mar," quoth he?
Gentlemen, can any of you tell me where I may find the
young Romeo?

ROMEO

I can tell you, but young Romeo will be older when you
have found him than he was when you sought him. I am the
105   youngest of that name, for fault of a worse.

NURSE

You say well.

MERCUTIO

Yea, is the worst well? Very well took, i' faith, wisely, wisely.

PETER

I'm at your service.

NURSE

Give me my fan, Peter.

MERCUTIO

Good Peter, give her her fan to hide her face. Her fan is prettier than her face.

NURSE

Good morning, gentlemen.

MERCUTIO

Good afternoon, fair lady.

NURSE

Is it now afternoon?

MERCUTIO

It's not earlier than that, I tell you. The lusty hand of the clock is now pricking noon.

Again, Mercutio's language is full of offensive sexual innuendo.

NURSE

Get out of here! What kind of man are you?

MERCUTIO

I'm a man, my lady, that God has made for himself to ruin.

NURSE

I swear, you speak the truth. "For himself to ruin," he says. Gentlemen, can any of you tell me where I can find young Romeo?

ROMEO

I can tell you, but young Romeo will be older when you find him than he was when you started looking for him. I am the youngest man by that name, because there is no one younger, or worse.

NURSE

You speak well.

MERCUTIO

Is the worst well? Very well taken, I believe, very wise.

NURSE
If you be he, sir, I desire some confidence with you.

BENVOLIO
She will indite him to some supper.

MERCUTIO
110   A bawd, a bawd, a bawd! So ho!

ROMEO
What hast thou found?

MERCUTIO
No hare, sir, unless a hare, sir, in a Lenten pie—that is,
something stale and hoar ere it be spent.

(sings)

          An old hare hoar,
115   *And an old hare hoar,*
              Is very good meat in Lent.
          But a hare that is hoar
          Is too much for a score
              When it hoars ere it be spent.

(speaks)
120   Romeo, will you come to your father's? We'll to dinner,
thither.

ROMEO
I will follow you.

MERCUTIO
Farewell, ancient lady. Farewell, lady, lady, lady.

                  Exeunt MERCUTIO *and* BENVOLIO

NURSE

The nurse means "conference," not confidence. This is a joke called a malapropism, where the right word is replaced by a similar-sounding word with a completely different meaning.

(to ROMEO*)* If you're the Romeo I'm looking for, sir, I would like to have a confidence with you.

BENVOLIO

Benvolio makes fun of the Nurse by saying "indite" instead of "invite."

She will indite him to some dinner party.

MERCUTIO

A pimp! A pimp! A pimp! I've found it out.

ROMEO

What have you found out?

MERCUTIO

She's not a prostitute unless she's using her ugliness to hide her promiscuity.

(he walks by them and sings)
> Old rabbit meat is good to eat,
> If you can't get anything else.
> But if it's so old,
> That it goes bad before you eat it,
> Then it was a waste of money.

(speaking)
Romeo, are you going to your father's for lunch? Let's go there.

ROMEO

I'll follow after you.

MERCUTIO

Mercutio mockingly sings a romantic song to the Nurse.

Goodbye, old lady. Goodbye, lady, lady, lady.

BENVOLIO *and* MERCUTIO *exit.*

NURSE

I pray you, sir, what saucy merchant was this that was so
full of his ropery?

ROMEO

A gentleman, Nurse, that loves to hear himself talk, and
will speak more in a minute than he will stand to in a month.

NURSE

An he speak any thing against me, I'll take him down, an he
were lustier than he is, and twenty such Jacks. And if I
cannot, I'll find those that shall. Scurvy knave! I am none of
his flirt-gills. I am none of his skains-mates. *(to* PETER*)* And
thou must stand by, too, and suffer every knave to use me at
his pleasure?

PETER

I saw no man use you at his pleasure. If I had, my weapon
should quickly have been out, I warrant you. I dare draw as
soon as another man if I see occasion in a good quarrel and
the law on my side.

NURSE

Now, afore God, I am so vexed that every part about me
quivers. Scurvy knave! *(to* ROMEO*)* Pray you, sir, a word.
And as I told you, my young lady bid me inquire you out.
What she bade me say, I will keep to myself. But first let me
tell ye, if ye should lead her into a fool's paradise, as they
say, it were a very gross kind of behavior, as they say. For the
gentlewoman is young, and therefore, if you should deal
double with her, truly it were an ill thing to be offered to any
gentlewoman, and very weak dealing.

ROMEO

Nurse, commend me to thy lady and mistress. I protest
unto thee—

NURSE

Please tell me, sir, who was that foulmouthed punk who was so full of crude jokes?

ROMEO

Nurse, he's a man who likes to hear the sound of his own voice. He says more in one minute than he does in a whole month.

NURSE

If he says anything against me, I'll humble him, even if he were stronger than he is—and twenty punks like him. If I can't do it myself, I'll find someone who can. That dirty rat! I'm not one of his sluts. I'm not one of his punk friends who carries a knife. *(to* PETER*)* And you just stand there letting every jerk make fun of me for kicks.

PETER

I didn't see anybody use you for kicks. If I had seen something like that, I would have quickly pulled out my weapon. Believe me, I'll draw my sword as quick as any other man if I see a fight starting and the law is on my side.

NURSE

Now, I swear, I'm so angry that I'm shaking all over. That rotten scoundrel! *(to* ROMEO*)* Now, please, may I have a word with you, sir? My young mistress asked me to find you. What she asked me to say I'll keep to myself. But let me tell you this first. If you lead her into a fool's paradise, as the saying goes, it would be an outrageous crime because the girl is so young. And if you try to trick her, it would be an evil thing to do to any woman and very poor behavior.

ROMEO

Nurse, give my regards to to your lady. I swear to you—

ACT TWO

NURSE
Good heart, and i' faith, I will tell her as much. Lord, Lord,
150   she will be a joyful woman.

ROMEO
What wilt thou tell her, Nurse? Thou dost not mark me.

NURSE
I will tell her, sir, that you do protest, which, as I take it, is
a gentlemanlike offer.

ROMEO
Bid her devise
155   Some means to come to shrift this afternoon.
And there she shall at Friar Lawrence' cell
Be shrived and married. *(gives her coins)* Here is for thy
        pains.

NURSE
No, truly, sir. Not a penny.

ROMEO
Go to. I say you shall.

NURSE
160   *(takes the money)* This afternoon, sir? Well, she shall be there.

ROMEO
And stay, good Nurse. Behind the abbey wall
Within this hour my man shall be with thee
And bring thee cords made like a tackled stair,
Which to the high top-gallant of my joy
165   Must be my convoy in the secret night.
Farewell. Be trusty, and I'll quit thy pains.
Farewell. Commend me to thy mistress.

NURSE
Now God in heaven bless thee! Hark you, sir.

ROMEO
What sayst thou, my dear Nurse?

NURSE

You have a good heart, and believe me, I'll tell her that. Lord, Lord, she'll be a happy woman.

ROMEO

What are you going to tell her, Nurse? You're not paying attention to me.

NURSE

Sir, I'll tell her that you protest to her, which I think is the gentlemanly thing to do.

Here the Nurse makes another malapropism, saying "protest" when she means "propose."

ROMEO

Tell her to devise a plan to get out of her house and come to confession at the abbey this afternoon. At Friar Lawrence's cell she can make confession and be married. *(giving her coins)* Here is a reward for your efforts.

NURSE

No, really, I won't take a penny.

ROMEO

Go on, I insist you take it.

NURSE

(taking the money) This afternoon, sir? She'll be there.

ROMEO

Wait good Nurse. Within an hour, one of my men will come to you behind the abbey wall and give you a rope ladder. I'll use the rope ladder to climb over the walls at night. Then I'll meet Juliet joyfully and in secret. Goodbye. Be honest and helpful, and I'll repay you for your efforts. Goodbye. Sing my praises to your mistress.

NURSE

May God in heaven bless you. Now please listen, sir.

ROMEO

What do you have to say, my dear Nurse?

NURSE

170   Is your man secret? Did you ne'er hear say,
       "Two may keep counsel, putting one away"?

ROMEO

       Warrant thee, my man's as true as steel.

NURSE

       Well, sir, my mistress is the sweetest lady.—Lord, Lord!
       when 'twas a little prating thing.—Oh, there is a nobleman
175   in town, one Paris, that would fain lay knife aboard, but she,
       good soul, had as lief see a toad, a very toad, as see him. I
       anger her sometimes and tell her that Paris is the properer
       man. But, I'll warrant you, when I say so, she looks as pale
       as any clout in the versal world. Doth not *rosemary* and
180   *Romeo* begin both with a letter?

ROMEO

       Ay, Nurse, what of that? Both with an *R*.

NURSE

       Ah, mocker, that's the dog's name. *R* is for the—No, I know
       it begins with some other letter, and she hath the prettiest
       sententious of it, of you and rosemary, that it would do you
185   good to hear it.

ROMEO

       Commend me to thy lady.

NURSE

       Ay, a thousand times.—Peter!

PETER

       Anon!

NURSE

       Before and apace.

                                              Exeunt

NURSE

Can your man keep a secret? Haven't you ever heard the saying, "Two can conspire to put one away"?

ROMEO

I assure you, my man is as true as steel.

NURSE

Well, sir, my mistress is the sweetest lady. Lord, Lord, when she was a little baby—Oh, there is one nobleman in the city, a guy named Paris, who would be happy to claim her as his own. Juliet would rather look at a toad than at him. I make her angry sometimes by saying that Paris is more handsome than you are. But when I say so, I swear she turns white as a sheet. Don't "rosemary" and "Romeo" begin with the same letter?

Rosemary was a token of remembrance between lovers and for the dead.

ROMEO

Yes, Nurse, what about that? They both begin with the letter "R."

NURSE

Ah, you jokester—that's the dog's name. "R" is for the—no, I know it begins with another letter. She says the most beautiful things about you and rosemary. It would be good for you to hear the things she says.

ROMEO

Give my compliments to your lady.

NURSE

Yes, a thousand times. Peter!

PETER

I'm ready.

NURSE

(giving PETER *her fan)* Go ahead. Go quickly.

They all exit.

ACT TWO, Scene 5

Enter JULIET

JULIET

The clock struck nine when I did send the Nurse.
In half an hour she promised to return.
Perchance she cannot meet him. That's not so.
Oh, she is lame! Love's heralds should be thoughts,
5   Which ten times faster glide than the sun's beams,
Driving back shadows over louring hills.
Therefore do nimble-pinioned doves draw love
And therefore hath the wind-swift Cupid wings.
Now is the sun upon the highmost hill
10   Of this day's journey, and from nine till twelve
Is three long hours, yet she is not come.
Had she affections and warm youthful blood,
She would be as swift in motion as a ball.
My words would bandy her to my sweet love,
15   And his to me.
But old folks, many feign as they were dead,
Unwieldy, slow, heavy, and pale as lead.

Enter NURSE *and* PETER

O God, she comes.—O honey Nurse, what news?
Hast thou met with him? Send thy man away.

NURSE

20   Peter, stay at the gate.

Exit PETER

JULIET

Now, good sweet Nurse— O Lord, why look'st thou sad?
Though news be sad, yet tell them merrily.
If good, thou shamest the music of sweet news
By playing it to me with so sour a face.

ACT TWO, Scene 5

JULIET *enters.*

JULIET

I sent the Nurse at nine o'clock. Maybe she can't find him. That can't be. Oh, she's slow! Love's messengers should be thoughts, which fly ten times faster than sunbeams. They should be strong enough to push shadows over the dark hills. That's the way doves carry Venus so fast, and that's why Cupid has wings that let him fly as fast as the wind. Now it's noon. That's three hours since nine o'clock, but she hasn't come back. If she was young and passionate, she'd move as fast as a ball. My words would bounce her to my sweet love, and his words would bounce her back to me. But a lot of old people act like they're already dead—sluggish, slow, fat, and colorless, like lead.

The NURSE *and* PETER *enter.*

Oh my God, here she comes! Oh sweet Nurse, what news do you bring? Have you spoken to him? Send your man away.

NURSE

Peter, wait for me at the gate.

PETER *exits.*

JULIET

Now, good sweet Nurse—Oh Lord, why do you look so sad? Even if the news is sad, tell me with a smile on your face. If the news is good, you're ruining the sweet news by playing a trick with a sour face like that.

NURSE

25   I am aweary. Give me leave awhile.
         Fie, how my bones ache! What a jaunt have I!

JULIET

         I would thou hadst my bones and I thy news.
         Nay, come, I pray thee, speak. Good, good Nurse, speak.

NURSE

         Jesu, what haste! Can you not stay awhile?
30   Do you not see that I am out of breath?

JULIET

         How art thou out of breath when thou hast breath
         To say to me that thou art out of breath?
         The excuse that thou dost make in this delay
         Is longer than the tale thou dost excuse.
35   Is thy news good, or bad? Answer to that.
         Say either, and I'll stay the circumstance.
         Let me be satisfied. Is 't good or bad?

NURSE

         Well, you have made a simple choice. You know not how to
         choose a man. Romeo! No, not he, though his face be better
40   than any man's, yet his leg excels all men's, and for a hand
         and a foot and a body, though they be not to be talked on, yet
         they are past compare. He is not the flower of courtesy, but,
         I'll warrant him, as gentle as a lamb. Go thy ways, wench.
         Serve God. What, have you dined at home?

JULIET

45   No, no. But all this did I know before.
         What says he of our marriage? What of that?

NURSE

         Lord, how my head aches! What a head have I!
         It beats as it would fall in twenty pieces.
         My back a' t' other side. Ah, my back, my back!

NURSE

I am tired. Leave me alone for a minute. Oh my, my bones ache so much. I've been running all over the place.

JULIET

I wish you had my bones, and I had your news. Come on now, I beg you, speak, good Nurse, speak.

NURSE

Sweet Jesus, you're in such a hurry! Can't you wait for a moment? Don't you see that I'm out of breath?

JULIET

How can you be out of breath when you have enough breath to tell me that you're out of breath? The excuse you make to delay the news is longer than the news itself. Is the news good or bad? Answer that question. Tell me if it's good or bad, and I'll wait for the details. Tell me so I can be satisfied. Is it good or bad?

NURSE

Well, you have made a foolish choice. You don't know how to pick a man. Romeo? No, not him, though his face is more handsome than any man's, and his legs are prettier, and as for his hands and feet and body, they're not much to speak of, and yet they're beyond compare. He's not the most polite man in the world, but, believe me, he's gentle as a lamb. Well, do what you want. Be good. Have you had lunch yet?

JULIET

No, I haven't had lunch. Everything you told me I already knew. What does he say about our marriage? What about that?

NURSE

Lord, what a headache I've got! My head is pounding. It feels like it'll break into twenty pieces. My back aches too—(JULIET *rubs her back*) Ooh, on the other

50   Beshrew your heart for sending me about,
        To catch my death with jaunting up and down!

JULIET
        I' faith, I am sorry that thou art not well.
        Sweet, sweet, sweet Nurse, tell me, what says my love?

NURSE
        Your love says, like an honest gentleman, and a
55   courteous, and a kind, and a handsome, and, I
        warrant, a virtuous—Where is your mother?

JULIET
        Where is my mother? Why, she is within.
        Where should she be? How oddly thou repliest!
        "Your love says, like an honest gentleman,
60   'Where is your mother?'"

NURSE
                        O God's lady dear,
        Are you so hot? Marry, come up, I trow.
        Is this the poultice for my aching bones?
        Henceforward do your messages yourself.

JULIET
        Here's such a coil. Come, what says Romeo?

NURSE
65   Have you got leave to go to shrift today?

JULIET
        I have.

NURSE
        Then hie you hence to Friar Lawrence's cell.
        There stays a husband to make you a wife.
        Now comes the wanton blood up in your cheeks.
70   They'll be in scarlet straight at any news.
        Hie you to church. I must another way
        To fetch a ladder, by the which your love
        Must climb a bird's nest soon when it is dark.

side—ah, my poor aching back! Curse your heart for sending me running all over town. I could get sick and die.

JULIET

Believe me, I'm sorry you're in pain. Sweet, sweet, sweet Nurse, tell me, what did my love Romeo say?

NURSE

Your love says, like an honorable gentleman, who is courteous, kind, handsome, and, I believe, virtuous— where is your mother?

JULIET

Where is my mother? Why, she's inside. Where else would she be? Your answer is so strange! "Your love says, like an honorable gentleman, 'Where is your mother?'"

NURSE

Oh holy Mary, mother of God! Are you this impatient? Come on, you're being ridiculous! Is this the cure for my aching bones? From now on, take care of your messages yourself.

JULIET

You're making such a fuss. Come on, what did Romeo say?

NURSE

Do you have permission to go out and take confession today?

JULIET

I do.

NURSE

Then hurry up and rush over to Friar Lawrence's cell. There's a husband there who's waiting to make you his wife. Now I see the blood rushing to your cheeks. You blush bright red as soon as you hear any news. Go to the church. I must go by a different path to get a rope ladder. Your love will use it to climb up to your window while it's dark. I do the drudge work for your

I am the drudge and toil in your delight,
75   But you shall bear the burden soon at night.
Go. I'll to dinner. Hie you to the cell.

JULIET
Hie to high fortune! Honest Nurse, farewell.

Exeunt

pleasure. But soon you'll be doing a wife's work all night long. Go. I'll go to lunch. You go to Friar Lawrence's cell.

JULIET

Wish me luck. Thank you, dear Nurse.

They exit.

ACT TWO, Scene 6

Enter FRIAR LAWRENCE *and* ROMEO

FRIAR LAWRENCE
So smile the heavens upon this holy act
That after-hours with sorrow chide us not.

ROMEO
Amen, amen. But come what sorrow can,
It cannot countervail the exchange of joy
5   That one short minute gives me in her sight.
Do thou but close our hands with holy words,
Then love-devouring death do what he dare;
It is enough I may but call her mine.

FRIAR LAWRENCE
These violent delights have violent ends
10   And in their triumph die, like fire and powder,
Which, as they kiss, consume. The sweetest honey
Is loathsome in his own deliciousness
And in the taste confounds the appetite.
Therefore love moderately. Long love doth so.
15   Too swift arrives as tardy as too slow.

Enter JULIET, *somewhat fast, and embraceth* ROMEO

Here comes the lady. Oh, so light a foot
Will ne'er wear out the everlasting flint.
A lover may bestride the gossamers
That idles in the wanton summer air,
20   And yet not fall. So light is vanity.

JULIET
Good even to my ghostly confessor.

FRIAR LAWRENCE
Romeo shall thank thee, daughter, for us both.

ACT TWO, Scene 6

FRIAR LAWRENCE *and* ROMEO *enter.*

FRIAR LAWRENCE
> May the heavens be happy with this holy act of mar-
> riage, so nothing unfortunate happens later to make
> us regret it.

ROMEO
> Amen, amen. But whatever misfortunes occur, they
> can't ruin the joy I feel with one look at her. All you
> have to do is join our hands with holy words, then
> love-destroying death can do whatever it pleases. It's
> enough for me if I can call her mine.

FRIAR LAWRENCE
> These sudden joys have sudden endings. They burn
> up in victory like fire and gunpowder. When they
> meet, as in a kiss, they explode. Too much honey is
> delicious, but it makes you sick to your stomach.
> Therefore, love each other in moderation. That is the
> key to long-lasting love. Too fast is as bad as too slow.

JULIET *enters in a rush and embraces* ROMEO.

> Here comes the lady. Oh, a footstep as light as hers will
> never endure the rocky road of life. Lovers are so light
> they can walk on a spiderweb floating on a summer
> breeze, and yet not fall. That's how flimsy and unreal
> pleasure is.

JULIET
> Good evening, my spiritual confessor.

FRIAR LAWRENCE
> Romeo will thank you, my girl, for both of us.

JULIET
> As much to him, else is his thanks too much.

ROMEO
> Ah, Juliet, if the measure of thy joy
25   Be heaped like mine, and that thy skill be more
> To blazon it, then sweeten with thy breath
> This neighbor air, and let rich music's tongue
> Unfold the imagined happiness that both
> Receive in either by this dear encounter.

JULIET
30   Conceit, more rich in matter than in words,
> Brags of his substance, not of ornament.
> They are but beggars that can count their worth.
> But my true love is grown to such excess
> I cannot sum up sum of half my wealth.

FRIAR LAWRENCE
35   Come, come with me, and we will make short work.
> For, by your leaves, you shall not stay alone
> Till holy church incorporate two in one.

Exeunt

JULIET

I'll give him equal thanks, so we're even.

ROMEO

Ah, Juliet if you're as happy as I am, and you're better with words, tell me about the happiness you imagine we'll have in our marriage.

JULIET

I can imagine more than I can say—I have more on my mind than words. Anyone who can count how much he has is poor. My true love has made me so rich that I can't count even half of my wealth.

FRIAR LAWRENCE

Come, come with me, and we'll do the job quickly. Because if you don't mind, I'm not leaving you two alone until you're united in marriage.

They exit.

ACT THREE

Scene 1

Enter MERCUTIO, BENVOLIO, *Mercutio's* PAGE, *and others*

BENVOLIO
I pray thee, good Mercutio, let's retire.
The day is hot; the Capulets, abroad;
And if we meet we shall not 'scape a brawl,
For now, these hot days, is the mad blood stirring.

MERCUTIO
5   Thou art like one of those fellows that, when he enters the
confines of a tavern, claps me his sword upon the table and
says "God send me no need of thee!" and, by the operation
of the second cup, draws it on the drawer when indeed there
is no need.

BENVOLIO
10   Am I like such a fellow?

MERCUTIO
Come, come, thou art as hot a Jack in thy mood as any in
Italy, and as soon moved to be moody, and as soon moody
to be moved.

BENVOLIO
And what to?

MERCUTIO
15   Nay, an there were two such, we should have none shortly,
for one would kill the other. Thou, why, thou wilt quarrel
with a man that hath a hair more or a hair less in his beard
than thou hast. Thou wilt quarrel with a man for cracking
nuts, having no other reason but because thou hast hazel
20   eyes. What eye but such an eye would spy out such a

ACT THREE

Scene 1

MERCUTIO, *his page, and* BENVOLIO *enter with other men.*

BENVOLIO

I'm begging you, good Mercutio, let's call it a day. It's hot outside, and the Capulets are wandering around. If we bump into them, we'll certainly get into a fight. When it's hot outside, people become angry and hot-blooded.

MERCUTIO

You're like one of those guys who walks into a bar, slams his sword on the table, and then says, "I pray I never have to use you." By the time he orders his second drink, he pulls his sword on the bartender for no reason at all.

BENVOLIO

Am I really like one of those guys?

MERCUTIO

Come on, you can be as angry as any guy in Italy when you're in the mood. When someone does the smallest thing to make you angry, you get angry. And when you're in the mood to get angry, you find something to get angry about.

BENVOLIO

And what about that?

MERCUTIO

If there were two men like you, pretty soon there'd be none because the two of you would kill each other. You would fight with a man if he had one more whisker or one less whisker in his beard than you have in your beard. You'll fight with a man who's cracking nuts just because you have hazelnut-colored eyes. Only you quarrel? Thy head is as full of quarrels as an egg is full of meat, and yet thy head hath been beaten as addle as an egg for quarreling. Thou hast quarreled with a man for coughing in the street because he hath wakened thy dog that hath lain asleep in the sun. Didst thou not fall out with a tailor for wearing his new doublet before Easter? With another, for tying his new shoes with old ribbon? And yet thou wilt tutor me from quarreling!

BENVOLIO
An I were so apt to quarrel as thou art, any man should buy the fee simple of my life for an hour and a quarter.

MERCUTIO
The fee simple? O simple!

Enter TYBALT, PETRUCHIO, *and other* CAPULETS

BENVOLIO
By my head, here comes the Capulets.

MERCUTIO
By my heel, I care not.

TYBALT
Follow me close, for I will speak to them.
Gentlemen, good e'en. A word with one of you.

MERCUTIO
And but one word with one of us? Couple it with something. Make it a word and a blow.

TYBALT
You shall find me apt enough to that, sir, an you will give me occasion.

MERCUTIO
Could you not take some occasion without giving?

TYBALT
Mercutio, thou consort'st with Romeo.

would look for a fight like that. Your head is as full of fights as an egg is full of yolk, but your head has been beaten like scrambled eggs from so much fighting. You started a fight with a man who coughed in the street because he woke up a dog that was sleeping in the sun. Didn't you argue it out with your tailor for wearing one of his new suits before the right season? And with another for tying the new shoes he made with old laces? And yet you're the one who wants to teach me about restraint!

BENVOLIO

If I were in the habit of fighting the way you are, my life insurance rates would be sky high.

MERCUTIO

Your life insurance? That's foolish.

TYBALT, PETRUCHIO, and CAPULETS enter.

BENVOLIO

Oh great, here come the Capulets.

MERCUTIO

Well, well, I don't care.

TYBALT

(to PETRUCCIO and others) Follow me closely, I'll talk to them. *(to the MONTAGUES)* Good afternoon, gentlemen. I'd like to have a word with one of you.

MERCUTIO

You just want one word with one of us? Put it together with something else. Make it a word and a blow.

TYBALT

You'll find me ready enough to do that, sir, if you give me a reason.

MERCUTIO

Can't you find a reason without my giving you one?

TYBALT

Mercutio, you hang out with Romeo.

MERCUTIO
Consort? What, dost thou make us minstrels? An thou
make minstrels of us, look to hear nothing but discords.
Here's my fiddlestick. Here's that shall make you dance.
45   Zounds, "consort"!

BENVOLIO
We talk here in the public haunt of men.
Either withdraw unto some private place,
And reason coldly of your grievances,
Or else depart. Here all eyes gaze on us.

MERCUTIO
50   Men's eyes were made to look and let them gaze.
I will not budge for no man's pleasure, I.

Enter ROMEO

TYBALT
Well, peace be with you, sir. Here comes my man.

MERCUTIO
But I'll be hanged, sir, if he wear your livery.
Marry, go before to field, he'll be your follower.
55   Your worship in that sense may call him "man."

TYBALT
Romeo, the love I bear thee can afford
No better term than this: thou art a villain.

ROMEO
Tybalt, the reason that I have to love thee
Doth much excuse the appertaining rage
60   To such a greeting. Villain am I none.
Therefore, farewell. I see thou know'st me not.

TYBALT
Boy, this shall not excuse the injuries
That thou hast done me. Therefore turn and draw.

MERCUTIO

"Hang out?" Who do you think we are, musicians in a band? If we look like musicians to you, you can expect to hear nothing but noise. *(touching the blade of his sword)* This is my fiddlestick. I'll use it to make you dance. Goddammit—"Hang out!"

BENVOLIO

We're talking here in a public place. Either go some-place private, or talk it over rationally, or else just go away. Out here everybody can see us.

MERCUTIO

Men's eyes were made to see things, so let them watch. I won't move to please anybody.

ROMEO *enters.*

TYBALT

Well, may peace be with you. Here comes my man, the man I'm looking for.

MERCUTIO

He's not your man. Alright, walk out into a field, and he'll chase you. In that sense you can call him your "man."

TYBALT

Romeo, there's only one thing I can call you. You're a villain.

ROMEO

Tybalt, I have a reason to love you that lets me put aside the rage I should feel and excuse that insult. I am no villain. So, goodbye. I can tell that you don't know who I am.

TYBALT

Boy, your words can't excuse the harm you've done to me. So now turn and draw your sword.

ROMEO
I do protest I never injured thee,
65 But love thee better than thou canst devise,
Till thou shalt know the reason of my love.
And so, good Capulet—which name I tender
As dearly as my own—be satisfied.

MERCUTIO
O calm dishonourable, vile submission!
70 *Alla stoccata* carries it away. *(draws his sword)*
Tybalt, you ratcatcher, will you walk?

TYBALT
What wouldst thou have with me?

MERCUTIO
Good King of Cats, nothing but one of your nine lives, that
I mean to make bold withal, and, as you shall use me
75 hereafter, dry-beat the rest of the eight. Will you pluck your
sword out of his pilcher by the ears? Make haste, lest mine
be about your ears ere it be out.

TYBALT
I am for you. *(draws his sword)*

ROMEO
Gentle Mercutio, put thy rapier up.

MERCUTIO
80 Come, sir, your *passado.*

  MERCUTIO *and* **TYBALT** *fight*

ROMEO
(draws his sword) Draw, Benvolio. Beat down their weapons.
Gentlemen, for shame! Forbear this outrage.
Tybalt, Mercutio! The Prince expressly hath
Forbidden bandying in Verona streets.
85 Hold, Tybalt! Good Mercutio!

ROMEO

I disagree. I've never done you harm. I love you more than you can understand until you know the reason why I love you. And so, good Capulet—which is a name I love like my own name—you should be satisfied with what I say.

MERCUTIO

This calm submission is dishonorable and vile. The thrust of a sword will end this surrender. *(draws his sword)* Tybalt, you rat-catcher, will you go fight me?

TYBALT

What do you want from me?

MERCUTIO

Good King of Cats, I want to take one of your nine lives. I'll take one, and, depending on how you treat me after that, I might beat the other eight out of you too. Will you pull your sword out of its sheath? Hurry up, or I'll smack you on the ears with my sword before you have yours drawn.

TYBALT

I'll fight you. *(he draws his sword)*

ROMEO

Noble Mercutio, put your sword away.

MERCUTIO

(to TYBALT*)* Come on, sir, perform your forward thrust, your *passado.*

MERCUTIO *and* TYBALT *fight.*

ROMEO

(drawing his sword) Draw your sword, Benvolio. Let's beat down their weapons. Gentlemen, stop this disgraceful fight. Tybalt, Mercutio, the Prince has banned fighting in the streets of Verona. Stop, Tybalt. Stop, good Mercutio.

ACT THREE

ROMEO *tries to break up the fight*
TYBALT *stabs* MERCUTIO *under* ROMEO'S *arm*

PETRUCHIO
　　Away, Tybalt.
　　　　　Exeunt TYBALT, PETRUCHIO, *and the other* CAPULETS

MERCUTIO
　　I am hurt.
　　A plague o' both your houses! I am sped.
　　Is he gone and hath nothing?
BENVOLIO
　　　　　　　　　　　　What, art thou hurt?
MERCUTIO
90　　Ay, ay, a scratch, a scratch. Marry, 'tis enough.
　　Where is my page?—Go, villain, fetch a surgeon.
　　　　　　　　　　　Exit MERCUTIO'S PAGE

ROMEO
　　Courage, man. The hurt cannot be much.
MERCUTIO
　　No, 'tis not so deep as a well nor so wide as a church-door,
　　but 'tis enough, 'twill serve. Ask for me tomorrow, and you
95　　shall find me a grave man. I am peppered, I warrant, for this
　　world. A plague o' both your houses! Zounds, a dog, a rat,
　　a mouse, a cat to scratch a man to death! A braggart, a rogue,
　　a villain that fights by the book of arithmetic! Why the devil
　　came you between us? I was hurt under your arm.

ROMEO
100　　I thought all for the best.

ROMEO *tries to break up the fight.* TYBALT *reaches under* ROMEO's *arm and stabs* MERCUTIO.

PETRUCHIO

Let's get away, Tybalt.

TYBALT, PETRUCHIO, *and the other* CAPULETS *exit.*

MERCUTIO

I've been hurt. May a plague curse both your families. I'm finished. Did he get away clean?

BENVOLIO

What, are you hurt?

MERCUTIO

Yes, yes. It's a scratch, just a scratch. But it's enough. Where is my page? Go, boy. Get me a doctor.

MERCUTIO'S PAGE *exits.*

ROMEO

Have courage, man. The wound can't be that bad.

MERCUTIO

No, it's not as deep as a well, or as wide as a church door, but it's enough. It'll do the job. Ask for me tomorrow, and you'll find me in a grave. I'm done for in this world, I believe. May a plague strike both your houses. Goddammit! I can't believe that dog, that rat, that mouse, that cat could scratch me to death! That braggart, punk villain who fights like he learned swordsmanship from a manual! Why the hell did you come in between us? He struck me from under your arm.

ROMEO

I thought it was the right thing to do.

ACT THREE

MERCUTIO
Help me into some house, Benvolio,
Or I shall faint. A plague o' both your houses!
They have made worms' meat of me. I have it,
And soundly too. Your houses!

Exeunt MERCUTIO *and* BENVOLIO

ROMEO
105   This gentleman, the Prince's near ally,
My very friend, hath got his mortal hurt
In my behalf. My reputation stained
With Tybalt's slander.—Tybalt, that an hour
Hath been my kinsman! O sweet Juliet,
110   Thy beauty hath made me effeminate
And in my temper softened valor's steel!

Enter BENVOLIO

BENVOLIO
O Romeo, Romeo, brave Mercutio is dead!
That gallant spirit hath aspired the clouds,
Which too untimely here did scorn the earth.

ROMEO
115   This day's black fate on more days doth depend.
This but begins the woe others must end.

Enter TYBALT

BENVOLIO
Here comes the furious Tybalt back again.

ROMEO
Alive in triumph—and Mercutio slain!
Away to heaven, respective lenity,
120   And fire-eyed fury be my conduct now.
Now, Tybalt, take the "villain" back again

MERCUTIO

Take me inside some house, Benvolio, or I'll pass out. May a plague strike both your families! They've turned me into food for worms. I'm done for. Curse your families!

MERCUTIO and BENVOLIO exit.

ROMEO

This gentleman Mercutio, a close relative of the Prince and my dear friend, was killed while defending me from Tybalt's slander—Tybalt, who had been my cousin for a whole hour! Oh, sweet Juliet, your beauty has made me weak like a woman, and you have softened my bravery, which before was as hard as steel.

BENVOLIO enters.

BENVOLIO

Oh Romeo, Romeo, brave Mercutio is dead! His brave spirit has floated up to heaven, but it was too early for him to leave life on earth.

ROMEO

The future will be affected by today's terrible events. Today is the start of a terror that will end in the days ahead.

TYBALT enters.

BENVOLIO

Here comes the furious Tybalt back again.

ROMEO

He's alive and victorious, and Mercutio's dead? Enough with mercy and consideration. It's time for rage to guide my actions. Now, Tybalt, you can call me "villain" the way you did before. Mercutio's soul is

ACT THREE

That late thou gavest me, for Mercutio's soul
Is but a little way above our heads,
Staying for thine to keep him company.
125   Either thou or I, or both, must go with him.

TYBALT
Thou, wretched boy, that didst consort him here
Shalt with him hence.

ROMEO
                  This shall determine that.

They fight. **TYBALT** *falls*

BENVOLIO
Romeo, away, be gone!
The citizens are up, and Tybalt slain.
130   Stand not amazed. The Prince will doom thee death
If thou art taken. Hence, be gone, away!

ROMEO
Oh, I am fortune's fool!

BENVOLIO
                Why dost thou stay?

                      Exit **ROMEO**

Enter **CITIZENS OF THE WATCH**

CITIZEN OF THE WATCH
Which way ran he that killed Mercutio?
Tybalt, that murderer, which way ran he?

BENVOLIO
135   There lies that Tybalt.

CITIZEN OF THE WATCH
(to **TYBALT***)* Up, sir, go with me.
I charge thee in the Prince's name, obey.

Enter **PRINCE, MONTAGUE, CAPULET, LADY MONTAGUE,
LADY CAPULET,** *and* **OTHERS**

floating right above our heads. He's waiting for you to keep him company on the way up to heaven. Either you, or I, or both of us have to go with him.

TYBALT

Wretched boy, you hung out with him here, and you're going to go to heaven with him.

ROMEO

This fight will decide who dies.

They fight. TYBALT *falls and dies.*

BENVOLIO

Romeo, get out of here. The citizens are around, and Tybalt is dead. Don't stand there shocked. The Prince will give you the death penalty if you get caught. So get out of here!

ROMEO

Oh, I have awful luck.

BENVOLIO

Why are you waiting?

ROMEO *exits.*

The CITIZENS OF THE WATCH *enter.*

CITIZEN OF THE WATCH

The man who killed Mercutio, which way did he go? Tybalt, that murderer, which way did he run?

BENVOLIO

Tybalt is lying over there.

CITIZEN OF THE WATCH

(to TYBALT*)* Get up, sir, and come with me. I command you, by the authority of the Prince, to obey me.

The PRINCE *enters with* MONTAGUE, CAPULET, LADY MONTAGUE, LADY CAPULET, *and* OTHERS.

PRINCE
Where are the vile beginners of this fray?

BENVOLIO
O noble prince, I can discover all
140 The unlucky manage of this fatal brawl.
There lies the man, slain by young Romeo,
That slew thy kinsman, brave Mercutio.

LADY CAPULET
Tybalt, my cousin! O my brother's child!
O Prince! O cousin! Husband! Oh, the blood is spilled
145 Of my dear kinsman! Prince, as thou art true,
For blood of ours shed blood of Montague.
O cousin, cousin!

PRINCE
                              Benvolio, who began this bloody fray?

BENVOLIO
Tybalt here slain, whom Romeo's hand did slay.
Romeo, that spoke him fair, bade him bethink
150 How nice the quarrel was and urged withal
Your high displeasure. All this uttered
With gentle breath, calm look, knees humbly bowed,
Could not take truce with the unruly spleen
Of Tybalt deaf to peace, but that he tilts
155 With piercing steel at bold Mercutio's breast,
Who, all as hot, turns deadly point to point,
And, with a martial scorn, with one hand beats
Cold death aside and with the other sends
It back to Tybalt, whose dexterity,
160 Retorts it. Romeo, he cries aloud,
"Hold, friends! Friends, part!" and, swifter than his
                    tongue,
His agile arm beats down their fatal points,
And 'twixt them rushes—underneath whose arm
An envious thrust from Tybalt hit the life
165 Of stout Mercutio, and then Tybalt fled.

PRINCE

Where are the evil men who started this fight?

BENVOLIO

Oh, noble prince, I can tell you everything about the unfortunate circumstances of this deadly fight. Over there Tybalt is lying dead. He killed your relative, brave Mercutio, and then young Romeo killed him.

LADY CAPULET

Tybalt was my nephew! He was my brother's son! Oh Prince, oh nephew, oh husband! Oh, my nephew is dead! Oh Prince, as you are a man of honor, take revenge for this murder by killing someone from the Montague family. Oh cousin, cousin!

PRINCE

Benvolio, who started this fight?

BENVOLIO

Tybalt started the fight before he was killed by Romeo. Romeo spoke to Tybalt politely and told him how silly this argument was. He mentioned that you would not approve of the fight. He said all of this gently and calmly, kneeling down out of respect. But he could not make peace with Tybalt, who was in an angry mood and wouldn't listen to talk about peace. Tybalt and Mercutio began to fight each other fiercely, lunging at one another and dodging each other's blows. Romeo cried out, "Stop, my friends. Break it up." Then he jumped in between them and forced them to put their swords down. But Tybalt reached under Romeo's arm and thrust his sword into brave Mercutio. Then Tybalt fled the scene.

ACT THREE

But by and by comes back to Romeo,
Who had but newly entertained revenge,
And to 't they go like lightning, for ere I
Could draw to part them was stout Tybalt slain.
170 And, as he fell, did Romeo turn and fly.
This is the truth, or let Benvolio die.

LADY CAPULET
He is a kinsman to the Montague.
Affection makes him false. He speaks not true.
Some twenty of them fought in this black strife,
175 And all those twenty could but kill one life.
I beg for justice, which thou, Prince, must give.
Romeo slew Tybalt. Romeo must not live.

PRINCE
Romeo slew him; he slew Mercutio.
Who now the price of his dear blood doth owe?

MONTAGUE
180 Not Romeo, Prince, he was Mercutio's friend.
His fault concludes but what the law should end,
The life of Tybalt.

PRINCE
                    And for that offence
Immediately we do exile him hence.
I have an interest in your hearts' proceeding.
185 My blood for your rude brawls doth lie a-bleeding.
But I'll amerce you with so strong a fine
That you shall all repent the loss of mine.
I will be deaf to pleading and excuses.
Nor tears nor prayers shall purchase out abuses,
190 Therefore use none. Let Romeo hence in haste,
Else, when he's found, that hour is his last.
Bear hence this body and attend our will.
Mercy but murders, pardoning those that kill.

Exeunt

But pretty soon he came back to meet Romeo, who was overcome with the desire for revenge. As quick as lightning, they started fighting. Before I could break up the fight, Tybalt was killed. Romeo ran away when Tybalt fell dead. I'm telling you the truth, I swear on my life.

LADY CAPULET

Benvolio is part of the Montague family. His loyalties to the Montagues make him tell lies. He's not telling the truth. There were twenty Montagues fighting in this awful riot, and together those twenty could only kill one man. I demand justice. You, Prince, are the man who can give me justice. Romeo killed Tybalt. Romeo must die.

PRINCE

Romeo killed Tybalt. Tybalt killed Mercutio. Who should now pay the price for Mercutio's life?

MONTAGUE

Not Romeo, Prince. He was Mercutio's friend. His crime did justice's job by taking Tybalt's life.

PRINCE

And for that crime, Romeo is hereby exiled from Verona. I'm involved in your rivalry. Mercutio was my relative, and he lies dead because of your bloody feud. I'll punish you so harshly that you'll regret causing me this loss. I won't listen to your pleas or excuses. You can't get out of trouble by praying or crying, so don't bother. Tell Romeo to leave the city immediately, or else, if he is found, he will be killed. Take away this body, and do what I say. Showing mercy by pardoning killers only causes more murders.

They exit.

ACT THREE, Scene 2

Enter JULIET alone

JULIET

    Gallop apace, you fiery-footed steeds,
    Toward Phoebus' lodging. Such a wagoner
    As Phaeton would whip you to the west
    And bring in cloudy night immediately.
5   Spread thy close curtain, love-performing night,
    That runaways' eyes may wink, and Romeo
    Leap to these arms, untalked of and unseen.
    Lovers can see to do their amorous rites
    By their own beauties, or, if love be blind,
10   It best agrees with night. Come, civil night,
    Thou sober-suited matron, all in black,
    And learn me how to lose a winning match
    Played for a pair of stainless maidenhoods.
    Hood my unmanned blood bating in my cheeks,
15   With thy black mantle, till strange love, grow bold,
    Think true love acted simple modesty.
    Come, night. Come, Romeo. Come, thou day in night,
    For thou wilt lie upon the wings of night
    Whiter than new snow upon a raven's back.
20   Come, gentle night, come, loving, black-browed night,
    Give me my Romeo. And when I shall die,
    Take him and cut him out in little stars,
    And he will make the face of heaven so fine
    That all the world will be in love with night
25   And pay no worship to the garish sun.
    Oh, I have bought the mansion of a love,
    But not possessed it, and though I am sold,
    Not yet enjoyed. So tedious is this day
    As is the night before some festival
30   To an impatient child that hath new robes
    And may not wear them.

ACT THREE, Scene 2

JULIET enters alone.

I wish the sun would hurry up and set and night would come immediately. When the night comes and everyone goes to sleep, Romeo will leap into my arms, and no one will know. Beauty makes it possible for lovers to see how to make love in the dark. Or else love is blind, and its best time is the night. I wish night would come, like a widow dressed in black, so I can learn how to submit to my husband and lose my virginity. Let the blood rushing to my cheeks be calmed. In the darkness, let me, a shy virgin, learn the strange act of sex so that it seems innocent, modest, and true. Come, night. Come, Romeo. You're like a day that comes during the night. You're whiter than snow on the black wings of a raven. Come, gentle night. Come, loving, dark night. Give me my Romeo. And when I die, turn him into stars and form a constellation in his image. His face will make the heavens so beautiful that the world will fall in love with the night and forget about the garish sun. Oh, I have bought love's mansion, but I haven't moved in yet. I belong to Romeo now, but he hasn't taken possession of me yet. This day is so boring that I feel like a child on the night before a holiday, waiting to put on my fancy new clothes.

Enter NURSE *with cords*

                         Oh, here comes my Nurse,
And she brings news, and every tongue that speaks
But Romeo's name speaks heavenly eloquence.—
Now, Nurse, what news? What hast thou there? The cords
35   That Romeo bid thee fetch?

NURSE
Ay, ay, the cords.

JULIET
Ay me, what news? Why dost thou wring thy hands?

NURSE
Ah, welladay! He's dead, he's dead, he's dead!
We are undone, lady, we are undone!
40   Alack the day! He's gone, he's killed, he's dead!

JULIET
Can heaven be so envious?

NURSE
                         Romeo can,
Though heaven cannot. O Romeo, Romeo!
Who ever would have thought it? Romeo!

JULIET
What devil art thou that dost torment me thus?
45   This torture should be roared in dismal hell.
Hath Romeo slain himself? Say thou but "ay,"
And that bare vowel *I* shall poison more
Than the death-darting eye of cockatrice.
I am not I if there be such an *I*,
50   Or those eyes shut that makes thee answer "ay."
If he be slain, say "ay," or if not, "no."
Brief sounds determine of my weal or woe.

NURSE
I saw the wound, I saw it with mine eyes—
God save the mark!—here on his manly breast.
55   A piteous corse, a bloody piteous corse.

The NURSE *enters with the rope ladder in her pouch.*

Oh, here comes my Nurse, and she brings news. Every voice that mentions Romeo's name sounds beautiful. Now, Nurse, what's the news? Is that the rope ladder Romeo told you to pick up?

NURSE

Yes, yes, this is the rope ladder.

JULIET

Oh my, what's the news? Why do you look so upset?

NURSE

Oh, it's a sad day! He's dead. He's dead. He's dead! We're ruined, lady, we're ruined! What an awful day! He's gone. He's been killed. He's dead!

JULIET

Can God be so jealous and hateful?

NURSE

Romeo is hateful, even though God isn't. Oh, Romeo, Romeo, who ever would have thought it would be Romeo?

JULIET

What kind of devil are you to torture me like this? This is as bad as the tortures of hell. Has Romeo killed himself? Just say "Yes" and I will turn more poisonous than the snake with the evil eye. I will no longer be myself if you tell me Romeo killed himself. If he's been killed, say "Yes." If not, say "No." These short words will determine my joy or my pain.

NURSE

I saw the wound. I saw it with my own eyes. God bless that wound, here on his manly chest. A pitiful corpse, a bloody, pitiful corpse.

Pale, pale as ashes, all bedaubed in blood,
All in gore blood. I swoonèd at the sight.

JULIET
O, break, my hear, poor bankrupt, break at once!
To prison, eyes, ne'er look on liberty.
60 Vile earth, to earth resign. End motion here,
And thou and Romeo press one heavy bier.

NURSE
O Tybalt, Tybalt, the best friend I had!
O courteous Tybalt! Honest gentleman!
That ever I should live to see thee dead.

JULIET
65 What storm is this that blows so contrary?
Is Romeo slaughtered, and is Tybalt dead?
My dearest cousin and my dearer lord?
Then, dreadful trumpet, sound the general doom!
For who is living if those two are gone?

NURSE
70 Tybalt is gone, and Romeo banishèd.
Romeo that killed him—he is banishèd.

JULIET
O God, did Romeo's hand shed Tybalt's blood?

NURSE
It did, it did. Alas the day, it did.

JULIET
O serpent heart hid with a flowering face!
75 Did ever dragon keep so fair a cave?
Beautiful tyrant! Fiend angelical!
Dove-feathered raven, wolvish-ravening lamb!
Despisèd substance of divinest show,
Just opposite to what thou justly seem'st.
80 A damnèd saint, an honorable villain!
O nature, what hadst thou to do in hell
When thou didst bower the spirit of a fiend
In moral paradise of such sweet flesh?

Pale as ashes and drenched in blood. All the dried blood was so gory. I fainted when I saw it.

JULIET

Oh, my heart is breaking. Oh, my bankrupt heart is breaking. I'll send my eyes to prison, and they'll never be free to look at anything again. I'll give my vile body back to the earth. I'll never move again. My body and Romeo's will lie together in one sad coffin.

NURSE

Oh, Tybalt, Tybalt, he was the best friend I had. Oh, polite Tybalt, he was an honorable gentleman. I wish I had not lived long enough to see him die.

JULIET

What disaster is this? Has Romeo been killed, and is Tybalt dead too? Tybalt was my dearest cousin. Romeo was even dearer to me as my husband. Let the trumpets play the song of doom, because who can be alive if those two are gone?

NURSE

Tybalt is dead, and Romeo has been banished. Romeo killed Tybalt, and his punishment was banishment.

JULIET

Oh God, did Romeo's hand shed Tybalt's blood?

NURSE

It did, it did. Curse the day this happened, but it did.

JULIET

Oh, he's like a snake disguised as a flower. Did a dragon ever hide in such a beautiful cave? He's a beautiful tyrant and a fiendish angel! He's a raven with the feathers of the dove. He's a lamb who hunts like a wolf! I hate him, yet he seemed the most wonderful man. He's turned out to be the exact opposite of what he seemed. He's a saint who should be damned. He's a villain who seemed honorable. Oh nature, what were you doing in hell? Why did you put the soul of a criminal in the perfect body of a man? Was there ever

ACT THREE

Was ever book containing such vile matter
85   So fairly bound? Oh, that deceit should dwell
In such a gorgeous palace!

NURSE
There's no trust,
No faith, no honesty in men. All perjured,
All forsworn, all naught, all dissemblers.
Ah, where's my man?—Give me some aqua vitae.—
90   These griefs, these woes, these sorrows make me old.
Shame come to Romeo!

JULIET
Blistered be thy tongue
For such a wish! He was not born to shame.
Upon his brow shame is ashamed to sit,
For 'tis a throne where honor may be crowned.
95   Sole monarch of the universal earth,
Oh, what a beast was I to chide at him!

NURSE
Will you speak well of him that killed your cousin?

JULIET
Shall I speak ill of him that is my husband?
Ah, poor my lord, what tongue shall smooth thy name,
100   When I, thy three hours' wife, have mangled it?
But wherefore, villain, didst thou kill my cousin?
That villain cousin would have killed my husband.
Back, foolish tears, back to your native spring.
Your tributary drops belong to woe,
105   Which you, mistaking, offer up to joy.
My husband lives, that Tybalt would have slain,
And Tybalt's dead, that would have slain my husband.
All this is comfort. Wherefore weep I then?
Some word there was, worser than Tybalt's death,
110   That murdered me. I would forget it fain,
But oh, it presses to my memory,
Like damnèd guilty deeds to sinners' minds.
"Tybalt is dead, and Romeo banishèd."

such an evil book with such a beautiful cover? Oh, I can't believe the deepest evil lurked inside something so beautiful!

NURSE

There is no trust, no faith, no honesty in men. All of them lie. All of them cheat. They're all wicked. Ah, where's my servant?—Give me some brandy.—These griefs, these pains, these sorrows make me old. Shame on Romeo!

JULIET

I hope sores cover your tongue for a wish like that! He was not born to be shameful. Shame does not belong with Romeo. He deserves only honor, complete honor. Oh, I was such a beast to be angry at him.

NURSE

Are you going to say good things about the man who killed your cousin?

JULIET

Am I supposed to say bad things about my own husband? Ah, my poor husband, who will sing your praises when I, your wife of three hours, have been saying awful things about you? But why, you villain, did you kill my cousin? Probably because my cousin the villain would have killed my husband. I'm not going to cry any tears. I would cry with joy that Romeo is alive, but I should cry tears of grief because Tybalt is dead. My husband, whom Tybalt wanted to kill, is alive. Tybalt, who wanted to kill my husband, is dead. All this is comforting news. Why, then, should I cry? There is news worse than the news that Tybalt is dead, news that makes me want to die. I would be glad to forget about it, but it weighs on my memory like sins linger in guilty minds. "Tybalt is dead, and Romeo has been banished."

ACT THREE

That "banishèd," that one word "banishèd"
115   Hath slain ten thousand Tybalts. Tybalt's death
Was woe enough, if it had ended there.
Or, if sour woe delights in fellowship
And needly will be ranked with other griefs,
Why followed not, when she said "Tybalt's dead,"
120   "Thy father" or "thy mother," nay, or both,
Which modern lamentations might have moved?
But with a rearward following Tybalt's death,
"Romeo is banishèd." To speak that word,
Is father, mother, Tybalt, Romeo, Juliet,
125   All slain, all dead. "Romeo is banishèd."
There is no end, no limit, measure, bound,
In that word's death. No words can that woe sound.
Where is my father and my mother, Nurse?

NURSE
Weeping and wailing over Tybalt's corse.
130   Will you go to them? I will bring you thither.

JULIET
Wash they his wounds with tears? Mine shall be spent
When theirs are dry, for Romeo's banishment.
Take up those cords.—Poor ropes, you are beguiled,
Both you and I, for Romeo is exiled.
135   He made you for a highway to my bed,
But I, a maid, die maiden-widowèd.
Come, cords.—Come, Nurse. I'll to my wedding bed.
And death, not Romeo, take my maidenhead!

NURSE
Hie to your chamber. I'll find Romeo
140   To comfort you. I wot well where he is.
Hark ye, your Romeo will be here at night.
I'll to him. He is hid at Lawrence' cell.

That banishment is worse than the murder of ten thousand Tybalts. Tybalt's death would be bad enough if that was all. Maybe pain likes to have company and can't come without bringing more pain. It would have been better if, after she said, "Tybalt's dead," she told me my mother or my father, or both, were gone. That would have made me make the normal cries of sadness. But to say that Tybalt's dead and then say, "Romeo has been banished." To say that is like saying that my father, my mother, Tybalt, Romeo, and Juliet have all been killed, they're all dead. "Romeo has been banished." That news brings infinite death. No words can express the pain. Where are my father and my mother, Nurse?

NURSE

They are crying and moaning over Tybalt's corpse. Are you going to join them? I'll bring you there.

JULIET

Are they washing out his wounds with their tears? I'll cry my tears for Romeo's banishment when their tears are dry. Pick up this rope ladder. This poor rope ladder, it's useless now, just like me, because Romeo has been exiled. He made this rope ladder to be a highway to my bed, but I am a virgin, and I will die a virgin and a widow. Let's go, rope ladder. Nurse, I'm going to lie in my wedding bed. And death, not Romeo, can take my virginity!

NURSE

Go to your bedroom. I'll find Romeo to comfort you. I know where he is. Listen, your Romeo will be here tonight. I'll go to him. He's hiding out in Friar Lawrence's cell.

JULIET
    (gives the NURSE *a ring)* O, find him! Give this ring to my
        true knight,
And bid him come to take his last farewell.

                              Exeunt

JULIET

(giving her a ring) Oh, find him! Give this ring to my true knight! And tell him to come here to say his last goodbye.

They exit.

ACT THREE, Scene 3

Enter FRIAR LAWRENCE

FRIAR LAWRENCE
Romeo, come forth. Come forth, thou fearful man.
Affliction is enamoured of thy parts,
And thou art wedded to calamity.

Enter ROMEO

ROMEO
Father, what news? What is the Prince's doom?
5   What sorrow craves acquaintance at my hand
That I yet know not?

FRIAR LAWRENCE
                Too familiar
Is my dear son with such sour company.
I bring thee tidings of the Prince's doom.

ROMEO
What less than doomsday is the Prince's doom?

FRIAR LAWRENCE
10   A gentler judgment vanished from his lips:
Not body's death, but body's banishment.

ROMEO
Ha, banishment! Be merciful, say "death,"
For exile hath more terror in his look,
Much more than death. Do not say "banishment."

FRIAR LAWRENCE
15   Hence from Verona art thou banishèd.
Be patient, for the world is broad and wide.

ROMEO
There is no world without Verona walls
But purgatory, torture, hell itself.
Hence "banishèd" is banished from the world,
20   And world's exile is death. Then "banishèd,"

ACT THREE, Scene 3

FRIAR LAWRENCE *enters.*

FRIAR LAWRENCE
Romeo, come out. Come out, you frightened man. Trouble likes you, and you're married to disaster.

ROMEO *enters.*

ROMEO
Father, what's the news? What punishment did the Prince announce? What suffering lies in store for me that I don't know about yet?

FRIAR LAWRENCE
You know too much about suffering. I have news for you about the Prince's punishment.

ROMEO
Is the Prince's punishment any less awful than doomsday?

FRIAR LAWRENCE
He made a gentler decision. You won't die, but you'll be banished from the city.

ROMEO
Ha, banishment? Be merciful and say "death." Exile is much worse than death. Don't say "banishment."

FRIAR LAWRENCE
From now on, you are banished from Verona. You should be able to endure this because the world is broad and wide.

ROMEO
There is no world for me outside the walls of Verona, except purgatory, torture, and hell itself. So to be banished from Verona is like being banished from the world, and being banished from the world is death.

Is death mistermed. Calling death "banishment,"
Thou cutt'st my head off with a golden ax
And smilest upon the stroke that murders me.

FRIAR LAWRENCE
O deadly sin! O rude unthankfulness!
25   Thy fault our law calls death, but the kind Prince,
Taking thy part, hath rushed aside the law,
And turned that black word "death" to "banishment."
This is dear mercy, and thou seest it not.

ROMEO
'Tis torture and not mercy. Heaven is here,
30   Where Juliet lives, and every cat and dog
And little mouse, every unworthy thing,
Live here in heaven and may look on her,
But Romeo may not. More validity,
More honorable state, more courtship lives
35   In carrion flies than Romeo. They may seize
On the white wonder of dear Juliet's hand
And steal immortal blessing from her lips,
Who even in pure and vestal modesty,
Still blush, as thinking their own kisses sin.
40   But Romeo may not. He is banishèd.
Flies may do this, but I from this must fly.
They are free men, but I am banishèd.
And sayst thou yet that exile is not death?
Hadst thou no poison mixed, no sharp-ground knife,
45   No sudden mean of death, though ne'er so mean,
But "banishèd" to kill me?—"Banishèd"!
O Friar, the damnèd use that word in hell.
Howling attends it. How hast thou the heart,
Being a divine, a ghostly confessor,
50   A sin-absolver, and my friend professed,
To mangle me with that word "banishèd"?

FRIAR LAWRENCE
Thou fond mad man, hear me a little speak.

ACT THREE, SCENE 3

Banishment is death by the wrong name. Calling death banishment is like cutting off my head with a golden ax and smiling while I'm being murdered.

FRIAR LAWRENCE

Oh, deadly sin! Oh, rude and unthankful boy! You committed a crime that is punishable by death, but our kind Prince took sympathy on you and ignored the law when he substituted banishment for death. This is kind mercy, and you don't realize it.

ROMEO

It's torture, not mercy. Heaven is here because Juliet lives here. Every cat and dog and little mouse, every unworthy animal that lives here can see her, but Romeo can't. Flies are healthier and more honorable and better suited for romance than Romeo. They can take hold of Juliet's wonderful white hand and they can kiss her sweet lips. Even while she remains a pure virgin, she blushes when her lips touch each other because she thinks it's a sin. But Romeo can't kiss her or hold her hand because he's been banished. Flies can kiss her, but I must flee the city. Flies are like free men, but I have been banished. And yet you say that exile is not death? Did you have no poison, no sharp knife, no weapon you could use to kill me quickly, nothing so disgraceful, except banishment? Oh Friar, damned souls use the word banishment to describe hell. They howl about banishment. If you're a member of a divine spiritual order of men who forgive sins, and you say you're my friend, how do you have the heart to mangle me with the word banishment?

FRIAR LAWRENCE

You foolish madman, listen to me for a moment.

MODERN TEXT   **193**

ROMEO
Oh, thou wilt speak again of banishment.

FRIAR LAWRENCE
I'll give thee armor to keep off that word—
55 Adversity's sweet milk, philosophy—
To comfort thee though thou art banishèd.

ROMEO
Yet "banishèd"? Hang up philosophy!
Unless philosophy can make a Juliet,
Displant a town, reverse a prince's doom,
60 It helps not, it prevails not. Talk no more.

FRIAR LAWRENCE
Oh, then I see that madmen have no ears.

ROMEO
How should they, when that wise men have no eyes?

FRIAR LAWRENCE
Let me dispute with thee of thy estate.

ROMEO
Thou canst not speak of that thou dost not feel.
65 Wert thou as young as I, Juliet thy love,
An hour but married, Tybalt murderèd,
Doting like me, and like me banishèd,
Then mightst thou speak, then mightst thou tear thy hair
And fall upon the ground, as I do now,
70 Taking the measure of an unmade grave.

Knocking from within

FRIAR LAWRENCE
Arise. One knocks. Good Romeo, hide thyself.

ROMEO

Oh, you're just going to talk about banishment again.

FRIAR LAWRENCE

I'll give you protection from that word. I'll give you the antidote for trouble: philosophy. Philosophy will comfort you even though you've been banished.

ROMEO

You're still talking about "banished?" Forget about philosophy! Unless philosophy can create a Juliet, or pick up a town and put it somewhere else, or reverse a prince's punishment, it doesn't do me any good. Don't say anything else.

FRIAR LAWRENCE

Oh, so madmen like you are also deaf.

ROMEO

How should madmen hear, if wise men can't even see?

FRIAR LAWRENCE

Let me talk to you about your situation.

ROMEO

You can't talk about something that you don't feel. If you were as young as I am, if you were in love with Juliet, if you had just married her an hour ago, if then you murdered Tybalt, if you were lovesick like me, and if you were banished, then you might talk about it. You might also tear your hair out of your head and collapse to the ground the way I do right now. *(ROMEO falls on the ground)* You might kneel down and measure the grave that hasn't yet been dug.

Knocking from offstage.

FRIAR LAWRENCE

Get up. Somebody's knocking. Hide yourself, good Romeo.

ROMEO
Not I, unless the breath of heartsick groans,
Mistlike, infold me from the search of eyes.

Knocking

FRIAR LAWRENCE
Hark, how they knock!—Who's there?—Romeo, arise.
75   Thou wilt be taken.—Stay awhile.—Stand up.

Knocking

Run to my study.—By and by!—God's will,
What simpleness is this!—I come, I come.

Knocking

Who knocks so hard? Whence come you? What's your will?

NURSE
(from within) Let me come in, and you shall know my errand.
80   I come from Lady Juliet.

FRIAR LAWRENCE
                              (opens the door) Welcome then.

Enter **NURSE**

NURSE
O holy Friar, O, tell me, holy Friar,
Where is my lady's lord? Where's Romeo?

ROMEO

I won't hide unless all the mist from my heartsick groans envelopes me like fog and conceals me from people's searching eyes.

Knocking.

FRIAR LAWRENCE

Listen, they're still knocking!—*(to the person at the door)* Who's there?—*(to* ROMEO*)* Romeo, get up. They'll arrest you.—*(to the person at the door)* Hold on a moment.—*(to* ROMEO*)* Get up.

Knocking.

Run and hide in my study.—Just a minute—For the love of God, why are you being so stupid? I'm coming. I'm coming.

Knocking.

Why are you knocking so hard? Where do you come from? What do you want?

NURSE

(from offstage) Let me come in, and I'll tell you why I came. I come from Lady Juliet.

FRIAR LAWRENCE

(opening the door) Welcome, then.

The NURSE *enters.*

NURSE

Oh, holy Friar, Oh, tell me, holy Friar, where is my lady's husband? Where's Romeo?

FRIAR LAWRENCE
There on the ground, with his own tears made drunk.

NURSE
Oh, he is even in my mistress' case,
85   Just in her case. O woeful sympathy,
Piteous predicament! Even so lies she,
Blubbering and weeping, weeping and blubbering.
Stand up, stand up. Stand, an you be a man.
For Juliet's sake, for her sake, rise and stand.
90   Why should you fall into so deep an O?

ROMEO
Nurse!

NURSE
Ah sir, ah sir. Death's the end of all.

ROMEO
Spakest thou of Juliet? How is it with her?
Doth she not think me an old murderer,
95   Now I have stained the childhood of our joy
With blood removed but little from her own?
Where is she? And how doth she? And what says
My concealed lady to our canceled love?

NURSE
Oh, she says nothing, sir, but weeps and weeps,
100   And now falls on her bed, and then starts up,
And "Tybalt" calls, and then on Romeo cries,
And then down falls again.

ROMEO
                As if that name,
Shot from the deadly level of a gun,
Did murder her, as that name's cursed hand
105   Murdered her kinsman. O, tell me, Friar, tell me,
In what vile part of this anatomy
Doth my name lodge? Tell me, that I may sack
The hateful mansion. *(draws his dagger)*

FRIAR LAWRENCE

He's there on the ground. He's been getting drunk on his own tears.

NURSE

Oh, he's acting just like Juliet, just like her. Oh painful sympathy! What a pitiful problem! She's lying on the ground just like him, blubbering and weeping, weeping and blubbering. Stand up. Stand up. Stand up if you're really a man. For Juliet's sake, for her sake, rise and stand up. Why should you fall into so deep a moan?

ROMEO

Nurse!

NURSE

Ah sir, ah sir. Well, death is the end for everybody.

ROMEO

Were you talking about Juliet? How is she? Does she think that I'm a practiced murderer because I tainted our newfound joy by killing one of her close relatives? Where is she? How is she doing? What does my hidden wife say about our ruined love?

NURSE

Oh, she doesn't say anything, sir. She just weeps and weeps. She falls on her bed and then starts to get up. Then she calls out Tybalt's name and cries "Romeo," and then she falls down again.

ROMEO

She's calling out my name as if I were a bullet murdering her, just like I murdered her relative. Tell me, Friar, in what part of my body is my name embedded? Tell me, so I can cut it out of myself. *(he draws his dagger)*

FRIAR LAWRENCE Hold thy desperate hand.
Art thou a man? Thy form cries out thou art.
110 Thy tears are womanish. Thy wild acts denote
The unreasonable fury of a beast.
Unseemly woman in a seeming man,
And ill-beseeming beast in seeming both!
Thou hast amazed me. By my holy order,
115 I thought thy disposition better tempered.
Hast thou slain Tybalt? Wilt thou slay thyself,
And slay thy lady that in thy life lives
By doing damnèd hate upon thyself?
Why rail'st thou on thy birth, the heaven, and earth?
120 Since birth and heaven and earth, all three do meet
In thee at once, which thou at once wouldst lose?
Fie, fie, thou shamest thy shape, thy love, thy wit,
Which, like a usurer, abound'st in all
And usest none in that true use indeed
125 Which should bedeck thy shape, thy love, thy wit.
Thy noble shape is but a form of wax,
Digressing from the valor of a man;
Thy dear love sworn but hollow perjury,
Killing that love which thou hast vowed to cherish;
130 Thy wit, that ornament to shape and love,
Misshapen in the conduct of them both,
Like powder in a skill-less soldier's flask,
Is set afire by thine own ignorance;
And thou dismembered with thine own defence.
135 What, rouse thee, man! Thy Juliet is alive,
For whose dear sake thou wast but lately dead—
There art thou happy. Tybalt would kill thee,
But thou slew'st Tybalt—there art thou happy.
The law that threatened death becomes thy friend
140 And turns it to exile—there art thou happy.
A pack of blessings light upon thy back,
Happiness courts thee in her best array,

FRIAR LAWRENCE

Hold on, and don't act out of desperation. Are you a man? You look like a man, but your tears make you look like a woman. Your wild actions resemble the irrational fury of a beast. You're a shameful woman who looks like a man or else an ugly creature who's half-man, half-beast. You have amazed me. I swear by my holy order, I thought you were smarter and more rational than this. Have you killed Tybalt? Will you kill yourself? And would you also kill your wife, who shares your life, by committing the sin of killing yourself? Why do you complain about your birth, the heavens, and the earth? Life is the union of soul in body through the miracle of birth, but you would throw all that away. You bring shame to your body, your love, and your mind. You have so much natural talent, but like someone who hoards money, you use none of your talent for the right purpose—not your body, not your love, not your mind. Your body is just a wax figure, without the honor of a man. The love that you promised was a hollow lie. You're killing the love that you vowed to cherish. Your mind, which aids both your body and your love, has mishandled both of them. You're like a stupid soldier whose gunpowder explodes because he's careless. The things you were supposed to use to defend yourself end up killing you. Get up, man! Your Juliet is alive. It was for her that you were almost killed earlier. Be happy that she's alive. Tybalt wanted to kill you, but you killed Tybalt. Be happy that you're alive. The law that threatened your life was softened into exile. Be happy about that. Your life is full of blessings. You have the best sorts of happiness to enjoy.

But, like a misbehaved and sullen wench,
Thou pout'st upon thy fortune and thy love.
145　Take heed, take heed, for such die miserable.
Go, get thee to thy love, as was decreed.
Ascend her chamber, hence, and comfort her.
But look thou stay not till the watch be set,
For then thou canst not pass to Mantua,
150　Where thou shalt live, till we can find a time
To blaze your marriage, reconcile your friends,
Beg pardon of the Prince, and call thee back
With twenty hundred thousand times more joy
Than thou went'st forth in lamentation.—
155　Go before, Nurse. Commend me to thy lady,
And bid her hasten all the house to bed,
Which heavy sorrow makes them apt unto.
Romeo is coming.

NURSE
O Lord, I could have stayed here all the night
160　To hear good counsel. Oh, what learning is!
My lord, I'll tell my lady you will come.

ROMEO
Do so, and bid my sweet prepare to chide.

NURSE
Here, sir, a ring she bid me give you, sir.
(gives **ROMEO** **JULIET**'s *ring)*
Hie you, make haste, for it grows very late.

Exit **NURSE**

ROMEO
165　How well my comfort is revived by this!

But like a misbehaved, sullen girl, you're whining about your bad luck and your love. Listen, listen, people who act like that die miserable. Go be with your love, as it was decided at your wedding. Climb up to her bedroom and comfort her. But get out of there before the night watchmen take their positions. Then you will escape to the city of Mantua, where you'll live until we can make your marriage public and make peace between your families. We'll ask the Prince to pardon you. Then we'll welcome you back with twenty thousand times more joy than you'll have when you leave this town crying. Go ahead, Nurse. Give my regards to your lady, and tell her to hurry everybody in the house to bed. I'm sure they're all so sad that they'll be ready to sleep. Romeo is coming.

NURSE

O Lord, I could stay here all night listening to such good advice. Educated men are so impressive! *(speaking to* ROMEO*)* My lord, I'll tell my lady you will come.

ROMEO

Do so, and tell my sweet to be ready to scold me.

NURSE

Here, sir, this is a ring she asked me to give you. Hurry up, it's getting late. *(she gives* ROMEO JULIET*'s ring)*
                              The NURSE *exits.*

ROMEO

This makes me feel so much better!

FRIAR LAWRENCE
Go hence. Good night. And here stands all your state:
Either be gone before the watch be set,
Or by the break of day disguised from hence.
Sojourn in Mantua. I'll find out your man,
170 And he shall signify from time to time
Every good hap to you that chances here.
Give me thy hand. 'Tis late. Farewell, good night.

ROMEO
But that a joy past joy calls out on me,
It were a grief so brief to part with thee.
175 Farewell.
                                        Exeunt

FRIAR LAWRENCE

Now get out of here. Good night. Everything depends on this: either be out of here before the night watchmen take their positions, or leave in disguise after daybreak. Take a little vacation in Mantua. I'll find your servant, and he'll update you now and then on your case as it stands here. Give me your hand. It's late. Farewell. Good night.

ROMEO

I'm off to experience the greatest joy of all, but still it's sad to leave you in such a rush. Farewell.

They exit.

ACT THREE, Scene 4

Enter CAPULET, LADY CAPULET, *and* PARIS

CAPULET
Things have fall'n out, sir, so unluckily,
That we have had no time to move our daughter.
Look you, she loved her kinsman Tybalt dearly,
And so did I. Well, we were born to die.
5 'Tis very late. She'll not come down tonight.
I promise you, but for your company,
I would have been abed an hour ago.

PARIS
These times of woe afford no time to woo.
Madam, good night. Commend me to your daughter.

LADY CAPULET
10 I will, and know her mind early tomorrow.
Tonight she is mewed up to her heaviness.

CAPULET
Sir Paris, I will make a desperate tender
Of my child's love. I think she will be ruled
In all respects by me. Nay, more, I doubt it not.—
15 Wife, go you to her ere you go to bed.
Acquaint her here of my son Paris' love,
And bid her, mark you me, on Wednesday next—
But, soft! What day is this?

PARIS
Monday, my lord.

CAPULET
20 Monday! Ha, ha. Well, Wednesday is too soon,
O' Thursday let it be.—O' Thursday, tell her,
She shall be married to this noble earl.—
Will you be ready? Do you like this haste?
We'll keep no great ado, a friend or two.

ACT THREE, Scene 4

Enter CAPULET, LADY CAPULET, *and* PARIS.

CAPULET

Things have turned out so unluckily, sir, that we haven't had time to convince our daughter to marry you. Listen, she loved her cousin Tybalt dearly, and so did I. Well, we were all born to die. It's very late, she won't be coming downstairs tonight. Believe me, if you weren't here visiting me, I myself would have gone to bed an hour ago.

PARIS

These times of pain are bad times for romance. Madam, good night. Give my regards to your daughter.

LADY CAPULET

I will. And I'll find out what she thinks about marriage early tomorrow. Tonight she is shut up in her room, alone with her sadness.

CAPULET

Sir Paris, I'll make a desperate argument for my child's love. I think she'll do whatever I say. No, I think she'll do all that and more. I have no doubt about it. Wife, visit her in her room before you go to bed. Tell her about my son Paris's love for her. And tell her, listen to me, on Wednesday—Wait—What day is today?

PARIS

Monday, my lord.

CAPULET

Monday! Ha, ha! Well, Wednesday is too soon. Let it be on Thursday. On Thursday, tell her, she'll be married to this noble earl. Will you be ready? Do you think it's a good idea to rush? We shouldn't have too big a celebration—we can invite a friend or two.

25 For, hark you, Tybalt being slain so late,
It may be thought we held him carelessly,
Being our kinsman, if we revel much.
Therefore we'll have some half a dozen friends,
And there an end. But what say you to Thursday?

PARIS

30 My lord, I would that Thursday were tomorrow.

CAPULET

Well get you gone. O' Thursday be it, then.—
Go you to Juliet ere you go to bed.
Prepare her, wife, against this wedding day.—
Farewell, my lord.—Light to my chamber, ho!
35 Afore me! It is so very late,
That we may call it early by and by.—
Good night.

Exeunt

Listen, because Tybalt was just killed, people might think that we don't care about his memory as our relative if we have too grand a party. Therefore we'll have about half a dozen friends to the wedding, and that's it. What do you think about Thursday?

PARIS

My lord, I wish Thursday were tomorrow.

CAPULET

Well go on home. Thursday it is, then. *(to* LADY CAPULET*)* Visit Juliet before you go to bed. Get her ready, my wife, for this wedding day. *(to* PARIS*)* Farewell, my lord. Now I'm off to bed. Oh my! It's so late that we might as well call it early. Good night.

They all exit.

ACT THREE, Scene 5

Enter ROMEO *and* JULIET *aloft*

JULIET
  Wilt thou be gone? It is not yet near day.
  It was the nightingale, and not the lark,
  That pierced the fearful hollow of thine ear.
  Nightly she sings on yon pomegranate tree.
  Believe me, love, it was the nightingale.

5 **ROMEO**
  It was the lark, the herald of the morn,
  No nightingale. Look, love, what envious streaks
  Do lace the severing clouds in yonder east.
  Night's candles are burnt out, and jocund day
  Stands tiptoe on the misty mountain tops.
10 I must be gone and live, or stay and die.

  JULIET
  Yon light is not daylight, I know it, I.
  It is some meteor that the sun exhales
  To be to thee this night a torchbearer,
  And light thee on thy way to Mantua.
15 Therefore stay yet. Thou need'st not to be gone.

  ROMEO
  Let me be ta'en. Let me be put to death.
  I am content, so thou wilt have it so.
  I'll say yon grey is not the morning's eye.
  'Tis but the pale reflex of Cynthia's brow.
20 Nor that is not the lark, whose notes do beat
  The vaulty heaven so high above our heads.
  I have more care to stay than will to go.
  Come, death, and welcome! Juliet wills it so.—
  How is 't, my soul? Let's talk. It is not day.

25

ACT THREE, Scene 5

ROMEO and JULIET enter above the stage.

JULIET

Are you going? It's still a long time until daybreak. Don't be afraid. That sound you heard was the nightingale, not the lark. Every night the nightingale chirps on that pomegranate tree. Believe me, my love, it was the nightingale.

The lark sings in the morning, the nightingale sings at night.

ROMEO

It was the lark, the bird that sings at dawn, not the nightingale. Look, my love, what are those streaks of light in the clouds parting in the east? Night is over, and day is coming. If I want to live, I must go. If I stay, I'll die.

JULIET

That light is not daylight, I know it. It's some meteor coming out of the sun to light your way to Mantua. So stay for a while. You don't have to go yet.

ROMEO

Let me be captured. Let me be put to death. I am con-tent, if that's the way you want it. I'll say the light over there isn't morning. I'll say it's the reflection of the moon. I'll say that sound isn't the lark ringing in the sky. I want to stay more than I want to go. Come, death, and welcome! Juliet wants it this way. How are you, my love? Let's talk. It's not daylight.

JULIET
It is, it is. Hie hence! Be gone, away!
It is the lark that sings so out of tune,
Straining harsh discords and unpleasing sharps.
Some say the lark makes sweet division.
30   This doth not so, for she divideth us.
Some say the lark and loathèd toad change eyes.
Oh, now I would they had changed voices too,
Since arm from arm that voice doth us affray,
Hunting thee hence with hunt's-up to the day.
35   O, now be gone. More light and light it grows.

ROMEO
More light and light, more dark and dark our woes!

Enter NURSE

NURSE
Madam.

JULIET
Nurse?

NURSE
Your lady mother is coming to your chamber.
40   The day is broke. Be wary, look about.

Exit NURSE

JULIET
Then, window, let day in and let life out.

ROMEO
Farewell, farewell. One kiss, and I'll descend.

Kiss. ROMEO *goes down*

JULIET

It is, it is. Get out of here, be gone, go away! It's the lark that sings so out of tune, making such harsh noise. Some say the lark makes a sweet division between day and night. It's not true because she separates us. Some say the lark traded its eyes with the toad. Oh, now I wish they had traded voices too! Because the lark's voice tears us out of each other's arms, and now there will be men hunting for you. Oh, go away now. I see more and more light.

A folktale said that the lark had gotten its ugly eyes from the toad, who had taken its pretty eyes from the lark.

ROMEO

More and more light. More and more pain for us.

The **NURSE** *enters.*

NURSE

Madam.

JULIET

Nurse?

NURSE

Your mother is coming to your bedroom. Day has broken. Be careful. Watch out.

The **NURSE** *exits.*

JULIET

Then the window lets day in, and life goes out the window.

ROMEO

Farewell, farewell! Give me one kiss, and I'll go down.

They kiss. **ROMEO** *drops the ladder and goes down.*

ACT THREE

JULIET
Art thou gone so, love, lord? Ay, husband, friend,
I must hear from thee every day in the hour,
45   For in a minute there are many days.
Oh, by this count I shall be much in years
Ere I again behold my Romeo.

ROMEO
                                         Farewell!
I will omit no opportunity
That may convey my greetings, love, to thee.

JULIET
50   Oh, think'st thou we shall ever meet again?

ROMEO
I doubt it not, and all these woes shall serve
For sweet discourses in our time to come.

JULIET
O God, I have an ill-divining soul.
Methinks I see thee now, thou art so low
55   As one dead in the bottom of a tomb.
Either my eyesight fails, or thou look'st pale.

ROMEO
And trust me, love, in my eye so do you.
Dry sorrow drinks our blood. Adieu, adieu!

                                         Exit ROMEO

JULIET
O fortune, fortune! All men call thee fickle.
60   If thou art fickle, what dost thou with him
That is renowned for faith? Be fickle, fortune,
For then, I hope, thou wilt not keep him long,
But send him back.

LADY CAPULET
(from within) Ho, daughter, are you up?

JULIET

Are you gone like that, my love, my lord? Yes, my husband, my friend! I must hear from you every day in the
hour. In a minute there are many days. Oh, by this
count I'll be many years older before I see my Romeo
again.

ROMEO

Farewell! I won't miss any chance to send my love to
you.

JULIET

Oh, do you think we'll ever meet again?

ROMEO

I have no doubts. All these troubles will give us stories
to tell each other later in life.

JULIET

Oh God, I have a soul that predicts evil things! Now
that you are down there, you look like someone dead
in the bottom of a tomb. Either my eyesight is failing
me, or you look pale.

ROMEO

And trust me, love, you look pale to me too. Sadness
takes away our color. Goodbye, Goodbye!

ROMEO *exits.*

JULIET

Oh luck, luck. Everyone says you can't make up your
mind. If you change your mind so much, what are you
going to do to Romeo, who's so faithful? Change your
mind, luck. I hope maybe then you'll send him back
home soon.

LADY CAPULET

(offstage) Hey, daughter! Are you awake?

ACT THREE

JULIET

65   Who is 't that calls? Is it my lady mother?
Is she not down so late or up so early?
What unaccustomed cause procures her hither?

Enter LADY CAPULET

LADY CAPULET
Why, how now, Juliet?

JULIET
                         Madam, I am not well.

LADY CAPULET
Evermore weeping for your cousin's death?
70   What, wilt thou wash him from his grave with tears?
An if thou couldst, thou couldst not make him live.
Therefore, have done. Some grief shows much of love,
But much of grief shows still some want of wit.

JULIET
Yet let me weep for such a feeling loss.

LADY CAPULET
75   So shall you feel the loss, but not the friend
Which you weep for.

JULIET
                    Feeling so the loss,
Cannot choose but ever weep the friend.

LADY CAPULET
Well, girl, thou weep'st not so much for his death,
As that the villain lives which slaughtered him.

JULIET
80   What villain, madam?

LADY CAPULET
                  That same villain, Romeo.

JULIET

Who's that calling? Is it my mother? Isn't she up very late? Or is she up very early? What strange reason could she have for coming here?

LADY CAPULET enters.

LADY CAPULET

What's going on, Juliet?

JULIET

Madam, I am not well.

LADY CAPULET

Will you cry about your cousin's death forever? Are you trying to wash him out of his grave with tears? If you could, you couldn't bring him back to life. So stop crying. A little bit of grief shows a lot of love. But too much grief makes you look stupid.

JULIET

Let me keep weeping for such a great loss.

LADY CAPULET

You will feel the loss, but the man you weep for will feel nothing.

JULIET

Feeling the loss like this, I can't help but weep for him forever.

LADY CAPULET

Well, girl, you're weeping not for his death as much as for the fact that the villain who killed him is still alive.

JULIET

What villain, madam?

LADY CAPULET

That villain, Romeo.

JULIET
> *(aside)* Villain and he be many miles asunder.
> *(to* **LADY CAPULET***)* God pardon him! I do, with all my heart,
> And yet no man like he doth grieve my heart.

LADY CAPULET
> That is because the traitor murderer lives.

JULIET
85
> Ay, madam, from the reach of these my hands.
> Would none but I might venge my cousin's death!

LADY CAPULET
> We will have vengeance for it, fear thou not.
> Then weep no more. I'll send to one in Mantua,
> Where that same banished runagate doth live,
90
> Shall give him such an unaccustomed dram
> That he shall soon keep Tybalt company.
> And then, I hope, thou wilt be satisfied.

JULIET
> Indeed, I never shall be satisfied
> With Romeo, till I behold him—dead—
95
> Is my poor heart for a kinsman vexed.
> Madam, if you could find out but a man
> To bear a poison, I would temper it,
> That Romeo should, upon receipt thereof,
> Soon sleep in quiet. Oh, how my heart abhors
100
> To hear him named, and cannot come to him.
> To wreak the love I bore my cousin
> Upon his body that slaughtered him!

LADY CAPULET
> Find thou the means, and I'll find such a man.
> But now I'll tell thee joyful tidings, girl.

JULIET
105
> And joy comes well in such a needy time.
> What are they, beseech your ladyship?

JULIET

(*speaking so that* LADY CAPULET *can't hear*) He's far from being a villain. *(to* LADY CAPULET*)* May God pardon him! I do, with all my heart. And yet no man could make my heart grieve like he does.

LADY CAPULET

That's because the murderer is alive.

JULIET

Yes, madam, he lies beyond my reach. I wish that no one could avenge my cousin's death except me!

LADY CAPULET

We'll have revenge for it. Don't worry about that. Stop crying. I'll send a man to Mantua, where that exiled rogue is living. Our man will poison Romeo's drink, and Romeo will join Tybalt in death. And then, I hope, you'll be satisfied.

JULIET

I'll never be satisfied with Romeo until I see him . . . dead—dead is how my poor heart feels when I think about my poor cousin. Madam, if you can find a man to deliver the poison, I'll mix it myself so that Romeo will sleep quietly soon after he drinks it. Oh, how I hate to hear people say his name and not be able to go after him. I want to take the love I had for my cousin and take it out on the body of the man who killed him.

LADY CAPULET

Find out the way, and I'll find the right man. But now I have joyful news for you, girl.

JULIET

And it's good to have joy in such a joyless time. What's the news? Please tell me.

LADY CAPULET
Well, well, thou hast a careful father, child.
One who, to put thee from thy heaviness,
Hath sorted out a sudden day of joy
110 That thou expect'st not, nor I looked not for.

JULIET
Madam, in happy time, what day is that?

LADY CAPULET
Marry, my child, early next Thursday morn,
The gallant, young, and noble gentleman,
The County Paris, at Saint Peter's Church,
115 Shall happily make thee there a joyful bride.

JULIET
Now, by Saint Peter's Church and Peter too,
He shall not make me there a joyful bride.
I wonder at this haste, that I must wed
Ere he, that should be husband, comes to woo.
120 I pray you, tell my lord and father, madam,
I will not marry yet. And when I do, I swear
It shall be Romeo, whom you know I hate,
Rather than Paris. These are news indeed!

LADY CAPULET
Here comes your father. Tell him so yourself,
125 And see how he will take it at your hands.

Enter CAPULET *and* NURSE

CAPULET
When the sun sets the air doth drizzle dew,
But for the sunset of my brother's son
It rains downright.
How now? A conduit, girl? What, still in tears,
130 Evermore showering? In one little body
Thou counterfeit'st a bark, a sea, a wind,
For still thy eyes, which I may call the sea,
Do ebb and flow with tears. The bark thy body is,

LADY CAPULET

> Well, well, you have a careful father, child. He has arranged a sudden day of joy to end your sadness. A day that you did not expect and that I did not seek out.

JULIET

> Madam, tell me quickly, what day is that?

LADY CAPULET

> Indeed, my child, at Saint Peter's Church early Thursday morning, the gallant, young, and noble gentleman Count Paris will happily make you a joyful bride.

JULIET

> Now, I swear by Saint Peter's Church and Peter too, he will not make me a joyful bride there. This is a strange rush. How can I marry him, this husband, before he comes to court me? Please, tell my father, madam, I won't marry yet. And, when I do marry, I swear, it will be Romeo, whom you know I hate, rather than Paris. That's really news!

LADY CAPULET

> Here comes your father. Tell him so yourself, and see how he takes the news.

CAPULET *and the* NURSE *enter.*

CAPULET

> When the sun sets, the air drizzles dew. But at the death of my brother's son, it rains a downpour. What are you, girl? Some kind of fountain? Why are you still crying? Will you cry forever? In one little body you seem like a ship, the sea, and the winds. Your eyes, which I call the sea, flow with tears. The ship is your body which is sailing on the salt flood of your tears.

Sailing in this salt flood. The winds thy sighs,
135   Who, raging with thy tears, and they with them,
Without a sudden calm will overset
Thy tempest-tossèd body.—How now, wife?
Have you delivered to her our decree?

LADY CAPULET
Ay, sir, but she will none, she gives you thanks.
140   I would the fool were married to her grave!

CAPULET
Soft, take me with you, take me with you, wife.
How, will she none? Doth she not give us thanks?
Is she not proud? Doth she not count her blessed,
Unworthy as she is, that we have wrought
145   So worthy a gentleman to be her bride?

JULIET
Not proud you have, but thankful that you have.
Proud can I never be of what I hate,
But thankful even for hate that is meant love.

CAPULET
How, how, how, how? Chopped logic! What is this?
150   "Proud," and "I thank you," and "I thank you not,"
And yet "not proud"? Mistress minion you,
Thank me no thankings, nor proud me no prouds,
But fettle your fine joints 'gainst Thursday next
To go with Paris to Saint Peter's Church,
155   Or I will drag thee on a hurdle thither.
Out, you green sickness, carrion! Out, you baggage!
You tallow face!

LADY CAPULET
             Fie, fie! What, are you mad?

JULIET
Good Father, I beseech you on my knees,
Hear me with patience but to speak a word.

The winds are your sighs. Your sighs and your tears are raging. Unless you calm down, tears and sighs will overwhelm your body and sink your ship. So where do things stand, wife? Have you told her our decision?

LADY CAPULET

Yes, sir, I told her. But she won't agree. She says thank you but refuses. I wish the fool were dead and married to her grave!

CAPULET

Wait! Hold on, wife. I don't understand. How can this be? She refuses? Isn't she grateful? Isn't she proud of such a match? Doesn't she realize what a blessing this is? Doesn't she realize how unworthy she is of the gentleman we have found to be her bridegroom?

JULIET

I am not proud of what you have found for me. But I am thankful that you have found it. I can never be proud of what I hate. But I can be thankful for something I hate, if it was meant with love.

CAPULET

What is this? What is this fuzzy logic? What is this? I hear you say "proud" and "I thank you," and then "no thank you" and "not proud," you spoiled little girl. You're not really giving me any thanks or showing me any pride. But get yourself ready for Thursday. You're going to Saint Peter's Church to marry Paris. And if you don't go on your own, I'll drag you there. You disgust me, you little bug! You worthless girl! You pale face!

LADY CAPULET

Shame on you! What, are you crazy?

JULIET

Good father, I'm begging you on my knees, be patient and listen to me say just one thing.

ACT THREE

CAPULET
160   Hang thee, young baggage! Disobedient wretch!
      I tell thee what: get thee to church o' Thursday,
      Or never after look me in the face.
      Speak not. Reply not. Do not answer me.
      My fingers itch.—Wife, we scarce thought us blest
165   That God had lent us but this only child,
      But now I see this one is one too much
      And that we have a curse in having her.
      Out on her, hilding!

NURSE
                    God in heaven bless her!
      You are to blame, my lord, to rate her so.

CAPULET
170   And why, my Lady Wisdom? Hold your tongue,
      Good prudence. Smatter with your gossips, go.

NURSE
      I speak no treason.

CAPULET
                 Oh, God 'i' good e'en.

NURSE
      May not one speak?

CAPULET
                 Peace, you mumbling fool!
      Utter your gravity o'er a gossip's bowl,
175   For here we need it not.

LADY CAPULET
                 You are too hot.

CAPULET
      God's bread! It makes me mad.
      Day, night, hour, tide, time, work, play,
      Alone, in company, still my care hath been
      To have her matched. And having now provided
180   A gentleman of noble parentage,
      Of fair demesnes, youthful, and nobly trained,
      Stuffed, as they say, with honorable parts,

CAPULET

Forget about you, you worthless girl! You disobedient wretch! I'll tell you what. Go to church on Thursday or never look me in the face again. Don't say anything. Don't reply. Don't talk back to me. *(JULIET rises)* I feel like slapping you. Wife, we never thought ourselves blessed that God only gave us this one child. But now I see that this one is one too many. We were cursed when we had her. She disgusts me, the little hussy!

NURSE

God in heaven bless her! My lord, you're wrong to berate her like that.

CAPULET

And why, wise lady? You shut up, old woman. Go blabber with your gossiping friends.

NURSE

I've said nothing wrong.

CAPULET

Oh, for God's sake.

NURSE

Can't I say something?

CAPULET

Be quiet, you mumbling fool! Say your serious things at lunch with your gossiping friends. We don't need to hear it.

LADY CAPULET

You're getting too angry.

CAPULET

Goddammit! It makes me mad. Day and night, hour after hour, all the time, at work, at play, alone, in company, my top priority has always been to find her a husband. Now I've provided a husband from a noble family, who is good-looking, young, well-educated. He's full of good qualities.

Proportioned as one's thought would wish a man—
And then to have a wretched puling fool,
185   A whining mammet, in her fortune's tender,
To answer "I'll not wed," "I cannot love,"
"I am too young," "I pray you, pardon me."—
But, an you will not wed, I'll pardon you.
Graze where you will, you shall not house with me.
190   Look to 't, think on 't, I do not use to jest.
Thursday is near. Lay hand on heart, advise.
An you be mine, I'll give you to my friend.
An you be not, hang, beg, starve, die in the streets,
For, by my soul, I'll ne'er acknowledge thee,
195   Nor what is mine shall never do thee good.
Trust to 't, bethink you. I'll not be forsworn.

Exit CAPULET

JULIET
Is there no pity sitting in the clouds
That sees into the bottom of my grief?—
O sweet my mother, cast me not away!
200   Delay this marriage for a month, a week.
Or, if you do not, make the bridal bed
In that dim monument where Tybalt lies.

LADY CAPULET
Talk not to me, for I'll not speak a word.
Do as thou wilt, for I have done with thee.

Exit LADY CAPULET

JULIET
205   O God!—O Nurse, how shall this be prevented?
My husband is on earth, my faith in heaven.
How shall that faith return again to earth,
Unless that husband send it me from heaven
By leaving earth? Comfort me. Counsel me.—
210   Alack, alack, that heaven should practice stratagems
Upon so soft a subject as myself.—

He's the man of any girl's dreams. But this wretched, whimpering fool, like a whining puppet, she looks at this good fortune and answers, "I won't get married. I can't fall in love. I'm too young. Please, excuse me." Well, if you won't get married, I'll excuse you. Eat wherever you want, but you can no longer live under my roof. Consider that. Think about it. I'm not in the habit of joking. Thursday is coming. Put your hand on your heart and listen to my advice. If you act like my daughter, I'll marry you to my friend. If you don't act like my daughter, you can beg, starve, and die in the streets. I swear on my soul, I will never take you back or do anything for you. Believe me. Think about it. I won't break this promise.

CAPULET *exits.*

JULIET

Is there no pity in the sky that can see my sadness? Oh, my sweet mother, don't throw me out! Delay this marriage for a month, or a week. Or, if you don't delay, make my wedding bed in the tomb where Tybalt lies.

LADY CAPULET

Don't talk to me, because I won't say a word. Do as you please, because I'm done worrying about you.

LADY CAPULET *exits.*

JULIET

Oh God!—Oh Nurse, how can this be stopped? My husband is alive on earth, my vows of marriage are in heaven. How can I bring those promises back down to earth, unless my husband sends them back down to me by dying and going to heaven? Give me comfort. Give me advice. Oh no! Oh no! Why does heaven play tricks on someone as weak as me? What do you say?

What sayst thou? Hast thou not a word of joy?
Some comfort, Nurse.

NURSE
                              Faith, here it is.
Romeo is banishèd, and all the world to nothing
215   That he dares ne'er come back to challenge you.
Or, if he do, it needs must be by stealth.
Then, since the case so stands as now it doth,
I think it best you married with the county.
Oh, he's a lovely gentleman.
220   Romeo's a dishclout to him. An eagle, madam,
Hath not so green, so quick, so fair an eye
As Paris hath. Beshrew my very heart,
I think you are happy in this second match,
For it excels your first. Or if it did not,
225   Your first is dead, or 'twere as good he were,
As living here and you no use of him.

JULIET
Speakest thou from thy heart?

NURSE
And from my soul too, else beshrew them both.

JULIET
Amen!

NURSE
230   What?

JULIET
Well, thou hast comforted me marvelous much.
Go in, and tell my lady I am gone,
Having displeased my father, to Lawrence's cell
To make confession and to be absolved.

NURSE
235   Marry, I will, and this is wisely done.

                                        Exit **NURSE**

Don't you have one word of joy? Give me some comfort, Nurse.

NURSE

This is what I have to say: Romeo has been banished. And it's a sure thing that he will never come back to challenge you. If he does come back, he'll have to sneak back undercover. Then, since things are the way they are, I think the best thing to do is to marry the count. Oh, he's a lovely gentleman! Romeo's a dishcloth compared to him. Madam, an eagle does not have eyes as green, as quick, and as fair as the eyes of Paris. Curse my very heart, but I think you should be happy in this second marriage, because it's better than your first. Even if it's not better, your first marriage is over. Or if Romeo is as good as Paris, Romeo doesn't live here, so you don't get to enjoy him.

JULIET

Are you speaking from your heart?

NURSE

I speak from my heart and from my soul too. If not, curse them both.

JULIET

Amen!

NURSE

What?

JULIET

Well, you have given me great comfort. Go inside and tell my mother that I'm gone. I made my father angry, so I went to Friar Lawrence's cell to confess and be forgiven.

NURSE

Alright, I will. This is a good idea.

The **NURSE** *exits.*

JULIET
    Ancient damnation! O most wicked fiend!
    Is it more sin to wish me thus forsworn,
    Or to dispraise my lord with that same tongue
    Which she hath praised him with above compare
240   So many thousand times? Go, counselor.
    Thou and my bosom henceforth shall be twain.
    I'll to the friar to know his remedy.
    If all else fail, myself have power to die.

                                        Exit

JULIET

That damned old lady! Oh, that most wicked fiend! Is it a worse sin for her to want me to break my vows or for her to say bad things about my husband after she praised him so many times before? Away with you and your advice, Nurse. From now on, I will never tell you what I feel in my heart. I'm going to the Friar to find out his solution. If everything else fails, at least I have the power to take my own life.

JULIET exits.

ACT FOUR

Scene 1

Enter FRIAR LAWRENCE *and* PARIS

FRIAR LAWRENCE
On Thursday, sir? The time is very short.

PARIS
My father Capulet will have it so,
And I am nothing slow to slack his haste.

FRIAR LAWRENCE
You say you do not know the lady's mind.
5   Uneven is the course. I like it not.

PARIS
Immoderately she weeps for Tybalt's death,
And therefore have I little talked of love,
For Venus smiles not in a house of tears.
Now, sir, her father counts it dangerous
10   That she do give her sorrow so much sway,
And in his wisdom hastes our marriage
To stop the inundation of her tears—
Which, too much minded by herself alone,
May be put from her by society.
15   Now do you know the reason of this haste.

FRIAR LAWRENCE
(aside) I would I knew not why it should be slowed.—
Look, sir, here comes the lady toward my cell.

Enter JULIET

PARIS
Happily met, my lady and my wife.

JULIET
That may be, sir, when I may be a wife.

ACT FOUR

Scene 1

FRIAR LAWRENCE *and* PARIS *enter.*

FRIAR LAWRENCE
On Thursday, sir? That's very soon.

PARIS
That's how my future father-in-law Capulet wants it, and I'm not dragging my feet.

FRIAR LAWRENCE
You say you don't know what the girl thinks. That's a rocky road to be riding. I don't like it.

PARIS
She's grieving too much over the death of Tybalt. So I haven't had the chance to talk to her about love. Romantic love doesn't happen when people are in mourning. Now, sir, her father thinks it's dangerous that she allows herself to become so sad. He's being smart by rushing our marriage to stop her from crying. She cries too much by herself. If she had someone to be with her, she would stop crying. Now you know the reason for the rush.

FRIAR LAWRENCE
(to himself) I wish I didn't know the reason why the marriage should be slowed down. Look, sir, here comes the lady walking toward my cell.

JULIET *enters.*

PARIS
I'm happy to meet you, my lady and my wife.

JULIET
That might be the case sir, *after* I'm married.

PARIS

20   That "may be" must be, love, on Thursday next.

JULIET

What must be shall be.

FRIAR LAWRENCE

That's a certain text.

PARIS

Come you to make confession to this Father?

JULIET

To answer that, I should confess to you.

PARIS

25   Do not deny to him that you love me.

JULIET

I will confess to you that I love him.

PARIS

So will ye, I am sure, that you love me.

JULIET

If I do so, it will be of more price

Being spoke behind your back than to your face.

PARIS

30   Poor soul, thy face is much abused with tears.

JULIET

The tears have got small victory by that,

For it was bad enough before their spite.

PARIS

Thou wrong'st it more than tears with that report.

JULIET

That is no slander, sir, which is a truth,

35   And what I spake, I spake it to my face.

PARIS

Thy face is mine, and thou hast slandered it.

JULIET

It may be so, for it is not mine own.—

Are you at leisure, holy Father, now,

Or shall I come to you at evening mass?

PARIS

That "may be" must be, love, on Thursday.

JULIET

What must be will be.

FRIAR LAWRENCE

That is a certain truth.

PARIS

Have you come to make confession to this father?

JULIET

If I answered that question, I'd be making confession to you.

PARIS

Don't deny to him that you love me.

JULIET

I'll confess to you that I love him.

PARIS

You will also confess, I'm sure, that you love me.

JULIET

If I do so, it will mean more if I say it behind your back than if I say it to your face.

PARIS

You poor soul, your face has suffered many tears.

JULIET

The tears haven't done much because my face looked bad enough before I started to cry.

PARIS

You're treating your face even worse by saying that.

JULIET

What I say isn't slander, sir. It's the truth. And what I said, I said to my face.

PARIS

Your face is mine, and you have slandered it.

JULIET

That may be the case, because my face doesn't belong to me.—Do you have time for me now, Father, or should I come to you at evening mass?

FRIAR LAWRENCE
40   My leisure serves me, pensive daughter, now.—
        My lord, we must entreat the time alone.

PARIS
        God shield I should disturb devotion!—
        Juliet, on Thursday early will I rouse ye.
        (kisses her) Till then, adieu, and keep this holy kiss.

                                                        Exit PARIS

JULIET
45   O, shut the door! And when thou hast done so,
        Come weep with me, past hope, past cure, past help.

FRIAR LAWRENCE
        O Juliet, I already know thy grief.
        It strains me past the compass of my wits.
        I hear thou must, and nothing may prorogue it,
50   On Thursday next be married to this county.

JULIET
        Tell me not, Friar, that thou hear'st of this,
        Unless thou tell me how I may prevent it.
        If in thy wisdom thou canst give no help,
        Do thou but call my resolution wise,
55   And with this knife I'll help it presently.
        (shows him a knife)
        God joined my heart and Romeo's, thou our hands.
        And ere this hand, by thee to Romeo sealed,
        Shall be the label to another deed,
        Or my true heart with treacherous revolt
60   Turn to another, this shall slay them both.
        Therefore out of thy long-experienced time,
        Give me some present counsel, or, behold,
        'Twixt my extremes and me this bloody knife
        Shall play the umpire, arbitrating that
65   Which the commission of thy years and art
        Could to no issue of true honor bring.
        Be not so long to speak. I long to die
        If what thou speak'st speak not of remedy.

FRIAR LAWRENCE

I have time for you now, my sad daughter. *(to* PARIS*)*
My lord, we must ask you to leave us alone.

PARIS

God forbid that I should prevent sacred devotion!
Juliet, I will wake you early on Thursday. *(kissing her)*
Until then, good-bye, and keep this holy kiss.

PARIS *exits.*

JULIET

Oh, shut the door, and after you shut it, come over
here and weep with me. This mess is beyond hope,
beyond cure, beyond help!

FRIAR LAWRENCE

Oh, Juliet, I already know about your sad situation.
It's a problem too hard for me to solve. I hear that you
must marry this count on Thursday, and that nothing
can delay it.

JULIET

Don't tell me that you've heard about this marriage,
Friar, unless you can tell me how to prevent it. If you
who are so wise can't help, please be kind enough to
call my solution wise. *(she shows him a knife)* And I'll
solve the problem now with this knife. God joined my
heart to Romeo's. You joined our hands. And before
I—who was married to Romeo by you—am married
to another man, I'll kill myself. You are wise and you
have so much experience. Give me some advice about
the current situation. Or watch. Caught between
these two difficulties, I'll act like a judge with my
bloody knife. I will truly and honorably resolve the
situation that you can't fix, despite your experience
and education. Don't wait long to speak. I want to die
if what you say isn't another solution.

FRIAR LAWRENCE
　　Hold, daughter. I do spy a kind of hope,
70　　Which craves as desperate an execution
　　As that is desperate which we would prevent.
　　If, rather than to marry County Paris,
　　Thou hast the strength of will to slay thyself,
　　Then is it likely thou wilt undertake
75　　A thing like death to chide away this shame,
　　That copest with death himself to 'scape from it.
　　An if thou darest, I'll give thee remedy.

JULIET
　　O, bid me leap, rather than marry Paris,
　　From off the battlements of yonder tower;
80　　Or walk in thievish ways; or bid me lurk
　　Where serpents are; chain me with roaring bears;
　　Or shut me nightly in a charnel house,
　　O'ercovered quite with dead men's rattling bones,
　　With reeky shanks and yellow chapless skulls;
85　　Or bid me go into a new-made grave
　　And hide me with a dead man in his shroud—
　　Things that, to hear them told, have made me tremble—
　　And I will do it without fear or doubt,
　　To live an unstained wife to my sweet love.

FRIAR LAWRENCE
90　　Hold, then. Go home, be merry. Give consent
　　To marry Paris. Wednesday is tomorrow.
　　Tomorrow night look that thou lie alone.
　　Let not the Nurse lie with thee in thy chamber.
　　(shows her a vial)
　　Take thou this vial, being then in bed,
95　　And this distillèd liquor drink thou off,
　　When presently through all thy veins shall run
　　A cold and drowsy humor, for no pulse
　　Shall keep his native progress, but surcease.
　　No warmth, no breath shall testify thou livest.
100　　The roses in thy lips and cheeks shall fade

FRIAR LAWRENCE

Hold on, daughter, I see some hope. But we must act boldly because the situation is so desperate. If you've made up your mind to kill yourself instead of marrying Count Paris, then you'll probably be willing to try something like death to solve this shameful problem. You can wrestle with death to escape from shame. And if you dare to do it, I'll give you the solution.

JULIET

Oh, you can tell me to jump off the battle posts of any tower, or to walk down the crime-ridden streets of a slum. Or tell me to sit in a field full of poisonous snakes. Chain me up with wild bears. Hide me every night in a morgue full of dead bodies with wet, smelly flesh and skulls without jawbones. Or tell me to climb down into a freshly dug grave, and hide me with a dead man in his tomb. All those ideas make me tremble when I hear them named. But I will do them without fear or dread in order to be a pure wife to my sweet love.

FRIAR LAWRENCE

Hold on, then. Go home, be cheerful, and tell them you agree to marry Paris. Tomorrow is Wednesday. Tomorrow night make sure that you are alone. Don't let the Nurse stay with you in your bedroom. *(showing her a vial)* When you're in bed, take this vial, mix its contents with liquor, and drink. Then a cold, sleep-inducing drug will run through your veins, and your pulse will stop. Your flesh will be cold, and you'll stop breathing. The red in your lips and your cheeks will turn pale, and your eyes will shut. It will seem like you're dead. You won't be able to move, and your body will be stiff like a corpse. You'll remain in this deathlike state for forty-two hours, and then you'll

To paly ashes, thy eyes' windows fall
Like death when he shuts up the day of life.
Each part, deprived of supple government,
Shall, stiff and stark and cold, appear like death.
105   And in this borrowed likeness of shrunk death
Thou shalt continue two and forty hours,
And then awake as from a pleasant sleep.
Now, when the bridegroom in the morning comes
To rouse thee from thy bed, there art thou dead.
110   Then, as the manner of our country is,
In thy best robes uncovered on the bier
Thou shalt be borne to that same ancient vault
Where all the kindred of the Capulets lie.
In the meantime, against thou shalt awake,
115   Shall Romeo by my letters know our drift,
And hither shall he come, and he and I
Will watch thy waking, and that very night
Shall Romeo bear thee hence to Mantua.
And this shall free thee from this present shame,
120   If no inconstant toy, nor womanish fear,
Abate thy valor in the acting it.

JULIET
Give me, give me! O, tell not me of fear!

FRIAR LAWRENCE
(gives her a vial) Hold. Get you gone. Be strong and
           prosperous
In this resolve. I'll send a friar with speed
125   To Mantua with my letters to thy lord.

JULIET
Love give me strength, and strength shall help afford.
Farewell, dear Father.
                 Exeunt, separately

wake up as if from a pleasant sleep. Now, when the bridegroom comes to get you out of bed on Thursday morning, you'll seem dead. Then, as tradition demands, you'll be dressed up in your best clothes, put in an open coffin, and carried to the Capulet family tomb. Meanwhile, I'll send Romeo word of our plan. He'll come here, and we'll keep a watch for when you wake up. That night, Romeo will take you away to Mantua. This plan will free you from the shameful situation that troubles you now as long as you don't change your mind, or become scared like a silly woman and ruin your brave effort.

JULIET

Give me the vial. Give it to me! Don't talk to me about fear.

FRIAR LAWRENCE

(giving her the vial) Now go along on your way. Be strong and successful in this decision. I'll send a friar quickly to Mantua with my letter for Romeo.

JULIET

Love will give me strength, and strength will help me accomplish this plan. Goodbye, dear Father.

They exit separately.

ACT FOUR, Scene 2

Enter CAPULET, LADY CAPULET, NURSE, *and two or three* SERVINGMEN

CAPULET
(gives paper to FIRST SERVINGMAN*)* So many guests invite as here are writ.

                          Exit FIRST SERVINGMAN

(to SECOND SERVINGMAN*)* Sirrah, go hire me twenty cunning cooks.

SECOND SERVINGMAN
5   You shall have none ill, sir, for I'll try if they can lick their fingers.

CAPULET
How canst thou try them so?

SECOND SERVINGMAN
Marry, sir, 'tis an ill cook that cannot lick his own fingers. Therefore he that cannot lick his fingers goes not with me.

CAPULET
10   Go, be gone.
We shall be much unfurnished for this time.

                       Exit SECOND SERVINGMAN

What, is my daughter gone to Friar Lawrence?

NURSE
Ay, forsooth.

CAPULET
Well, he may chance to do some good on her.
15   A peevish self-willed harlotry it is.

Enter JULIET

ACT FOUR, Scene 2

CAPULET *enters with* LADY CAPULET, *the* NURSE, *and two or three* SERVINGMEN.

CAPULET

(giving the FIRST SERVINGMAN *a piece of paper)* Invite all the guests on this list.

The FIRST SERVINGMAN *exits.*

(to SECOND SERVINGMAN*)* Boy, go hire twenty skilled cooks.

SECOND SERVINGMAN

You won't get any bad cooks from me. I'll test them by making them lick their fingers.

CAPULET

How can you test them like that?

SECOND SERVINGMAN

Easy, sir. It's a bad cook who can't lick his own fingers. So the cooks who can't lick their fingers aren't hired.

CAPULET

Go, get out of here.

The SECOND SERVINGMAN *exits.*

We're unprepared for this wedding celebration. *(to the* NURSE*)* What, has my daughter gone to see Friar Lawrence?

NURSE

Yes, that's true.

CAPULET

Well, there's a chance he may do her some good. She's a stubborn little brat.

JULIET *enters.*

NURSE
    See where she comes from shrift with merry look.

CAPULET
    How now, my headstrong? Where have you been gadding?

JULIET
    Where I have learned me to repent the sin
    Of disobedient opposition
20   To you and your behests, and am enjoined
    By holy Lawrence to fall prostrate here
    To beg your pardon. *(falls to her knees)*
    Pardon, I beseech you!
    Henceforward I am ever ruled by you.

CAPULET
25   Send for the county. Go tell him of this.
    I'll have this knot knit up tomorrow morning.

JULIET
    I met the youthful lord at Lawrence' cell,
    And gave him what becomèd love I might,
    Not stepping o'er the bounds of modesty.

CAPULET
30   Why, I am glad on 't. This is well. Stand up.

JULIET *stands up*

    This is as 't should be.—Let me see the county.
    Ay, marry, go, I say, and fetch him hither.—
    Now, afore God, this reverend holy friar!
    Our whole city is much bound to him.

JULIET
35   Nurse, will you go with me into my closet
    To help me sort such needful ornaments
    As you think fit to furnish me tomorrow?

NURSE

Look, she's come home from confession with a happy look on her face.

CAPULET

So, my headstrong daughter, where have you been?

JULIET

I went somewhere where I learned that being disobedient to my father is a sin. Holy Father Lawrence instructed me to fall on my knees and beg your forgiveness. *(she kneels down)* Forgive me, I beg you. From now on I'll do whatever you say.

CAPULET

Send for the Count. Go tell him about this. I'll make this wedding happen tomorrow morning.

JULIET

I met the young man at Lawrence's cell. I treated him with the proper love, as well as I could, while still being modest.

CAPULET

Well, I'm glad about this. This is good. Stand up.

JULIET *stands up.*

This is the way is should be. I want to see the count. Yes, alright, go, I say, and bring him here. Now, before God, our whole city owes this friar a great debt.

JULIET

Nurse, will you come with me to my closet and help me pick out the clothes and the jewelry I'll need to wear tomorrow?

ACT FOUR

LADY CAPULET
No, not till Thursday. There is time enough.

CAPULET
Go, Nurse. Go with her. We'll to church tomorrow.
Exeunt JULIET *and* NURSE

LADY CAPULET
40   We shall be short in our provision.
'Tis now near night.

CAPULET
Tush, I will stir about,
And all things shall be well, I warrant thee, wife.
Go thou to Juliet, help to deck up her.
I'll not to bed tonight. Let me alone.
45   I'll play the housewife for this once.
LADY CAPULET *exits.*

—What, ho?
They are all forth?—Well, I will walk myself
To County Paris, to prepare him up
Against tomorrow. My heart is wondrous light
Since this same wayward girl is so reclaimed.
Exit

LADY CAPULET

No, not until Thursday. There's plenty of time.

CAPULET

Go, Nurse, go with her. We'll have the wedding at the church tomorrow.

JULIET and the NURSE exit.

LADY CAPULET

Our supplies will be short for the party. It's already almost night.

CAPULET

Don't worry, I will set things in motion. And everything will be alright, I promise you, wife. You should go to Juliet and dress her up. I'm not going to bed tonight. Leave me alone. I'll pretend to be the housewife for once.

LADY CAPULET exits.

Hey! What? They're all gone? Well, I will walk by myself to Count Paris to get him ready for tomorrow. My heart is wonderfully happy because this troubled girl has been taken back and now will be married.

CAPULET exits.

ACT FOUR, Scene 3

Enter JULIET *and* NURSE

JULIET
    Ay, those attires are best. But, gentle Nurse,
    I pray thee, leave me to myself tonight,
    For I have need of many orisons
    To move the heavens to smile upon my state,
5   Which, well thou know'st, is cross and full of sin.

Enter LADY CAPULET

LADY CAPULET
    What, are you busy, ho? Need you my help?

JULIET
    No, madam. We have culled such necessaries
    As are behooveful for our state tomorrow.
    So please you, let me now be left alone,
10   And let the Nurse this night sit up with you.
    For, I am sure, you have your hands full all
    In this so sudden business.

LADY CAPULET
                Good night.
    Get thee to bed and rest, for thou hast need.
                Exeunt LADY CAPULET *and* NURSE

JULIET
    Farewell!—God knows when we shall meet again.
15   I have a faint cold fear thrills through my veins
    That almost freezes up the heat of life.
    I'll call them back again to comfort me.—
    Nurse!—What should she do here?

ACT FOUR, Scene 3

JULIET *and the* NURSE *enter.*

JULIET

Yes, those are the best clothes. But, gentle Nurse, please leave me alone tonight. I have to say a lot of prayers to make the heavens bless me. You know that my life is troubled and full of sin.

LADY CAPULET *enters.*

LADY CAPULET

What, are you busy? Do you need my help?

JULIET

No, madam, we've figured out the best things for me to wear tomorrow at the ceremony. So if it's okay with you, I'd like to be left alone now. Let the Nurse sit up with you tonight. I'm sure you have your hands full preparing for the sudden festivities.

LADY CAPULET

Good night. Go to bed and get some rest. I'm sure you need it.

LADY CAPULET *and the* NURSE *exit.*

JULIET

Good-bye. Only God knows when we'll meet again. There is a slight cold fear cutting through my veins. It almost freezes the heat of life. I'll call them back here to comfort me. Nurse!—Oh, what good would she do here? In my desperate situation, I have to act alone.

My dismal scene I needs must act alone.
20   Come, vial. *(holds out the vial)*
What if this mixture do not work at all?
Shall I be married then tomorrow morning?
No, no. This shall forbid it. Lie thou there.
(lays her knife down)
What if it be a poison, which the friar
25   Subtly hath ministered to have me dead,
Lest in this marriage he should be dishonored
Because he married me before to Romeo?
I fear it is. And yet, methinks, it should not,
For he hath still been tried a holy man.
30   How if, when I am laid into the tomb,
I wake before the time that Romeo
Come to redeem me? There's a fearful point.
Shall I not, then, be stifled in the vault
To whose foul mouth no healthsome air breathes in,
35   And there die strangled ere my Romeo comes?
Or, if I live, is it not very like
The horrible conceit of death and night,
Together with the terror of the place—
As in a vault, an ancient receptacle,
40   Where for these many hundred years the bones
Of all my buried ancestors are packed;
Where bloody Tybalt, yet but green in earth,
Lies festering in his shroud; where, as they say,
At some hours in the night spirits resort—?
45   Alack, alack, is it not like that I,
So early waking, what with loathsome smells,
And shrieks like mandrakes torn out of the earth,
That living mortals, hearing them, run mad—?

Alright, here's the vial. What if this mixture doesn't work at all? Will I be married tomorrow morning? No, no, this knife will stop it. Lie down right there. *(she lays down the knife)* What if the Friar mixed the potion to kill me? Is he worried that he will be disgraced if I marry Paris after he married me to Romeo? I'm afraid that it's poison. And yet, it shouldn't be poison because he is a trustworthy holy man. What if, when I am put in the tomb, I wake up before Romeo comes to save me? That's a frightening idea. Won't I suffocate in the tomb? There's no healthy air to breathe in there. Will I die of suffocation before Romeo comes? Or if I live, I'll be surrounded by death and darkness. It will be terrible. There will be bones hundreds of years old in that tomb, my ancestors' bones. Tybalt's body will be in there, freshly entombed, and his corpse will be rotting. They say that during the night the spirits are in tombs. Oh no, oh no. I'll wake up and smell awful odors. I'll hear screams that would drive people crazy.

Oh, if I wake, shall I not be distraught,
50   Environèd with all these hideous fears,
And madly play with my forefather's joints,
And pluck the mangled Tybalt from his shroud,
And, in this rage, with some great kinsman's bone,
As with a club, dash out my desperate brains?
55   Oh, look! Methinks I see my cousin's ghost
Seeking out Romeo, that did spit his body
Upon a rapier's point. Stay, Tybalt, stay!
Romeo, Romeo, Romeo! Here's drink. I drink to thee.

She drinks and falls down on the bed,
hidden by the bed curtains

If I wake up too early, won't I go insane with all these horrible, frightening things around me, start playing with my ancestors' bones, and pull Tybalt's corpse out of his death shroud? Will I grab one of my dead ancestor's bones and bash in my own skull? Oh, look! I think I see my cousin Tybalt's ghost. He's looking for Romeo because Romeo killed him with his sword. Wait, Tybalt, wait! Romeo, Romeo, Romeo! Here's a drink. I drink to you.

She drinks from the vial and falls on her bed, hidden by her bed curtains.

ACT FOUR, Scene 4

Enter LADY CAPULET *and* NURSE

LADY CAPULET
Hold, take these keys, and fetch more spices, Nurse.

NURSE
They call for dates and quinces in the pastry.

Enter CAPULET

CAPULET
Come, stir, stir, stir! The second cock hath crowed.
The curfew bell hath rung. 'Tis three o'clock.—
Look to the baked meats, good Angelica.
Spare not for the cost.

NURSE
               Go, you cot-quean, go.
Get you to bed, faith. You'll be sick tomorrow
For this night's watching.

CAPULET
No, not a whit, what. I have watched ere now
All night for lesser cause, and ne'er been sick.

LADY CAPULET
Ay, you have been a mouse-hunt in your time,
But I will watch you from such watching now.
           Exeunt LADY CAPULET *and* NURSE

CAPULET
A jealous hood, a jealous hood!

Enter three or four SERVINGMEN *with spits
and logs and baskets*
               Now, fellow,
What is there?

ACT FOUR, Scene 4

LADY CAPULET *and the* NURSE *enter.*

LADY CAPULET
> Wait. Take these keys and get more spices, Nurse.

NURSE
> They're calling for dates and quinces in the pastry kitchen.

CAPULET *enters.*

CAPULET
> Come on, wake up, wake up, wake up! The second cock crowed. The curfew-bell rang. It's three o'clock. Go get the baked meats, good Angelica. Don't worry about the cost.

NURSE
> Go, you old housewife, go. Go to bed, dear. You'll be sick tomorrow because you've stayed up all night.

CAPULET
> No, not at all. What? I've stayed up all night many times before for less important matters, and I've never gotten sick.

LADY CAPULET
> Yes, you've been a ladies' man in your time. But I'll make sure you don't stay up any later now.

> > LADY CAPULET *and the* NURSE *exit.*

CAPULET
> A jealous woman, a jealous woman!

Three or four SERVINGMEN *enter with spits, logs, and baskets.*

> Now, fellow, what have you got there?

FIRST SERVINGMAN
15   Things for the cook, sir, but I know not what.

CAPULET
     Make haste, make haste, sirrah.

Exit **FIRST SERVINGMAN**

     (to **SECOND SERVINGMAN***)* Fetch drier logs.
     Call Peter. He will show thee where they are.

SECOND SERVINGMAN
     I have a head, sir, that will find out logs,
20   And never trouble Peter for the matter.

Exit **SECOND SERVINGMAN**

CAPULET
     Mass, and well said. A merry whoreson, ha!
     Thou shalt be loggerhead.—Good faith, 'tis day.
     The county will be here with music straight,
     For so he said he would. I hear him near.—

Music plays within

25   Nurse! Wife! What, ho? What, Nurse, I say!

Enter **NURSE**

     Go waken Juliet. Go and trim her up.
     I'll go and chat with Paris. Hie, make haste,
     Make haste. The bridegroom he is come already.
     Make haste, I say.

Exeunt

FIRST SERVINGMAN

Things for the cook, sir. But I don't know what they are.

CAPULET

Hurry up, hurry up.

The **FIRST SERVINGMAN** *exits.*

(to **SECOND SERVINGMAN***)* You, fetch logs that are drier than these. Call Peter, he'll show you where they are.

SECOND SERVINGMAN

I'm smart enough to find the logs myself without bothering Peter.

The **SECOND SERVINGMAN** *exits.*

CAPULET

Right, and well said. That guy's funny. He's got a head full of logs. Goodness, it's daylight. The count will be here soon with music. At least he said he would. I hear him coming near.

Music plays offstage.

Nurse! Wife! What? Hey, Nurse!

The **NURSE** *returns.*

Go wake Juliet. Go and get her dressed. I'll go and chat with Paris. Hey, hurry up, hurry up! The bridegroom is already here. Hurry up, I say.

They exit.

ACT FOUR, Scene 5

Enter NURSE

NURSE
Mistress! What, mistress! Juliet!—Fast, I warrant her,
    she.—
Why, lamb! Why, lady! Fie, you slug-a-bed.
Why, love, I say. Madam! Sweet-heart! Why, bride!
What, not a word? You take your pennyworths now.
5 Sleep for a week, for the next night, I warrant,
The County Paris hath set up his rest
That you shall rest but little.—God forgive me,
Marry, and amen. How sound is she asleep!
I must needs wake her.—Madam, madam, madam!
10 Ay, let the county take you in your bed.
He'll fright you up, i' faith. Will it not be?
(opens the bed curtains)
What, dressed and in your clothes, and down again?
I must needs wake you. Lady, lady, lady!—
Alas, alas! Help, help! My lady's dead!—
15 Oh, welladay, that ever I was born!—
Some aqua vitae, ho!—My lord! My lady!

Enter LADY CAPULET

LADY CAPULET
What noise is here?

NURSE
                 O lamentable day!

LADY CAPULET
What is the matter?

NURSE
                 Look, look. O heavy day!

ACT FOUR, Scene 5

The NURSE *enters.*

NURSE

Mistress! Hey, mistress! Juliet! I bet she's fast asleep.
Hey, lamb! Hey, lady! Hey, you lazy bones! Hey, love,
I say! Madam! Sweetheart! Hey, bride! What, you
don't say a word? You take your beauty sleep now. Get
yourself a week's worth of sleep. Tomorrow night, I
bet, Count Paris won't let you get much rest. God forgive me. Alright, and amen. How sound asleep she is!
I must wake her up. Madam, madam, madam! Yes, let
the count take you in your bed. He'll wake you up, I
bet. Won't he? *(she opens the bed curtains)* What?
You're still dressed in all your clothes. But you're still
asleep. I must wake you up. Lady! Lady! Lady! Oh
no, oh no! Help, help! My lady's dead! Oh curse the
day that I was born! Ho! Get me some brandy! My
lord! My lady!

LADY CAPULET *enters.*

LADY CAPULET
What's all the noise in here?

NURSE
Oh, sad day!

LADY CAPULET
What is the matter?

NURSE
Look, look! Oh, what a sad day!

LADY CAPULET
O me, O me! My child, my only life,
20   Revive, look up, or I will die with thee!—
Help, help! Call help.

Enter CAPULET

CAPULET
For shame, bring Juliet forth. Her lord is come.

NURSE
She's dead, deceased, she's dead. Alack the day!

LADY CAPULET
Alack the day. She's dead, she's dead, she's dead!

CAPULET
25   Ha? Let me see her. Out, alas! She's cold.
Her blood is settled, and her joints are stiff.
Life and these lips have long been separated.
Death lies on her like an untimely frost
Upon the sweetest flower of all the field.

NURSE
30   O lamentable day!

LADY CAPULET
                    O woeful time.

CAPULET
Death, that hath ta'en her hence to make me wail,
Ties up my tongue and will not let me speak.

Enter FRIAR LAWRENCE, *County* PARIS, *and* MUSICIANS

FRIAR LAWRENCE
Come, is the bride ready to go to church?

CAPULET
Ready to go, but never to return.
35   O son! The night before thy wedding day
Hath death lain with thy wife. There she lies,
Flower as she was, deflowered by him.

LADY CAPULET

Oh my, Oh my! My child, my reason for living, wake up, look up, or I'll die with you! Help, help! Call for help.

CAPULET *enters.*

CAPULET

For shame, bring Juliet out here. Her bridegroom is here.

NURSE

She's dead, deceased, she's dead. Curse the day!

LADY CAPULET

Curse the day! She's dead, she's dead, she's dead!

CAPULET

No! Let me see her. Oh no! She's cold. Her blood has stopped, and her joints are stiff. She's been dead for some time. She's dead, like a beautiful flower, killed by an unseasonable frost.

NURSE

Oh, sad day!

LADY CAPULET

Oh, this is a painful time!

CAPULET

Death, which has taken her away to make me cry, now ties up my tongue and won't let me speak.

FRIAR LAWRENCE *and* PARIS *enter with* MUSICIANS.

FRIAR LAWRENCE

Come, is the bride ready to go to church?

CAPULET

She's ready to go, but she'll never return. *(to* PARIS*)* Oh son! On the night before your wedding day, death has taken your wife. There she lies. She was a flower, but death deflowered her.

Death is my son-in-law. Death is my heir.
My daughter he hath wedded. I will die,
40 And leave him all. Life, living, all is Death's.

PARIS
Have I thought long to see this morning's face,
And doth it give me such a sight as this?

LADY CAPULET
Accursed, unhappy, wretched, hateful day!
Most miserable hour that e'er time saw
45 In lasting labor of his pilgrimage.
But one, poor one, one poor and loving child,
But one thing to rejoice and solace in,
And cruel death hath catched it from my sight!

NURSE
O woe! O woeful, woeful, woeful day!
50 Most lamentable day, most woeful day
That ever, ever, I did yet behold!
O day, O day, O day, O hateful day!
Never was seen so black a day as this.
O woeful day, O woeful day!

PARIS
55 Beguiled, divorcèd, wrongèd, spited, slain!
Most detestable Death, by thee beguiled,
By cruel, cruel thee quite overthrown!
O love! O life! Not life, but love in death.

CAPULET
Despised, distressèd, hated, martyred, killed!
60 Uncomfortable time, why camest thou now
To murder, murder our solemnity?
O child, O child! My soul, and not my child!
Dead art thou! Alack, my child is dead,
And with my child my joys are buried.

FRIAR LAWRENCE
65 Peace, ho, for shame! Confusion's cure lives not
In these confusions. Heaven and yourself
Had part in this fair maid. Now heaven hath all,

Death is my son-in-law. Death is my heir. My daughter married death. I will die and leave Death everything. Life, wealth, everything belongs to Death.

PARIS

Have I waited so long to see this morning, only to see this?

LADY CAPULET

Accursed, unhappy, wretched, hateful day! This is the most miserable hour of all time! I had only one child, one poor child, one poor and loving child, the one thing I had to rejoice and comfort myself, and cruel Death has stolen it from me!

NURSE

Oh pain! Oh painful, painful, painful day! The saddest day, most painful day that I ever, ever did behold! Oh day! Oh day! Oh day! Oh hateful day! There has never been so black a day as today. Oh painful day, Oh painful day!

PARIS

She was tricked, divorced, wronged, spited, killed! Death, the most despicable thing, tricked her. Cruel, cruel Death killed her. Oh love! Oh life! There is no life, but my love is dead!

CAPULET

Despised, distressed, hated, martyred, killed! Why did this have to happen now? Why did Death have to ruin our wedding? Oh child! Oh child! My soul and not my child! You are dead! Oh no! My child is dead. My child will be buried, and so will my joys.

FRIAR LAWRENCE

Be quiet, for shame! The cure for confusion is not yelling and screaming. You had this child with the help of heaven. Now heaven has her.

And all the better is it for the maid.
Your part in her you could not keep from death,
70   But heaven keeps his part in eternal life.
The most you sought was her promotion,
For 'twas your heaven she should be advanced.
And weep ye now, seeing she is advanced
Above the clouds, as high as heaven itself?
75   Oh, in this love, you love your child so ill
That you run mad, seeing that she is well.
She's not well married that lives married long,
But she's best married that dies married young.
Dry up your tears and stick your rosemary
80   On this fair corse, and, as the custom is,
And in her best array, bear her to church.
For though some nature bids us all lament,
Yet nature's tears are reason's merriment.

CAPULET
All things that we ordained festival
85   Turn from their office to black funeral.
Our instruments to melancholy bells,
Our wedding cheer to a sad burial feast.
Our solemn hymns to sullen dirges change,
Our bridal flowers serve for a buried corse,
90   And all things change them to the contrary.

FRIAR LAWRENCE
Sir, go you in, and, madam, go with him;
And go, Sir Paris. Every one prepare
To follow this fair corse unto her grave.
The heavens do lour upon you for some ill.
95   Move them no more by crossing their high will.

Exeunt CAPULET, LADY CAPULET,
PARIS, *and* FRIAR LAWRENCE

FIRST MUSICIAN
Faith, we may put up our pipes and be gone.

She is in a better place. You could not prevent her from dying someday, but heaven will give her eternal life. The most you hope for was for her to marry wealthy and rise up the social ladder—that was your idea of heaven. And now you cry, even though she has risen up above the clouds, as high as heaven itself? Oh, in this love, you love your child so badly, that you go mad, even though she is in heaven. It is best to marry well and die young, better than to be married for a long time. Dry up your tears, and put your rosemary on this beautiful corpse. And, in accordance with custom, carry her to the church in her best clothes. It's natural for us to shed tears for her, but the truth is, we should be happy for her.

CAPULET

All the things that we prepared for the wedding party will now be used for the funeral. Our happy music will now be sad. Our wedding banquet will become a sad burial feast. Our celebratory hymns will change to sad funeral marches. Our bridal flowers will cover a buried corpse. And everything will be used for the opposite purpose from what we intended.

FRIAR LAWRENCE

Sir, you go in. And, madam, go with him. And you go too, Sir Paris. Everyone prepare to take this beautiful corpse to her grave. The heavens hang threateningly over you for some past sin. Don't disturb the heavens any more by trying to go against heaven's will.

CAPULET, LADY CAPULET, PARIS,
and FRIAR LAWRENCE *exit*.

FIRST MUSICIAN

Well, we can put away our pipes and go home.

ACT FOUR

NURSE
Honest good fellows, ah, put up, put up,
For, well you know, this is a pitiful case.

Exit

FIRST MUSICIAN
Ay, by my troth, the case may be amended.

Enter PETER

PETER
100   Musicians, O musicians, "Heart's Ease," "Heart's Ease."
O, an you will have me live, play "Heart's Ease."

FIRST MUSICIAN
Why "Heart's ease?"

PETER
O musicians, because my heart itself plays "My Heart is
Full." O, play me some merry dump to comfort me.

FIRST MUSICIAN
105   Not a dump, we. 'Tis no time to play now.

PETER
You will not then?

FIRST MUSICIAN
No.

PETER
I will then give it you soundly.

FIRST MUSICIAN
What will you give us?

PETER
110   No money, on my faith, but the gleek. I will give you the
minstrel.

FIRST MUSICIAN
Then I will give you the serving creature.

NURSE

Honest good boys, ah, put 'em away, put 'em away. As you know, this is a sad case.

The **NURSE** *exits.*

FIRST MUSICIAN

Yes, well, things could get better.

PETER *enters.*

PETER

Musicians, oh, musicians, play "Heart's Ease," "Heart's Ease." Oh, I'll die if you don't play "Heart's Ease."

FIRST MUSICIAN

Why "Heart's Ease"?

PETER

Oh, musicians, because my heart is singing "My Heart is Full of Woe." Oh, play me some happy sad song to comfort me.

FIRST MUSICIAN

No, not a sad song. It's not the right time to play.

PETER

You won't, then?

FIRST MUSICIAN

No.

PETER

Then I'll really give it to you.

FIRST MUSICIAN

What will you give us?

PETER

No money, I swear. But I'll play a trick on you. I'll call you a minstrel.

FIRST MUSICIAN

Then I'll call you a serving-creature.

PETER
Then will I lay the serving creature's dagger on your pate.
I will carry no crotchets. I'll *re* you, I'll *fa* you. Do you note
115 me?

FIRST MUSICIAN
An you *re* us and *fa* us, you note us.

SECOND MUSICIAN
Pray you, put up your dagger and put out your wit.

PETER
Then have at you with my wit. I will dry-beat you
with an iron wit and put up my iron dagger. Answer
120 me like men.

(sings)
   When griping grief the heart doth wound
   And doleful dumps the mind oppress,
   Then music with her silver sound—

(speaks) Why "silver sound"? Why "music with her silver
125 sound"? What say you, Simon Catling?

FIRST MUSICAN
Marry, sir, because silver hath a sweet sound.

PETER
Prates.—What say you, Hugh Rebeck?

SECOND MUSICIAN
I say, "silver sound" because musicians sound for silver.

PETER
Prates too.—What say you, James Soundpost?

THIRD MUSICIAN
130 Faith, I know not what to say.

PETER

Then I'll smack you on the head with the serving-creature's knife. I won't mess around. I'll make you sing. Do you hear me?

FIRST MUSICIAN

If you make us sing, you'll hear us.

SECOND MUSICIAN

Please, put down your knife and stop kidding around.

PETER

So you don't like my kidding around! I'll kid you to death, and then I'll put down my knife. Answer me like men.

(sings)

> *When sadness wounds your heart,*
> *And pain takes over your mind,*
> *Then music with her silver sound—*

Catling = a violin string

(speaks) Why the line "silver sound"? What do they mean, "music with her silver sound"? What do you say, Simon Catling?

FIRST MUSICIAN

Well, sir, because silver has a sweet sound.

PETER

Rebeck = a fiddle

That's a stupid answer! What do you say, Hugh Rebeck?

SECOND MUSICIAN

I say "silver sound," because musicians play to earn silver.

PETER

Soundpost = part of a violin

Another studpid answer! What do you say, James Soundpost?

THIRD MUSICIAN

Well, I don't know what to say.

PETER
Oh, I cry you mercy, you are the singer. I will say for you.
It is "music with her silver sound" because musicians have
no gold for sounding.

(sings)
> *Then music with her silver sound*
135 > *With speedy help doth lend redress.*

Exit PETER

FIRST MUSICIAN
What a pestilent knave is this same!

SECOND MUSICIAN
Hang him, Jack! Come, we'll in here, tarry for the mourners
and stay dinner.

Exeunt

PETER

Oh, I beg your pardon. You're the singer. I'll answer for you. It is "music with her silver sound," because musicians have no gold to use to make sounds.

(sings)

> *Then music with her silver sound*
> *makes you feel just fine.*

PETER exits.

FIRST MUSICIAN

What an annoying man, this guy is!

SECOND MUSICIAN

Forget about him, Jack! Come, we'll go in there. We'll wait for the mourners and stay for dinner.

The MUSICIANS exit.

ACT FIVE

Scene 1

Enter ROMEO

ROMEO
If I may trust the flattering truth of sleep,
My dreams presage some joyful news at hand.
My bosom's lord sits lightly in his throne,
And all this day an unaccustomed spirit
5   Lifts me above the ground with cheerful thoughts.
I dreamt my lady came and found me dead—
Strange dream, that gives a dead man leave to think—
And breathed such life with kisses in my lips
That I revived and was an emperor.
10   Ah me! How sweet is love itself possessed
When but love's shadows are so rich in joy!

Enter ROMEO'S *man* BALTHASAR

News from Verona!—How now, Balthasar?
Dost thou not bring me letters from the friar?
How doth my lady? Is my father well?
15   How fares my Juliet? That I ask again,
For nothing can be ill if she be well.

BALTHASAR
Then she is well, and nothing can be ill.
Her body sleeps in Capels' monument,
And her immortal part with angels lives.
20   I saw her laid low in her kindred's vault
And presently took post to tell it you.
O, pardon me for bringing these ill news,
Since you did leave it for my office, sir.

ACT FIVE

Scene 1

ROMEO *enters.*

ROMEO

If I can trust my dreams, then some joyful news is coming soon. Love rules my heart, and all day long a strange feeling has been making me cheerful. I had a dream that my lady came and found me dead. It's a strange dream that lets a dead man think! She came and brought me back to life by kissing my lips. I rose from the dead and was an emperor. Oh my! How sweet it it would be to actually have the woman I love, when merely thinking about love makes me so happy.

ROMEO's *servant* BALTHASAR *enters.*

Do you have news from Verona!—What is it, Balthasar? Do you bring me a letter from the friar? How is my wife? Is my father well? How is my Juliet? I ask that again because nothing can be wrong if she is well.

BALTHASAR

Then she is well, and nothing is wrong. Her body sleeps in the Capulet tomb, and her immortal soul lives with the angels in heaven. I saw her buried in her family's tomb, and then I came here to tell you the news. Oh, pardon me for bringing this bad news, but you told me it was my job, sir.

ROMEO
    Is it e'en so? Then I defy you, stars!
25   Thou know'st my lodging. Get me ink and paper,
    And hire post horses. I will hence tonight.

BALTHASAR
    I do beseech you, sir, have patience.
    Your looks are pale and wild, and do import
    Some misadventure.

ROMEO
30   Tush, thou art deceived.
    Leave me and do the thing I bid thee do.
    Hast thou no letters to me from the friar?

BALTHASAR
    No, my good lord.

ROMEO
    No matter. Get thee gone,
35   And hire those horses. I'll be with thee straight.

                    Exit **BALTHASAR**

    Well, Juliet, I will lie with thee tonight.
    Let's see for means. O mischief, thou art swift
    To enter in the thoughts of desperate men!
    I do remember an apothecary—
40   And hereabouts he dwells—which late I noted
    In tattered weeds, with overwhelming brows,
    Culling of simples. Meager were his looks,
    Sharp misery had worn him to the bones,
    And in his needy shop a tortoise hung,
45   An alligator stuffed, and other skins
    Of ill-shaped fishes; and about his shelves
    A beggarly account of empty boxes,
    Green earthen pots, bladders and musty seeds,
    Remnants of packthread and old cakes of roses,
50   Were thinly scattered to make up a show.

ROMEO

Is it really true? Then I rebel against you, stars! You know where I live. Get me some ink and paper, and hire some horses to ride. I will leave here for Verona tonight.

BALTHASAR

Please, sir, have patience. You look pale and wild as if you're going to hurt yourself.

ROMEO

Tsk, you're wrong. Leave me and do what I told you to do. Don't you have a letter for me from the friar?

BALTHASAR

No, my good lord.

ROMEO

No matter. Get on your way and hire those horses. I'll be with you right away.

BALTHASAR exits.

Well, Juliet, I'll lie with you tonight. Let's see how. Destructive thoughts come quickly to the minds of desperate men! I remember a pharmacist who lives nearby. I remember he wears shabby clothes and has bushy eyebrows. He makes drugs from herbs. He looks poor and miserable and worn out to the bone. He had a tortoise shell hanging up in his shop as well as a stuffed alligator and other skins of strange fish. There were a few empty boxes on his shelves, as well as green clay pots, and some musty seeds. There were a few strands of string and mashed rose petals on display.

Noting this penury, to myself I said,
"An if a man did need a poison now"—
Whose sale is present death in Mantua—
"Here lives a caitiff wretch would sell it him."
55   Oh, this same thought did but forerun my need,
And this same needy man must sell it me.
As I remember, this should be the house.
Being holiday, the beggar's shop is shut.
What, ho! Apothecary!

Enter APOTHECARY

APOTHECARY
                              Who calls so loud?

ROMEO
60   Come hither, man. I see that thou art poor.
Hold, there is forty ducats. Let me have
A dram of poison, such soon-speeding gear
As will disperse itself through all the veins
That the life-weary taker may fall dead,
65   And that the trunk may be discharged of breath
As violently as hasty powder fired
Doth hurry from the fatal cannon's womb.

APOTHECARY
Such mortal drugs I have, but Mantua's law
Is death to any he that utters them.

ROMEO
70   Art thou so bare and full of wretchedness,
And fear'st to die? Famine is in thy cheeks.
Need and oppression starveth in thine eyes.
Contempt and beggary hangs upon thy back.
The world is not thy friend nor the world's law.
75   The world affords no law to make thee rich.
Then be not poor, but break it, and take this.
(holds out money)

Noticing all this poverty, I said to myself, "If a man needed some poison"—which they would immediately kill you for selling in Mantua—"here is a miserable wretch who'd sell it to him." Oh, this idea came before I needed the poison. But this same poor man must sell it to me. As I remember, this should be the house. Today's a holiday, so the beggar's shop is shut. Hey! Pharmacist!

The APOTHECARY *enters.*

APOTHECARY

Who's that calling so loud?

ROMEO

Come here, man. I see that you are poor. Here are forty ducats. Let me have a shot of poison, something that works so fast that the person who takes it will die as fast as gunpowder exploding in a canon.

APOTHECARY

I have lethal poisons like that. But it's against the law to sell them in Mantua, and the penalty is death.

ROMEO

You're this poor and wretched and still afraid to die? Your cheeks are thin because of hunger. I can see in your eyes that you're starving. Anyone can see that you're a beggar. The world is not your friend, and neither is the law. The world doesn't make laws to make you rich. So don't be poor. Break the law, and take this money. *(he holds out money)*

APOTHECARY
My poverty, but not my will, consents.

ROMEO
I pay thy poverty and not thy will.

APOTHECARY
(gives ROMEO *poison)* Put this in any liquid thing you will
80   And drink it off; and, if you had the strength
Of twenty men, it would dispatch you straight.

ROMEO
(gives APOTHECARY *money)*
There is thy gold, worse poison to men's souls,
Doing more murder in this loathsome world,
Than these poor compounds that thou mayst not sell.
85   I sell thee poison. Thou hast sold me none.
Farewell. Buy food, and get thyself in flesh.—
Come, cordial and not poison, go with me
To Juliet's grave, for there must I use thee.

Exeunt

APOTHECARY

I agree because I'm poor, not because I want to.

ROMEO

I pay you because you're poor, not because you want me to buy this.

APOTHECARY

(gives ROMEO *poison)* Put this in any kind of liquid you want and drink it down. Even if you were as strong as twenty men, it would kill you immediately.

ROMEO

(gives APOTHECARY *money)* There is your gold. Money is a worse poison to men's souls, and commits more murders in this awful world, than these poor poisons that you're not allowed to sell. I've sold *you* poison. You haven't sold me any. Goodbye. Buy yourself food, and put some flesh on your bones. I'll take this mixture, which is a medicine, not a poison, to Juliet's grave. That's where I must use it.

They exit.

ACT FIVE, Scene 2

Enter FRIAR JOHN

FRIAR JOHN
Holy Franciscan Friar! Brother, ho!

Enter FRIAR LAWRENCE

FRIAR LAWRENCE
This same should be the voice of Friar John.
Welcome from Mantua. What says Romeo?
Or, if his mind be writ, give me his letter.

FRIAR JOHN
5   Going to find a barefoot brother out,
One of our order, to associate me,
Here in this city visiting the sick,
And finding him, the searchers of the town,
Suspecting that we both were in a house
10   Where the infectious pestilence did reign,
Sealed up the doors and would not let us forth.
So that my speed to Mantua there was stayed.

FRIAR LAWRENCE
Who bare my letter, then, to Romeo?

FRIAR JOHN
I could not send it—here it is again—
(gives FRIAR LAWRENCE *a letter)*
15   Nor get a messenger to bring it thee,
So fearful were they of infection.

FRIAR LAWRENCE
Unhappy fortune! By my brotherhood,
The letter was not nice but full of charge,
Of dear import, and the neglecting it
20   May do much danger. Friar John, go hence.
Get me an iron crow and bring it straight
Unto my cell.

ACT FIVE, Scene 2

FRIAR JOHN *enters.*

FRIAR JOHN
Holy Franciscan Friar! Brother, hey!

FRIAR LAWRENCE *enters.*

FRIAR LAWRENCE
That sounds like the voice of Friar John. Welcome back from Mantua. What does Romeo say? Or, if he wrote down his thoughts, give me his letter.

FRIAR JOHN
I went to find another poor friar from our order to accompany me. He was here in this city visiting the sick. When I found him, the town health officials suspected that we were both in a house that had been hit with the plague. They quarantined the house, sealed up the doors, and refused to let us out. I couldn't go to Mantua because I was stuck there.

FRIAR LAWRENCE
Then who took my letter to Romeo?

FRIAR JOHN
I couldn't send it. Here it is. *(he gives* FRIAR LAWRENCE *a letter)* I couldn't get a messenger to bring it to you either because they were scared of spreading the infection.

FRIAR LAWRENCE
Unhappy fortune! By my brotherhood, the letter was not just a nice greeting. It was full of very important information. It's very dangerous that it hasn't been sent. Friar John, go and get me an iron crowbar. Bring it straight back to my cell.

FRIAR JOHN
Brother, I'll go and bring it thee.

Exit **FRIAR JOHN**

FRIAR LAWRENCE
Now must I to the monument alone.
Within this three hours will fair Juliet wake.
25   She will beshrew me much that Romeo
Hath had no notice of these accidents.
But I will write again to Mantua,
And keep her at my cell till Romeo come.
Poor living corse, closed in a dead man's tomb!

Exit

FRIAR JOHN
>Brother, I'll go and bring it to you.

>*FRIAR JOHN exits.*

FRIAR LAWRENCE
>Now I must go to the tomb alone. Within three hours Juliet will wake up. She'll be very angry with me that Romeo doesn't know what happened. But I'll write again to Mantua, and I'll keep her in my cell until Romeo comes. That poor living corpse. She's shut inside a dead man's tomb!

>*FRIAR LAWRENCE exits.*

ACT FIVE, Scene 3

Enter PARIS *and his* PAGE

PARIS
Give me thy torch, boy. Hence, and stand aloof.
Yet put it out, for I would not be seen.
Under yon yew trees lay thee all along,
Holding thine ear close to the hollow ground—
5   So shall no foot upon the churchyard tread,
Being loose, unfirm, with digging up of graves,
But thou shalt hear it. Whistle then to me,
As signal that thou hear'st something approach.
Give me those flowers. Do as I bid thee, go.

PAGE *extinguishes torch, gives* PARIS *flowers*

PAGE
10   (*aside*) I am almost afraid to stand alone
Here in the churchyard. Yet I will adventure.

PAGE *moves aside*

PARIS
(*scatters flowers at* JULIET'S *closed tomb*)
Sweet flower, with flowers thy bridal bed I strew—
O woe! Thy canopy is dust and stones—
Which with sweet water nightly I will dew.
15   Or, wanting that, with tears distilled by moans,
The obsequies that I for thee will keep
Nightly shall be to strew thy grave and weep.

PAGE *whistles*

The boy gives warning something doth approach.
What cursèd foot wanders this way tonight

ACT FIVE, Scene 3

Give me your torch, boy. Go away and stay apart from me. Put the torch out, so I can't be seen. Hide under the yew-trees over there. Listen to make sure no one is coming through the graveyard. If you hear any one, whistle to me to signal that someone is approaching. Give me those flowers. Do as I tell you. Go.

The PAGE *puts out the torch and gives* PARIS *the flowers.*

PAGE

(to himself) I am almost afraid to stand alone here in the graveyard, but I'll take the risk.

The PAGE *moves aside.*

PARIS

(he scatters flowers at JULIET*'s closed tomb)* Sweet flower, I'm spreading flowers over your bridal bed. Oh, pain! Your canopy is dust and stones. I'll water these flowers every night with sweet water. Or, if I don't do that, my nightly rituals to remember you will be to put flowers on your grave and weep.

The PAGE *whistles.*

The boy is warning me that someone approaches. Who could be walking around here tonight? Who's

20   To cross my obsequies and true love's rite?
      What with a torch! Muffle me, night, awhile.

      PARIS *moves away from the tomb*
      Enter ROMEO *and* BALTHASAR

ROMEO
      Give me that mattock and the wrenching iron.
      (takes them from BALTHASAR*)*
      Hold, take this letter. Early in the morning
      See thou deliver it to my lord and father.
      (gives letter to BALTHASAR*)*
25   Give me the light.
      (takes torch from BALTHASAR*)*
                          Upon thy life I charge thee,
      Whate'er thou hear'st or seest, stand all aloof,
      And do not interrupt me in my course.
      Why I descend into this bed of death
      Is partly to behold my lady's face,
30   But chiefly to take thence from her dead finger
      A precious ring, a ring that I must use
      In dear employment. Therefore hence, be gone.
      But if thou, jealous, dost return to pry
      In what I farther shall intend to do,
35   By heaven, I will tear thee joint by joint
      And strew this hungry churchyard with thy limbs.
      The time and my intents are savage, wild,
      More fierce and more inexorable far
      Than empty tigers or the roaring sea.
BALTHASAR
40   I will be gone, sir, and not trouble you.
ROMEO
      So shalt thou show me friendship. Take thou that.
      (gives BALTHASAR *money)*
      Live and be prosperous, and farewell, good fellow.

ruining my rituals of true love? It's someone with a torch! I must hide in the darkness for awhile.

PARIS *hides in the darkness.*
ROMEO *and* BALTHASAR *enter with a torch,*
a pickax, and an iron crowbar.

ROMEO

Give me that pickax and the crowbar. *(he takes them from* BALTHASAR*)* Here, take this letter. Early in the morning deliver it to my father. *(he gives the letter to* BALTHASAR*)* Give me the light. *(he takes the torch from* BALTHASAR*)* Swear on your life, I command you, whatever you hear or see, stay away from me and do not interrupt me in my plan. I'm going down into this tomb of the dead, partly to behold my wife's face. But my main reason is to take a precious ring from her dead finger. I must use that ring for an important purpose. So go on your way. But if you get curious and return to spy on me, I swear I'll tear you apart limb by limb and spread your body parts around to feed the hungry animals in the graveyard. My plan is wild and savage. I am more fierce in this endeavor than a hungry tiger or the raging sea.

BALTHASAR

I'll go, sir, and I won't bother you.

ROMEO

That's the way to show me friendship. Take this. *(he gives* BALTHASAR *money)* Live and be prosperous. Farewell, good fellow.

ACT FIVE

BALTHASAR
(aside) For all this same, I'll hide me hereabout.
His looks I fear, and his intents I doubt.

BALTHASAR *moves aside, falls asleep*

ROMEO
45   Thou detestable maw, thou womb of death,
Gorged with the dearest morsel of the earth,
Thus I enforce thy rotten jaws to open,
And in despite I'll cram thee with more food!
(begins to opens the tomb with his tools)

PARIS
(aside) This is that banished haughty Montague,
50   That murdered my love's cousin, with which grief,
It is supposed the fair creature died.
And here is come to do some villainous shame
To the dead bodies. I will apprehend him.
(to ROMEO*)* Stop thy unhallowed toil, vile Montague!
55   Can vengeance be pursued further than death?
Condemnèd villain, I do apprehend thee.
Obey and go with me, for thou must die.

ROMEO
I must indeed, and therefore came I hither.
Good gentle youth, tempt not a desperate man.
60   Fly hence and leave me. Think upon these gone.
Let them affright thee. I beseech thee, youth,
Put not another sin upon my head
By urging me to fury. O, be gone!
By heaven, I love thee better than myself,
65   For I come hither armed against myself.
Stay not, be gone. Live, and hereafter say
A madman's mercy bid thee run away.

BALTHASAR

(*speaking so that only* PARIS *can hear*) Despite what I said, I'll hide nearby. I'm frightened by the look on his face, and I have doubts about his intentions.

BALTHASAR *moves aside and falls asleep.*

ROMEO

(*speaking to the tomb*) You horrible mouth of death! You've eaten up the dearest creature on Earth. Now I'm going to force open your rotten jaws and make you eat another body. (ROMEO *begins to open the tomb with his tools*)

PARIS

(*speaking so that* ROMEO *can't hear*) It's that arrogant Montague, the one who's been banished. He's the one who murdered my love's cousin Tybalt. They think she died with grief for that cousin. This guy has come here to commit awful crimes against the dead bodies. I'll catch him.

(*to* ROMEO) Stop your evil work, vile Montague! Can you take revenge on dead bodies? Condemned villain, I've caught you. Obey and come with me. You must die.

ROMEO

I must indeed. That's why I came here. Good and noble young man, don't mess with someone who's desperate. Get away from here and leave me. Think about the ones who have died. Let them put fear in your heart. Please, young man, don't make me angry. I don't want to commit another crime. Oh, go away! I swear, I love you more than I love myself. For I've come here with weapons to use against myself. Don't stay here, go away. Live, and from now on, say a madman mercifully told you to run away.

PARIS
I do defy thy commination
And apprehend thee for a felon here.

ROMEO
70   Wilt thou provoke me? Then have at thee, boy!

ROMEO *and* PARIS *fight*

PAGE
O Lord, they fight! I will go call the watch.

Exit PAGE

PARIS
(falls) Oh, I am slain! If thou be merciful,
Open the tomb. Lay me with Juliet.

PARIS *dies*

ROMEO
In faith, I will.—Let me peruse this face.
75   Mercutio's kinsman, noble County Paris.
What said my man, when my betossèd soul
Did not attend him as we rode? I think
He told me Paris should have married Juliet.
Said he not so? Or did I dream it so?
80   Or am I mad, hearing him talk of Juliet,
To think it was so?—O, give me thy hand,
One writ with me in sour misfortune's book.
I'll bury thee in a triumphant grave.

ROMEO *opens the tomb to reveal* JULIET *inside*

A grave? Oh, no. A lantern, slaughtered youth,
85   For here lies Juliet, and her beauty makes
This vault a feasting presence full of light.
Death, lie thou there, by a dead man interred.
(lays PARIS *in the tomb)*

PARIS

> I refuse your request. I'm arresting you as a criminal.

ROMEO

> Are you going to provoke me? Alright, let's fight, boy!

ROMEO *and* PARIS *fight.*

PAGE

> Oh Lord, they're fighting! I'll go call the watch.
>
> *The* PAGE *exits.*

PARIS

> *(he falls)* Oh, I've been killed! If you are merciful, open the tomb and lay me next to Juliet.

PARIS *dies.*

ROMEO

> Alright, I will. Let me look at this face. It's Mercutio's relative, noble Count Paris! What did my man say? I was worried, so I wasn't listening to him while we were riding. I think he told me Paris was about to marry Juliet. Isn't that what he said? Or was I dreaming? Or am I crazy? Did I hear him say something about Juliet and jump to conclusions? Oh, give me your hand. Both of us had such bad luck! I'll bury you in a magnificent grave.

ROMEO *opens the tomb to reveal* JULIET *inside.*

> A grave? Oh no! This is a lantern, dead Paris. Juliet lies here, and her beauty fills this tomb with light. Dead men, lie there. You are being buried by another dead man. *(he lays* PARIS *in the tomb)*

ACT FIVE

How oft when men are at the point of death
Have they been merry, which their keepers call
90   A lightning before death! Oh, how may I
Call this a lightning?—O my love, my wife!
Death, that hath sucked the honey of thy breath,
Hath had no power yet upon thy beauty.
Thou art not conquered. Beauty's ensign yet
95   Is crimson in thy lips and in thy cheeks,
And death's pale flag is not advancèd there.—
Tybalt, liest thou there in thy bloody sheet?
O, what more favor can I do to thee,
Than with that hand that cut thy youth in twain
100 To sunder his that was thine enemy?
Forgive me, cousin.—Ah, dear Juliet,
Why art thou yet so fair? Shall I believe
That unsubstantial death is amorous,
And that the lean abhorrèd monster keeps
105 Thee here in dark to be his paramour?
For fear of that, I still will stay with thee,
And never from this palace of dim night
Depart again. Here, here will I remain
With worms that are thy chamber maids. Oh, here
110 Will I set up my everlasting rest,
And shake the yoke of inauspicious stars
From this world-wearied flesh. Eyes, look your last.
Arms, take your last embrace. And, lips, O you
The doors of breath, seal with a righteous kiss
115 A dateless bargain to engrossing death.
(kisses JULIET, *takes out the poison)*
Come, bitter conduct, come, unsavoury guide.
Thou desperate pilot, now at once run on
The dashing rocks thy seasick, weary bark.
Here's to my love! *(drinks the poison)* O true apothecary,
120 Thy drugs are quick. Thus with a kiss I die.

ROMEO *dies*

How often are men happy right before they die! They call it the lightness before death. Oh, how can I call this lightness? Oh, my love! My wife! Death has sucked the honey from your breath, but it has not yet ruined your beauty. You haven't been conquered. There is still red in your lips and in your cheeks. Death has not yet turned them pale. Tybalt, are you lying there in your bloody death shroud? Oh, what better favor can I do for you than to kill the man who killed you with the same hand that made you die young. Forgive me, cousin! Ah, dear Juliet, why are you still so beautiful? Should I believe that death is in love with you, and that the awful monster keeps you here to be his mistress? I don't like that idea, so I'll stay with you. And I will never leave this tomb. Here, here I'll remain with worms that are your chamber-maids. Oh, I'll rest here forever. I'll forget about all the bad luck that has troubled me. Eyes, look out for the last time! Arms, make your last embrace! And lips, you are the doors of breath. Seal with a righteous kiss the deal I have made with death forever. (ROMEO *kisses* JULIET *and takes out the poison*) Come, bitter poison, come, unsavory guide! You desperate pilot, let's crash this sea-weary ship into the rocks! Here's to my love!

ROMEO *drinks the poison.*

Oh, that pharmacist was honest! His drugs work quickly. So I die with a kiss.

ROMEO *dies.*

ACT FIVE

Enter FRIAR LAWRENCE *with lantern, crow, and spade*

FRIAR LAWRENCE
Saint Francis be my speed! How oft tonight
Have my old feet stumbled at graves!—Who's there?

BALTHASAR
Here's one, a friend, and one that knows you well.

FRIAR LAWRENCE
Bliss be upon you! Tell me, good my friend,
125   What torch is yond that vainly lends his light
To grubs and eyeless skulls? As I discern,
It burneth in the Capels' monument.

BALTHASAR
It doth so, holy sir, and there's my master,
One that you love.

FRIAR LAWRENCE
                    Who is it?

BALTHASAR
                              Romeo.

FRIAR LAWRENCE
130   How long hath he been there?

BALTHASAR
                                 Full half an hour.

FRIAR LAWRENCE
Go with me to the vault.

BALTHASAR
                         I dare not, sir.
My master knows not but I am gone hence,
And fearfully did menace me with death
If I did stay to look on his intents.

FRIAR LAWRENCE
135   Stay, then. I'll go alone. Fear comes upon me.
Oh, much I fear some ill unthrifty thing.

FRIAR LAWRENCE *enters with a lantern, crowbar, and shovel.*

FRIAR LAWRENCE
> Saint Francis, help me! How often tonight have my old feet stumbled on gravestones! Who's there?

BALTHASAR
> I'm a friend, a friend who knows you well.

FRIAR LAWRENCE
> God bless you! Tell me, my good friend, what is that light over there? The one that vainly lights up the darkness for worms and skulls without eyes? It looks to me like it's burning in the Capulet tomb.

BALTHASAR
> That is where it's burning, father. My master is there. The one you love.

FRIAR LAWRENCE
> Who is it?

BALTHASAR
> Romeo.

FRIAR LAWRENCE
> How long has he been there?

BALTHASAR
> For a full half hour.

FRIAR LAWRENCE
> Go with me to the tomb.

BALTHASAR
> I don't dare, sir. My master doesn't know I'm still here. He threatened me with death if I stayed to look at what he was doing.

FRIAR LAWRENCE
> Stay, then. I'll go alone. I'm suddenly afraid. Oh, I'm very scared something awful has happened.

ACT FIVE

BALTHASAR
As I did sleep under this yew tree here,
I dreamt my master and another fought,
And that my master slew him.

FRIAR LAWRENCE
(approaches the tomb)
                    Romeo!—

140
Alack, alack, what blood is this, which stains
The stony entrance of the sepulcher?
What mean these masterless and gory swords
To lie discolored by this place of peace?
(looks inside the tomb)
Romeo! O, pale!—Who else? What, Paris too?

145
And steeped in blood?—Ah, what an unkind hour
Is guilty of this lamentable chance!
The lady stirs.

JULIET *wakes*

JULIET
O comfortable Friar! Where is my lord?
I do remember well where I should be,

150
And there I am. Where is my Romeo?

A noise sounds from outside the tomb

FRIAR LAWRENCE
I hear some noise. Lady, come from that nest
Of death, contagion, and unnatural sleep.
A greater power than we can contradict
Hath thwarted our intents. Come, come away.

155
Thy husband in thy bosom there lies dead,
And Paris too. Come, I'll dispose of thee
Among a sisterhood of holy nuns.
Stay not to question, for the watch is coming.
Come, go, good Juliet. I dare no longer stay.

BALTHASAR

As I slept under this yew-tree here, I had a dream that my master and someone else were fighting and that my master killed him.

FRIAR LAWRENCE

(approaching the tomb) Romeo! Oh no! What is this blood that stains the stony entrance of this tomb? Why are these bloody swords lying here, abandoned by their masters? Next to this place of peace? *(he looks inside the tomb)* Romeo! Oh, he's pale! Who else? What, Paris too? And he's covered in blood? Ah, when did these horrible things happen? The lady's moving.

JULIET *wakes up.*

JULIET

Oh friendly friar! Where is my husband? I remember very well where I should be, and here I am. Where is my Romeo?

A noise sounds from outside the tomb.

FRIAR LAWRENCE

I hear some noise. Lady, come out of the tomb. A greater power than we can fight has ruined our plan. Come, come away. Your husband lies dead there, and Paris too. Come, I'll place you among the sisterhood of holy nuns. Don't wait to ask questions. The watch is coming. Come, let's go, good Juliet, I don't dare stay any longer.

ACT FIVE

JULIET

160   Go, get thee hence, for I will not away.—

Exit **FRIAR LAWRENCE**

What's here? A cup, closed in my true love's hand?
Poison, I see, hath been his timeless end.—
O churl, drunk all, and left no friendly drop
To help me after? I will kiss thy lips.
165   Haply some poison yet doth hang on them,
To make me die with a restorative.
(kisses **ROMEO***)*
Thy lips are warm.

Enter **WATCHMEN** *and* **PARIS'S PAGE**

CHIEF WATCHMAN

(to **PAGE***)* Lead, boy. Which way?

JULIET

Yea, noise? Then I'll be brief. O happy dagger,
170   This is thy sheath. There rust and let me die.
(stabs herself with **ROMEO***'s dagger and dies)*

PAGE

This is the place. There, where the torch doth burn.

CHIEF WATCHMAN

The ground is bloody.—Search about the churchyard.
Go, some of you. Whoe'er you find, attach.

Exeunt some **WATCHMEN**

Pitiful sight! Here lies the county slain,
175   And Juliet bleeding, warm and newly dead,
Who here hath lain these two days buried.—
Go, tell the Prince. Run to the Capulets.
Raise up the Montagues. Some others search.

Exeunt more **WATCHMEN**

JULIET

Go, get out of here. I'm not going anywhere.

FRIAR LAWRENCE exits.

What's this here? It's a cup, closed in my true love's hand? Poison, I see, has been the cause of his death. How rude! He drank it all, and didn't leave any to help me afterward. I will kiss your lips. Perhaps there's still some poison on them, to make me die with a medicinal kiss. *(she kisses ROMEO)* Your lips are warm.

WATCHMEN and PARIS's PAGE enter.

CHIEF WATCHMAN

(coming to the PAGE) Lead, boy. Which way?

JULIET

Oh, noise? Then I'll be quick. Oh, good, a knife! My body will be your sheath. Rust inside my body and let me die. *(she stabs herself with ROMEO's dagger and dies)*

PAGE

This is the place. There, where the torch is burning.

CHIEF WATCHMAN

The ground is bloody. Search the graveyard. Go, some of you, arrest whoever you find.

Some WATCHMEN exit.

This is a pitiful sight! The count is dead. Juliet is bleeding. Her body is warm, and she seems to have been dead only a short time, even though she has been buried for two days. Go, tell the Prince. Run to the Capulets. Wake up the Montagues. Have some others search.

Some other WATCHMEN exit in several directions.

ACT FIVE

We see the ground whereon these woes do lie,
180 But the true ground of all these piteous woes
We cannot without circumstance descry.

Reenter SECOND WATCHMAN *with* ROMEO'S *man* BALTHASAR

SECOND WATCHMAN
Here's Romeo's man. We found him in the churchyard.

CHIEF WATCHMAN
Hold him in safety till the Prince come hither.

Reenter THIRD WATCHMAN *with* FRIAR LAWRENCE

THIRD WATCHMAN
Here is a friar that trembles, sighs and weeps.
185 We took this mattock and this spade from him
As he was coming from this churchyard's side.

CHIEF WATCHMAN
A great suspicion. Stay the friar too.

Enter the PRINCE *with* ATTENDANTS

PRINCE
What misadventure is so early up
That calls our person from our morning rest?

Enter CAPULET *and* LADY CAPULET

CAPULET
190 What should it be that is so shrieked abroad?

LADY CAPULET
Oh, the people in the street cry "Romeo,"
Some "Juliet," and some "Paris," and all run
With open outcry toward our monument.

We see the cause of all this pain. But we'll have to investigate to discover the whole story.

The SECOND WATCHMAN *reenters with* BALTHASAR.

SECOND WATCHMAN
Here's Romeo's man. We found him in the churchyard.

CHIEF WATCHMAN
Hold him in custody until the Prince gets here.

The THIRD WATCHMAN *reenters with* FRIAR LAWRENCE.

THIRD WATCHMAN
Here is a friar who's trembling, sighing and weeping. We took this pickax and this shovel from him, as he was walking from this side of the graveyard.

CHIEF WATCHMAN
Very suspicious. Hold the friar too.

The PRINCE *enters with* ATTENDANTS.

PRINCE
What crimes happen so early in the morning that I have to wake up before the usual time?

CAPULET *and* LADY CAPULET *enter.*

CAPULET
What's the problem, that they cry out so loud?

LADY CAPULET
Some people in the street are crying "Romeo." Some are crying "Juliet," and some are crying "Paris." They're all running in an open riot toward our tomb.

PRINCE
What fear is this which startles in our ears?

CHIEF WATCHMAN
195   Sovereign, here lies the County Paris slain,
And Romeo dead, and Juliet, dead before,
Warm and new killed.

PRINCE
Search, seek, and know how this foul murder comes.

CHIEF WATCHMAN
Here is a friar, and slaughtered Romeo's man,
200   With instruments upon them fit to open
These dead men's tombs.

CAPULET
O heavens! O wife, look how our daughter bleeds!
This dagger hath mista'en—for, lo, his house
Is empty on the back of Montague,
205   And it mis-sheathèd in my daughter's bosom.

LADY CAPULET
O me! This sight of death is as a bell,
That warns my old age to a sepulcher.

Enter MONTAGUE

PRINCE
Come, Montague, for thou art early up
To see thy son and heir now early down.

MONTAGUE
210   Alas, my liege, my wife is dead tonight.
Grief of my son's exile hath stopped her breath.
What further woe conspires against mine age?

PRINCE
Look, and thou shalt see.

MONTAGUE
(to ROMEO*)* O thou untaught! What manners is in this,
215   To press before thy father to a grave?

PRINCE

What's this awful thing that everyone's crying about?

CHIEF WATCHMAN

Prince, here lies Count Paris killed. And Romeo dead. And Juliet. She was dead before, but now she's warm and hasn't been dead for long.

PRINCE

Investigate how this foul murder came about.

CHIEF WATCHMAN

Here is a friar, and dead Romeo's man. They've got tools on them—tools they could use to open these tombs.

CAPULET

Oh heavens! Oh wife, look at how our daughter bleeds! That knife should be in its sheath on that Montague's back, but instead it's mis-sheathed in my daughter's breast.

LADY CAPULET

Oh my! This sight of death is like a bell that warns me I'm old and I'll die soon.

MONTAGUE *enters.*

PRINCE

Come, Montague. You're up early to see your son down early.

MONTAGUE

Oh, my liege, my wife died tonight. Sadness over my son's exile stopped her breath. What further pain must I endure in my old age?

PRINCE

Look, and you'll see.

MONTAGUE

(seeing ROMEO's *body)* Oh, you undisciplined boy! Where are your manners? It's not right for a son to push past his father on his way to the grave.

PRINCE
Seal up the mouth of outrage for a while,
Till we can clear these ambiguities
And know their spring, their head, their true descent,
And then will I be general of your woes,
220 And lead you even to death. Meantime forbear,
And let mischance be slave to patience.—
Bring forth the parties of suspicion.

FRIAR LAWRENCE
I am the greatest, able to do least,
Yet most suspected, as the time and place
225 Doth make against me, of this direful murder.
And here I stand, both to impeach and purge,
Myself condemnèd and myself excused.

PRINCE
Then say at once what thou dost know in this.

FRIAR LAWRENCE
I will be brief, for my short date of breath
230 Is not so long as is a tedious tale.
Romeo, there dead, was husband to that Juliet,
And she, there dead, that Romeo's faithful wife.
I married them, and their stol'n marriage day
Was Tybalt's doomsday, whose untimely death
235 Banished the new-made bridegroom from the city—
For whom, and not for Tybalt, Juliet pined.
You, to remove that siege of grief from her,
Betrothed and would have married her perforce
To County Paris. Then comes she to me,
240 And with wild looks bid me devise some mean
To rid her from this second marriage,
Or in my cell there would she kill herself.
Then gave I her, so tutored by my art,
A sleeping potion, which so took effect
245 As I intended, for it wrought on her
The form of death.

PRINCE

Be quiet and hold back your remarks of outrage, until we can clear up these questions. We want to know how it started and what really happened. And then I'll be the leader of pain, and maybe I'll lead you as far as death. In the meantime, hold on, and be patient. Bring forth the men under suspicion.

FRIAR LAWRENCE

I am the greatest, but I was able to do the least. I am under the most suspicion, because I was here at the time of this awful murder. And here I stand, you can question me and punish me. I have already condemned and excused myself.

PRINCE

Tell us what you know about this affair.

FRIAR LAWRENCE

I will be brief because I'm not going to live long enough to tell a boring story. Romeo, who lies there dead, was the husband of that Juliet. And she, who lies there dead, was that Romeo's faithful wife. I married them; their secret wedding day was the day Tybalt died. His untimely death caused the bridegroom to be banished from the city. Juliet was sad because Romeo was gone, not because of Tybalt's death. To cure her sadness, you arranged a marriage for her with Count Paris. Then she came to me, and, looking wild, she asked me to devise a plan to get her out of this second marriage. She threatened to kill herself in my cell if I didn't help her. So I gave her a sleeping potion that I had mixed with my special skills. It worked as planned. She seemed to everyone to be dead.

ACT FIVE

Meantime I writ to Romeo,
That he should hither come as this dire night,
To help to take her from her borrowed grave,
Being the time the potion's force should cease.
250 But he which bore my letter, Friar John,
Was stayed by accident, and yesternight
Returned my letter back. Then all alone
At the prefixèd hour of her waking
Came I to take her from her kindred's vault,
255 Meaning to keep her closely at my cell
Till I conveniently could send to Romeo,
But when I came, some minute ere the time
Of her awakening, here untimely lay
The noble Paris and true Romeo dead.
260 She wakes, and I entreated her come forth,
And bear this work of heaven with patience.
But then a noise did scare me from the tomb,
And she, too desperate, would not go with me,
But, as it seems, did violence on herself.
265 All this I know, and to the marriage
Her Nurse is privy. And if aught in this
Miscarried by my fault, let my old life
Be sacrificed some hour before his time
Unto the rigor of severest law.

PRINCE
270 We still have known thee for a holy man.—
Where's Romeo's man? What can he say in this?

BALTHASAR
I brought my master news of Juliet's death,
And then in post he came from Mantua
To this same place, to this same monument.
275 *(shows a letter)* This letter he early bid me give his father,
And threatened me with death, going in the vault,
If I departed not and left him there.

In the meantime I wrote to Romeo and told him to come here on this awful night to help remove her from her temporary grave when the sleeping potion wore off. But the man who carried my letter, Friar John, was held up by an accident. Last night he gave me the letter back. So I came here alone at the hour when she was supposed to wake up. I came to take her out of her family's tomb, hoping to hide her in my cell until I could make contact with Romeo. But by the time I got here, just a few minutes before Juliet woke up, Paris and Romeo were already dead. She woke up, and I asked her to come out of the tomb with me and endure this tragedy with patience. But then a noise sent me running scared from the tomb. She was too desperate to come with me, and it seems that she killed herself. I know all of this. And her Nurse knows about the marriage too. If any part of this tragedy is my fault, let my old life be sacrificed and let me suffer the most severe punishment.

PRINCE

We have always known you to be a holy man. Where's Romeo's man? What does he have to say about this?

BALTHASAR

I brought my master news of Juliet's death. And then he rode from Mantua here to this tomb. *(he shows a letter)* Earlier this morning he asked me to give this letter to his father. When he went into the vault, he threatened me with death if I didn't leave him alone there.

PRINCE
Give me the letter. I will look on it.
(takes letter from BALTHASAR*)*
Where is the county's page, that raised the watch?—
280   Sirrah, what made your master in this place?

PAGE
He came with flowers to strew his lady's grave,
And bid me stand aloof, and so I did.
Anon comes one with light to ope the tomb,
And by and by my master drew on him,
285   And then I ran away to call the watch.

PRINCE
(skims the letter) This letter doth make good the friar's
                words,
Their course of love, the tidings of her death.
And here he writes that he did buy a poison
Of a poor 'pothecary, and therewithal
290   Came to this vault to die and lie with Juliet.
Where be these enemies?—Capulet! Montague!
See what a scourge is laid upon your hate,
That heaven finds means to kill your joys with love!
And I, for winking at your discords, too
295   Have lost a brace of kinsmen. All are punished.

CAPULET
O brother Montague, give me thy hand.
This is my daughter's jointure, for no more
Can I demand.

MONTAGUE
                But I can give thee more,
For I will raise her statue in pure gold,
300   That whiles Verona by that name is known,
There shall no figure at such rate be set
As that of true and faithful Juliet.

CAPULET
As rich shall Romeo's by his lady's lie,
Poor sacrifices of our enmity.

PRINCE

Give me the letter. I'll look at it. *(he takes the letter from* BALTHASAR*)* Where is the count's page, the one who called the watch? Boy, what was your master doing here?

PAGE

He came with flowers to spread on his lady's grave. And he asked me to stand far away and leave him alone, and so I did. Then someone with a torch came to open the tomb. So my master drew on him. And then I ran away to call the watch.

PRINCE

(skimming the letter) This letter confirms the friar's account. It describes the course of their love and mentions the news of her death. Here he writes that he bought poison from a poor pharmacist. He brought that poison with him to this vault to die and lie with Juliet. Where are these enemies? Capulet! Montague! Do you see what a great evil results from your hate? Heaven has figured out how to kill your joys with love. Because I looked the other way when your feud flared up, I've lost several members of my family as well. Everyone is punished.

CAPULET

Oh, brother Montague, give me your hand. This is my daughter's dowry. I can ask you for nothing more.

MONTAGUE

But I can give you more. I'll raise her statue in pure gold. As long as this city is called Verona, there will be no figure praised more than that of true and faithful Juliet.

ACT FIVE

PRINCE

305 A glooming peace this morning with it brings.
The sun, for sorrow, will not show his head.
Go hence, to have more talk of these sad things.
Some shall be pardoned, and some punishèd.
For never was a story of more woe
310 Than this of Juliet and her Romeo.

Exeunt

CAPULET

The statue I will make of Romeo to lie beside his Juliet will be just as rich. They were poor sacrifices of our rivalry!

PRINCE

We settle a dark peace this morning. The sun is too sad to show itself. Let's go, to talk about these sad things some more. Some will be pardoned, and some will be punished. There was never a story more full of pain than the story of Romeo and Juliet.

They all exit.

ACT FIVE

PART III

STUDY
GUIDE

6

THEMATIC QUESTIONS

1. What effect does the accelerated time scheme have on the play's development? Is it plausible that a love story of this magnitude could take place so quickly? Does the play seem to take place over as little time as it actually occupies?

Because of the intensity of the relationship between Romeo and Juliet and the complex development of events during the few days of the play's action, the story can certainly seem to take place over a time span much longer than the one it actually occupies. By compressing all the events of the love story into just a few days, Shakespeare adds weight to every moment, and gives the sense that the action is happening so quickly that characters barely have time to react, and, by the end, that matters are careening out of control. This rush heightens the sense of pressure that hangs in the atmosphere of the play. While it may not seem plausible for a story such as *Romeo and Juliet* to take place over a span of only four days in the real world, this abbreviated time scheme makes sense in the universe of the play.

2. Compare and contrast the characters of Romeo and Juliet. How do they develop throughout the play? What makes them fall in love with one another?

Romeo is a passionate, extreme, excitable, intelligent, and moody young man, well-liked and admired throughout Verona. He is loyal to his friends, but his behavior is somewhat unpredictable. At the beginning of the play, he mopes over his hopeless unrequited love for Rosaline. In Juliet, Romeo finds a legitimate object for the extraordinary passion that he is capable of feeling, and his unyielding love for her takes control of him.

The attraction between Romeo and Juliet is immediate and overwhelming, and neither of the young lovers comments on or pretends to understand its cause. Each mentions the other's beauty, but it seems that destiny, rather than any particular character trait, has drawn them together. Their love for one another is so undeniable that neither they nor the audience feels the need to question or explain it.

Juliet, on the other hand, is an innocent girl, a child at the beginning of the play, and is startled by the sudden power of her love for Romeo. Guided by her feelings for him, she develops very quickly into a determined, capable, mature, and loyal woman who tempers her extreme feelings of love with sober-mindedness.

3. Compare and contrast the characters of Tybalt and Mercutio. Why does Mercutio hate Tybalt?

As Mercutio tells Benvolio, he hates Tybalt for being a slave to fashion and vanity, one of "such antic, lisping, affecting fantasmines, these new tuners of accents! . . . these fashion-mongers, these 'pardon-me's'" (II. iv.). Mercutio is so insistent that the reader feels compelled to accept this description of Tybalt's character as definitive. Tybalt does prove Mercutio's words true: he demonstrates himself to be as witty, vain, and prone to violence as he is fashionable, easily insulted, and defensive. To the self-possessed Mercutio, Tybalt seems a caricature; to Tybalt, the brilliant, earthy, and unconventional Mercutio is probably incomprehensible. (It might be interesting to compare Mercutio's comments about Tybalt to Hamlet's description of the foppish Osric in Act V, scene ii of *Hamlet*.)

7

KEY QUESTIONS
AND ANSWERS

1. Do Romeo and Juliet have sex?

Shakespeare would not have been allowed to show the lovers having sex, or to mention it directly, but it's very strongly implied that Romeo and Juliet have sex on their wedding night. Juliet looks forward to Romeo's arrival in daringly explicit language: "learn me how to lose a winning match / Played for a pair of stainless maidenhoods" (III.ii.). At the beginning of Act III, scene v, the lovers exchange lines in which they wish it wasn't morning yet. Shakespeare's audience would have recognized these lines as an "aubade," a kind of poem that traditionally describes a sexual relationship. Most importantly of all, a marriage that wasn't "consummated" with sex wasn't considered a legal marriage in Shakespeare's day, so it would be very surprising indeed if these two newlyweds didn't have sex on their wedding night.

2. Is Juliet too young to get married?

We don't know the exact ages of most of Shakespeare's characters, but we're repeatedly told that Juliet is only thirteen, which suggests that her age was significant to Elizabethan audiences. In Shakespeare's England it would have been extremely unusual for a girl to marry at thirteen, although aristocratic girls might sometimes be "betrothed," or engaged, when they were even younger.

Juliet's mother suggests that it's not uncommon for Veronese women to marry at Juliet's age, but her father says that she is too young to marry (although he changes his mind later in the play). Juliet's language shows that in some ways she is emotionally and even sexually mature. She talks intelligently and passionately about her feelings, using some of the most erotic language Shakespeare ever wrote. Shakespeare's audiences would probably have seen Juliet as a girl on the cusp of becoming a young woman. Her tragedy is that she dies before she can enter fully into adult life.

3. Who is Rosaline?

Romeo begins the play in love with a woman called Rosaline. He complains to Benvolio that he has been unable to seduce her: she has told Romeo that she wants to remain a virgin. Rosaline never appears onstage. Her role is to help us understand Romeo's character. His hopeless crush on Rosaline creates a sense that he feels trapped by his circumstances, which helps us to understand that when he meets and falls in love with Juliet, he feels liberated. Romeo's infatuation with Rosaline also serves as a contrast to his more mature passion for Juliet. Romeo describes his feelings for Rosaline in clichéd poetic lines that make Benvolio and Mercutio (and the audience) laugh at him. When he meets Juliet, Romeo describes his love for her in original and genuinely poetic imagery: "Oh, she doth teach the torches to burn bright!" (I.v.). The change in Romeo's language shows the audience that his passion for Juliet is more authentic than his feelings for Rosaline.

4. Is Juliet rebelling against her parents?

One of Juliet's main goals is to escape her parents' household on her own terms. When her mother tells her she should consider marrying Paris, her response is almost defiant: "I'll look to like if looking liking move" (I.iii.). At the ball where she is supposed to meet Paris, she kisses Romeo instead. When she discovers that Romeo is a Montague, she quickly moves on from wishing he wasn't to deciding that it doesn't matter, because "I'll no longer be a Capulet" (II.ii.). Juliet's determination to free herself from her family suggests that although she loves Romeo, she also sees him as an opportunity for freedom. At the same time, Romeo is also introduced as a character who longs to be free of his circumstances, so Juliet's longing for freedom shows us that she and Romeo are kindred spirits.

5. Why does Mercutio fight Tybalt?

In Act III, scene I, Tybalt calls Romeo a "villain." In Shakespeare's England (and in Renaissance Italy) insulting another young man was a common way to provoke a duel. It was considered dishonorable to ignore the insult instead of offering to fight. When Romeo ignores Tybalt's insult, Mercutio feels that Romeo has dishonored himself: "dishonourable, vile submission!" (III.i.). Mercutio steps in to preserve Romeo's reputation and his own reputation as Romeo's friend. However, several of Mercutio's earlier speeches suggest that he also dislikes Tybalt and envies his reputation as a fighter: "Oh, he's the courageous captain of compliments. He fights as you sing prick-song, keeps time, distance, and proportion" (II.iv.).

8

THEMES, MOTIFS, AND SYMBOLS

Themes

Themes are the fundamental and often universal ideas explored in a literary work.

THE FORCEFULNESS OF LOVE

Romeo and Juliet is the most famous love story in the English literary tradition. Love is naturally the play's dominant and most important theme. The play focuses on romantic love, specifically the intense passion that springs up at first sight between Romeo and Juliet. In *Romeo and Juliet*, love is a violent, ecstatic, overpowering force that supersedes all other values, loyalties, and emotions. In the course of the play, the young lovers are driven to defy their entire social world: families ("Deny thy father and refuse thy name," Juliet says. "Or, if thou wilt not, be but sworn my love, / And I'll no longer be a Capulet" II.ii.); friends (Romeo abandons Mercutio and Benvolio after the feast in order to go to Juliet's garden in Act II, scene ii); and ruler (Romeo returns to Verona for Juliet's sake after being exiled by the Prince on pain of death in Act III, scene i). Love is the overriding theme of the play, but a reader should always remember that Shakespeare is uninterested in portraying a prettied-up, dainty version of the emotion, the kind that bad poets write about, and whose bad poetry Romeo reads while pining for Rosaline. Love in *Romeo and Juliet* is a brutal, powerful emotion that captures individuals and catapults them against their world, and, at times, against themselves.

The powerful nature of love can be seen in the way it is described, or, more accurately, the way descriptions of it so consistently fail to capture its entirety. At times love is described in the terms of religion, as in the fourteen lines when Romeo and Juliet first meet. At others it is described as a sort of magic: "Alike bewitchèd by the charm of looks" (II.Prologue). Juliet, perhaps, most perfectly describes her love for Romeo by refusing to describe it: "But my true love is grown to such excess / I cannot sum up sum of half my wealth" (II.vi.). Love, in other words, resists any single metaphor because it is too powerful to be so easily contained or understood.

Romeo and Juliet does not make a specific moral statement about the relationships between love and society, religion, and family; rather, it portrays the chaos and passion of being in love, combining images of love, violence, death, religion, and family in an impressionistic rush leading to the play's tragic conclusion.

LOVE AS A CAUSE OF VIOLENCE

The themes of death and violence permeate *Romeo and Juliet*, and they are always connected to passion, whether that passion is love or hate. The connection between hate, violence, and death seems obvious. But the connection between love and violence requires further investigation.

Love, in *Romeo and Juliet*, is a grand passion, and as such it is blinding; it can overwhelm a person as powerfully and completely as hate can. The passionate love between Romeo and Juliet is linked from the moment of its inception with death: Tybalt notices that Romeo has crashed the feast and determines to kill him just as Romeo catches sight of Juliet and falls instantly in love with her. From that point on, love seems to push the lovers closer to love and violence, not farther from it. Romeo and Juliet are plagued with thoughts of suicide, and a willingness to experience it: in Act III, scene iii, Romeo brandishes a knife in Friar Lawrence's cell and threatens to kill himself after he has been banished from Verona and his love. Juliet also pulls a knife in order to take her own life in Friar Lawrence's presence just three scenes later. After Capulet decides that Juliet will marry Paris, Juliet says, "If all else fail, myself have power to die" (III.v.). Finally, each imagines that the other looks dead the morning after their first, and only, sexual experience ("Methinks I see thee . . . ," Juliet says, ". . . as one dead in the bottom of a tomb" (III.v.). This theme continues until its inevitable conclusion: double suicide. This tragic choice is the highest, most potent expression of love that Romeo and Juliet can make. It is only through death that they can preserve their love, and their love is so profound that they are willing to end their lives in its defense. In the play, love emerges as an amoral thing, leading as much to destruction as to happiness. But in its extreme passion, the love that Romeo and Juliet experience also appears so exquisitely beautiful that few would want, or be able, to resist its power.

THE INDIVIDUAL VERSUS SOCIETY

Much of *Romeo and Juliet* involves the lovers' struggles against public and social institutions that either explicitly or implicitly oppose the existence of their love. Such structures range from the concrete to the abstract: families and the placement of familial power in the father; law and the desire for public order; religion; and the social importance placed on masculine honor. These institutions often come into conflict with each other. The importance of honor, for example, time and again results in brawls that disturb the public peace.

Though they do not always work in concert, each of these societal institutions in some way present obstacles for Romeo and Juliet. The enmity between their families, coupled with the emphasis placed on loyalty and honor to kin, combine to create a profound conflict for Romeo and Juliet, who must rebel against their heritages. Further, the patriarchal power structure inherent in Renaissance families, wherein the father controls the action of all other family members, particularly women, places Juliet in an extremely vulnerable position. Her heart, in her family's mind, is not hers to give. The law and the emphasis on social civility demands terms of conduct with which the blind passion of love cannot comply. Religion similarly demands priorities that Romeo and Juliet cannot abide by because of the intensity of their love. Though in most situations the lovers uphold the traditions of Christianity (they wait to marry before consummating their love), their love is so powerful that they begin to think of each other in blasphemous terms. For example, Juliet calls Romeo "the god of my idolatry," elevating Romeo to level of God (II.ii.). The couple's final act of suicide is likewise un-Christian. The maintenance of masculine honor forces Romeo to commit actions he would prefer to avoid. But the social emphasis placed on masculine honor is so profound that Romeo cannot simply ignore it.

It is possible to see *Romeo and Juliet* as a battle between the responsibilities and actions demanded by social institutions and those demanded by the private desires of the individual. Romeo and Juliet's appreciation of night, with its darkness and privacy, and their renunciation of their names, with its attendant loss of obligation, make sense in the context of individuals who wish to escape the public world. But the lovers cannot stop the night from becoming day. And Romeo cannot cease being a Montague simply because he wants to; the rest of the world will not let him. The lovers' suicides can be understood as the ultimate night, the ultimate privacy.

THE INEVITABILITY OF FATE

In its first address to the audience, the Chorus states that Romeo and Juliet are "star-crossed"—that is to say that fate (a power often vested in the movements of the stars) controls them (Prologue). This sense of fate permeates the play, and not just for the audience. The characters also are quite aware of it: Romeo and Juliet constantly see omens. When Romeo believes that Juliet is dead, he cries out, "Then I defy you, stars!" completing the idea that the love between Romeo and Juliet is in opposition to the decrees of destiny (V.i.). Of course, Romeo's defiance itself plays into the hands of fate, and his determination to spend eternity with Juliet results in their deaths. The mechanism of fate works in all of the events surrounding the lovers: the feud between their families (it is worth noting that this hatred is never explained; rather, the reader must accept it as an undeniable aspect of the world of the play); the horrible series of accidents that ruin Friar Lawrence's seemingly well-intentioned plans at the end of the play; and the tragic timing of Romeo's suicide and Juliet's awakening. These events are not mere coincidences, but rather manifestations of fate that help bring about the unavoidable outcome of the young lovers' deaths.

The concept of fate described above is the most commonly accepted interpretation. There are other possible readings of fate in the play: as a force determined by the powerful social institutions that influence Romeo and Juliet's choices, as well as fate as a force that emerges from Romeo and Juliet's very personalities.

Motifs

Motifs are recurring structures, contrasts, and literary devices that can help to develop and inform the text's major themes.

LIGHT/DARK IMAGERY

One of the play's most consistent visual motifs is the contrast between light and dark, often in terms of night/day imagery. This contrast is not given a particular metaphoric meaning—light is not always good, and dark is not always evil. On the contrary, light and dark are generally used to provide a sensory contrast and to hint at opposed alternatives. One of the more important instances of this motif is Romeo's lengthy meditation on the sun and the moon during the balcony scene, in which Juliet, metaphorically described as the sun, is seen as banishing the "envious moon" and transforming the night into day (II.ii.). A similar blurring of night and day occurs in the early morning hours after the lovers' only night together. Romeo, forced to leave for exile in the morning, and Juliet, not wanting him to leave her room, both try to pretend that it is still night, and that the light is actually darkness: "More light and light, more dark and dark our woes!" (III.v.).

OPPOSITE POINTS OF VIEW

Shakespeare includes numerous speeches and scenes in *Romeo and Juliet* that hint at alternative ways to evaluate the play. Shakespeare uses two main devices in this regard: Mercutio and servants. Mercutio consistently skewers the viewpoints of all the other characters in play: he sees Romeo's devotion to love as a sort of blindness that robs Romeo from himself; similarly, he sees Tybalt's devotion to honor as blind and stupid. His punning and the Queen Mab speech can be interpreted as undercutting virtually every passion evident in the play. Mercutio serves as a critic of the delusions of righteousness and grandeur held by the characters around him.

Where Mercutio is a nobleman who openly criticizes other nobles, the views offered by servants in the play are less explicit. There is the Nurse who lost her baby and husband, the servant Peter who cannot read, the musicians who care about their lost wages and their lunches, and the Apothecary who cannot afford to make the moral choice; the lower classes present a second tragic world to counter that of the nobility. The nobles' world is full of grand tragic gestures. The servants' world, in contrast, is characterized by simple needs, and early deaths brought about by disease and poverty rather than dueling and grand passions. Where the nobility almost seem to revel in their capacity for drama, the servants' lives are such that they cannot afford tragedy of the epic kind.

Symbols

Symbols are objects, characters, figures, and colors used to represent abstract ideas or concepts.

POISON

In his first appearance, in Act II, scene iii, Friar Lawrence remarks that every plant, herb, and stone has its own special properties, and that nothing exists in nature that cannot be put to both good and bad uses. Thus, poison is not intrinsically evil, but is instead a natural substance made lethal by human hands. Friar Lawrence's words prove true over the course of the play. The sleeping potion he gives Juliet is concocted to cause the appearance of death, not death itself, but through circumstances beyond the Friar's control, the potion does bring about a fatal result: Romeo's suicide. As this example shows, human beings tend to cause death even without intending to. Similarly, Romeo suggests that society is to blame for the Apothecary's criminal selling of poison, because while there are laws prohibiting the apothecary from selling poison, there are no laws that would help the apothecary make money. Poison symbolizes human society's tendency to poison good things and make them fatal, just as the pointless Capulet-Montague feud turns Romeo and Juliet's love to poison. After all, unlike many of the other tragedies, this play does not have an evil villain, but rather people whose good qualities are turned to poison by the world in which they live.

THUMB-BITING

In Act I, scene I, the buffoonish Samson begins a brawl between the Montagues and Capulets by flicking his thumbnail from behind his upper teeth, an insulting gesture known as biting the thumb. He engages in this juvenile and vulgar display because he wants to get into a fight with the Montagues but doesn't want to be accused of starting the fight by making an explicit insult. Because of his timidity, he settles for being annoying rather than challenging. The thumb-biting, as an essentially meaningless gesture, represents the foolishness of the entire Capulet/Montague feud and the stupidity of violence in general.

QUEEN MAB

In Act I, scene iv, Mercutio delivers a dazzling speech about the fairy Queen Mab, who rides through the night on her tiny wagon bringing dreams to sleepers. One of the most noteworthy aspects of Queen Mab's ride is that the dreams she brings generally do not bring out the best sides of the dreamers, but instead serve to confirm them in whatever vices they are addicted to—for example, greed, violence, or lust. Another important aspect of Mercutio's description of Queen Mab is that it is complete nonsense, albeit vivid and highly colorful. Nobody believes in a fairy pulled about by "a small gray-coated gnat" whipped with a cricket's bone (I.iv.). Finally, it is worth noting that the description of Mab and her carriage goes to extravagant lengths to emphasize how tiny she and her accoutrements are. Queen Mab and her carriage do not merely symbolize the insubstantial dreams of sleepers, they also symbolize the power of waking fantasies, daydreams, and desires. Through the Queen Mab imagery, Mercutio suggests that all desires and fantasies are as nonsensical and fragile as Mab, and that they are basically corrupting. This point of view contrasts starkly with that of Romeo and Juliet, who see their love as real and ennobling.

9

QUOTES AND ANALYSIS
BY THEME

LOVE

> *Alas, that love, whose view is muffled still,*
> *Should, without eyes, see pathways to his will! (I.i.)*

Romeo begins the play in love with Rosaline, but his language in these opening scenes shows us that his first love is less mature than the love he will develop for Juliet. This couplet combines two ideas that were already clichés in Shakespeare's day: "love is blind" and "love will find a way." The clichéd expressions and obvious rhymes which Romeo uses to express his love for Rosaline would have been ridiculous to a contemporary audience, and Benvolio and Mercutio repeatedly make fun of them.

> *My only love sprung from my only hate!*
> *Too early seen unknown, and known too late!*
> *Prodigious birth of love it is to me,*
> *That I must love a loathèd enemy. (I.v.)*

Juliet speaks these lines after learning that Romeo is a Montague. The language of *Romeo and Juliet* insists that opposites can never be entirely separated: the lovers will never be allowed to forget that they are also enemies. Significantly Juliet blames herself for seeing Romeo "too early." Everything in this play happens too early: we learn what will happen at the end in the opening lines, Juliet is married too young, and Romeo kills himself moments before Juliet wakes. In *Romeo and Juliet*, love is a force which can—and does—move too fast.

With love's light wings did I o'erperch these walls,

For stony limits cannot hold love out (II.ii.)

Juliet wants to know how Romeo got into the walled garden of the Capulet house: these lines are his response. For Romeo, true love is a liberating force. Love gives him not just wings, but "light wings" and the power to overcome all "stony limits." Romeo answers Juliet's serious and practical question with a flight of romantic fantasy. Throughout the play, Juliet is more grounded in the real world than Romeo. For her, the freedom that love brings is the freedom to leave her parents' house and to have sex.

SEX

Now art thou what thou art—by art as well as by

nature, for this driveling love is like a great natural

that runs lolling up and down to hide his bauble in

a hole. (II.iv.)

Mercutio is pleased that Romeo is exchanging jokes with him instead of moping for his love. He dismisses love as foolish: a "natural" is a fool, and a "bauble" is the stick a professional fool carries. The image of the fool trying to "hide his bauble in a hole" also implies sexual intercourse. Mercutio's point is that at its root, love is really just sexual desire. As far as Mercutio is concerned, all of Romeo's romantic longing is just "driveling" and "lolling" brought on by sexual frustration. Mercutio's cynical point of view challenges the idealistic romance of the two lovers.

Come, gentle night, come, loving, black-browed night,

Give me my Romeo. And when I shall die,

Take him and cut him out in little stars (III.ii.)

Juliet yearns for her wedding night. The repetition of the word "come" shows us the strength of her desire. There's no ambiguity about what Juliet is yearning for. "Die" was Elizabethan slang for "orgasm." The image that follows, of Romeo "cut . . . out in little stars," is a subtle metaphor for the sexual ecstasy Juliet anticipates. At the same time, the image suggests childhood play, reminding us again that Juliet is very young. The words "die" and "cut" also have violent undertones. In this play, sex and violence are never far apart.

VIOLENCE

My naked weapon is out. Quarrel! I will back thee. (I.i.)

The action of *Romeo and Juliet* opens with Samson boasting that he is a violent man. When some Montague servants appear, he draws his sword and asks his companion Gregory to start a quarrel that might lead to a fight. This opening establishes that Verona is a place where violence can break out over nothing. Samson and Gregory and their Montague opponents are all afraid of breaking the law, which reminds us that the punishment for fighting is every bit as violent as the fighting itself. From the beginning of the play, all the young men involved in the feud are trapped between two threats of violence: the violence of their enemies and the violence of the Prince, who has threatened to execute anyone who continues the feud. This helps create the play's sense of confinement.

He rests his minim rests—one, two, and the third

in your bosom. The very butcher of a silk button, a

duelist, a duelist (II.iv.)

Mercutio makes fun of Tybalt's fighting style. At the time Shakespeare was writing, a new style of fencing (swordfighting) had recently been imported from Italy. Tybalt fences in this style, which allows Shakespeare to add a bit of local Italian color to his Verona. At the same time, in these lines of Mercutio's, Shakespeare pokes fun at the new trend in England. Even though Mercutio is mocking Tybalt, we sense an underlying admiration for Tybalt's ability as a fighter. It does not come as a surprise when Mercutio is tempted to test his own skill against Tybalt's, with fatal results.

They have made worms' meat of me. (III.i.)

Mercutio fights Tybalt and receives a fatal wound. As he dies, he continues to talk with his usual cynical wit. He imagines himself after his death in strictly physical and very unromantic terms: as meat for worms. This marks a turning point in the play. Up until now, violence has only been threatened, and for the characters and the audience alike it's been more a source of excitement than grief. Now, one of the play's most appealing characters is dying. From this point forward, the play's violence will be brutal and unrelenting. Tybalt will die, then Paris, and finally Romeo and Juliet.

YOUTH

My child is yet a stranger in the world.

She hath not seen the change of fourteen years. (I.ii.)

Capulet begins the play by denying Paris's request to marry Juliet, on the grounds that she is too young. Juliet is thirteen, but the word "thirteen" never appears in *Romeo and Juliet*. Instead we are repeatedly told that she is not yet fourteen. The fact that Juliet's father is looking forward to a birthday she will never reach emphasizes that Juliet's life is cut very short. Capulet's description of Juliet as "a stranger in the world" introduces us to an important aspect of her character. Her father means that she is inexperienced, which she is, but Juliet is also a "stranger in the world" because she prefers the transcendent experience she shares with Romeo to the compromises and practicalities of everyday life, even to the extent of choosing to die rather than live in a world without Romeo.

Come Lammas Eve at night shall she be fourteen.

Susan and she—God rest all Christian souls!—

Were of an age. (I.iii.)

The Nurse recalls that her own daughter, Susan, was the same age as Juliet, as she reminds us that Juliet is not yet fourteen. Susan died as a baby, and the Nurse's grief foreshadows the grief Capulet and Lady Capulet will feel at the end of the play, when they too lose their young daughter. The Nurse identifies Juliet's birthday as Lammas Eve. Lammas Eve was celebrated at the beginning of August, and we know that the play takes place in summer, so Juliet is a month or two from her birthday. This creates a dramatic irony: the Nurse and the Capulets are counting down to Juliet's fourteenth birthday, while the audience is counting down to her death.

> So tedious is this day
>
> As is the night before some festival
>
> To an impatient child that hath new robes
>
> And may not wear them. (III.ii.)

Here Juliet expresses her impatience for her wedding night. By comparing herself to a child, Juliet reminds us that she is almost a child herself. Her metaphor also points to an important aspect of Juliet's character. Throughout the play, Juliet is impatient to grow up. As soon as she meets Romeo she wants to marry him. She gets married even though her father thinks she is at least two years too young, and she can hardly contain her impatience for her wedding night. To the audience, Juliet's rush to grow up is tragic, because we know she will die only a few days after her marriage.

FATE

> From forth the fatal loins of these two foes
>
> A pair of star-crossed lovers take their life (Prologue)

The play's opening lines tell us that Romeo and Juliet will die, and that their tragic end is fated. "Star-crossed" means "opposed by the stars." In Shakespeare's day as in ours, some people believed that the course of your life was determined by the motion and position of the stars. "Take their life" is a pun: it means that the lovers were born from the "fatal loins" of their parents, and it also means that the lovers will kill themselves. Their births and deaths are described in the same short phrase, which again suggests that their deaths were fated from the moment they were born.

I fear too early, for my mind misgives

Some consequence yet hanging in the stars

Shall bitterly begin his fearful date (I.iv.)

Before he goes to the masque where he will meet Juliet, Romeo has a feeling that the consequences of his decision to go will be "bitter." He suspects that this is his fate—"hanging in the stars"—and his use of the word "stars" reminds the audience that he is "star-crossed" (Prologue). Romeo's fear that he will arrive at the masque "too early" points to an important theme of the play (I.iv.). Almost every event in the play happens too early. Tybalt finds Romeo too early, before the news of Romeo's marriage has been announced. Juliet's marriage to Paris is decided too early, before Romeo can return from exile. The lovers die too young.

10

QUOTES AND ANALYSIS
BY CHARACTER

ROMEO

But soft! What light through yonder window breaks?

It is the east, and Juliet is the sun. (II.ii.)

As Romeo approaches Juliet's bedroom, he describes her in language drawn from astrology: suns, moons, and stars. This grand imagery suggests that Romeo believes his love for Juliet is not earthbound but transcendent. Juliet herself is a force as powerful as the sun, the literal center of the universe. Astrological imagery also reminds the audience, however, that Romeo and Juliet are "star-crossed," in other words, fated to die. The following lines read "arise, fair sun, and kill the envious moon," suggesting that Romeo's love for Juliet has supplanted his previous, weaker infatuation with Rosaline.

With love's light wings did I o'erperch these walls,

For stony limits cannot hold love out (II.ii.)

Juliet asks Romeo how he has managed to reach her bedroom: this is his reply. His language is always less practical than Juliet's, but these lines also show that for Romeo, love is freedom. As a lover, he can ignore the boundaries set by the feud between Montagues and Capulets.

O sweet Juliet,

Thy beauty hath made me effeminate

And in my temper softened valor's steel! (III.i.)

When Tybalt kills Mercutio, Romeo regrets not fighting Tybalt himself. This is a turning point in Romeo's story. Up until now, Romeo has been trying to free himself from the feud between Montagues and Capulets, and the masculine code of honor which keeps the feud going. When he blames Juliet for making him "effeminate," he is embracing the masculine code once more.

> *Let's talk. It is not day. (III.v.)*

This line is the first moment in the play when it seems Romeo and Juliet might have a chance to talk about something besides their love for one another. The chance never comes, because Romeo has to escape from Verona. This moment emphasizes that Romeo and Juliet's love is new and immature. Part of the play's tragedy is that the lovers will never have the chance to have an adult relationship.

> *Then I defy you, stars! (V.i.)*

Romeo refuses to accept Juliet's death. He decides to return to Verona, but his attempt to defy the "stars" only succeeds in bringing about his tragic fate, which emphasizes that the lovers' destiny is inescapable. Because the Prologue references the lovers' "star-crossed destiny," every subsequent reference to the stars, or to the heavens in general, reminds the audience of the sad fate awaiting the lovers, and their inability to avoid it, try though they might.

JULIET

> *O Romeo, Romeo! Wherefore art thou Romeo? (II.ii)*

This line may be one of the most frequently quoted, and frequently misunderstood, lines in all of Shakespeare. Though Juliet is standing on her balcony, unaware of Romeo below her, the line doesn't mean she's asking *where* he is. Wherefore means *why*, so Juliet is asking why Romeo is who he is—namely, a Montague, and therefore her sworn enemy.

My bounty is as boundless as the sea,

My love as deep. The more I give to thee,

The more I have, for both are infinite. (II.ii.)

Like Romeo, Juliet sees love as a kind of freedom, "boundless" and "infinite." The suggestion that Juliet will "give" her "bounty" to Romeo is the most explicitly erotic moment in their conversation so far. Throughout the play, Juliet takes the lead in the sexual side of their relationship.

Hist! Romeo, hist!—Oh, for a falconer's voice,

To lure this tassel-gentle back again! (II.ii.)

Earlier in this scene, Romeo imagined himself with "light wings." In these lines, Juliet picks up on this image to picture Romeo as a tame falcon and herself as a falconer. Juliet's image suggests she feels she has power over him. The fact that she takes Romeo's metaphor and bends it to her own purposes also suggests her sense of power in their relationship.

O God, I have an ill-divining soul.

Methinks I see thee now, thou art so low

As one dead in the bottom of a tomb. (III.v.)

Just before Romeo and Juliet met, Romeo had an intuition that his life was about to take a tragic turn. In this scene, which is the lovers' last scene alive together, it is Juliet's turn to foresee their tragic fate. These two moments bookend the lovers' relationship and show that from beginning to end, Romeo and Juliet share a single fate and experience it together.

I will kiss thy lips.

Haply some poison yet doth hang on them,

To make me die with a restorative. (V.iii.)

These are Juliet's last words. She imagines the poison that has killed Romeo as a "restorative," a medicine that can put an end to her suffering. One of the play's major themes is the inseparability of good and evil, love and hate, poison and cure. Juliet's death is tragic, but she also celebrates it as a way of escaping a life without her beloved.

MERCUTIO

> *True, I talk of dreams,*
>
> *Which are the children of an idle brain,*
>
> *Begot of nothing but vain fantasy (I.iv.)*

Mercutio's "Queen Mab" speech introduces us to an important aspect of his character. He is a cynical realist, who finds dreams and fantasies ridiculous. Throughout the play, Mercutio makes fun of Romeo's fantasy of perfect romantic love, which invites the audience to question the seriousness and maturity of Romeo's feelings for Juliet.

> *Appear thou in the likeness of a sigh!*
>
> *Speak but one rhyme, and I am satisfied.*
>
> *Cry but "Ay me!" Pronounce but "love" and "dove."*
>
> *(II.i.)*

Mercutio makes fun of Romeo for using language drawn from the love poetry that was popular in Shakespeare's day. He draws attention to the fact that Romeo's romantic language is clichéd, suggesting that Romeo's feelings might be inauthentic or immature.

> *A plague o' both your houses!*
>
> *They have made worms' meat of me. (III.i)*

When Mercutio is fatally injured, he turns his cynical and realist eye on his own situation. He points out that the feud which has caused his death is pointless. While Romeo and Benvolio talk about Mercutio's "soul" and "gallant spirit," Mercutio himself describes his death in strictly physical and unromantic terms: he will be "worms' meat."

FRIAR LAWRENCE

For this alliance may so happy prove

To turn your households' rancor to pure love (II.iii.)

Friar Lawrence agrees to marry Romeo and Juliet, and these lines explain his motive. He hopes that the lovers' marriage will put an end to the feud between their families. However, these lines serve to remind the audience that according to the Prologue it is not the lovers' "alliance" but their deaths which will "end their parents' strife."

For, by your leaves, you shall not stay alone

Till holy church incorporate two in one. (II.vi.)

With these lines, the Friar leads Romeo and Juliet to their marriage ceremony. *Romeo and Juliet* is obsessed with pairs coming together to function as one: Montague and Capulet, sex and violence, poison and cure, Mercutio and Tybalt. The play's central pairing, of course, is the pairing of the two lovers. These lines explicitly remind us that by marrying, Romeo and Juliet become one in the eyes of God and the law.

NURSE

Come Lammas Eve at night shall she be fourteen.

Susan and she—God rest all Christian souls!—

Were of an age. (I.iii.)

The Nurse is introduced as someone who cares for Juliet almost like a parent. She is counting down the days to Juliet's birthday. Juliet reminds her of her own daughter, Susan, who died young, which foreshadows Juliet's own premature death.

> *"Yea," quoth he, "Dost thou fall upon thy face?*
> *Thou wilt fall backward when thou hast more wit,*
> *Wilt thou not, Jule?" (I.iii.)*

The Nurse fondly recounts a joke her husband once made about Juliet. The joke suggests that sex and harm are closely related, which in Juliet's case is true. Her first sexual relationship will result in her death.

> *I think it best you married with the county.*
> *Oh, he's a lovely gentleman.*
> *Romeo's a dishclout to him. (III.v.)*

One of the Nurse's roles in *Romeo and Juliet* is to highlight the development of Juliet's character. When Romeo is banished, the Nurse suggests that Juliet would be just as happy with Paris, because he's better looking. Juliet disagrees, which shows that her passion for Romeo is no longer merely physical, and also that she has outgrown her former trusted friend, the Nurse.

NOTES

11

WHAT DOES
THE ENDING MEAN?

AT THE END OF *ROMEO AND JULIET*, Romeo returns to Verona because he believes Juliet is dead. When he arrives at her tomb she appears lifeless, due to the sleeping potion given to her by Friar Lawrence, so he kills himself by drinking poison. Moments later Juliet wakes, finds Romeo dead, and kills herself with his sword. This ending replays in miniature the structure of the play as a whole. Throughout their story, the lovers have been pulled together and pushed apart: pulled together by their love and pushed apart by the hatred and violence between their families. In the play's final moments, the love they share and the violence that separates them become one and the same. Romeo rushes to Juliet's side because he loves her, and Juliet fakes her death because she loves Romeo, but the result of these actions is that both lovers die violently. They cause each other's deaths out of love for one another.

Some readers have suggested that Romeo and Juliet believe they will be together in the afterlife, since most people believed in heaven when Shakespeare was writing. Seen from this point of view, the lovers' suicide is a way of freeing themselves from the society which has trapped them in their roles as each other's enemies. Other readers have pointed out, however, that neither Romeo nor Juliet mentions the afterlife before they commit suicide. Instead, Romeo says that "Here, here will I remain / With worms that are thy chamber maids" (V.iii.), which suggests he is picturing their corpses remaining together rather than their souls. Throughout the play, the lovers have been united by their love but simultaneously kept apart by their family's feud. In death, the lovers are united forever, because they will be buried together. At the same time, they are divided forever, because they will never see each other alive again.

STUDY GUIDE

12

HOW TO WRITE LITERARY ANALYSIS

WHEN YOU READ FOR PLEASURE, your only goal is enjoyment. You might find yourself reading to get caught up in an exciting story, to learn about an interesting time or place, or just to pass the time. Maybe you're looking for inspiration, guidance, or a reflection of your own life. There are as many different, valid ways of reading a book as there are books in the world.

When you read a work of literature in an English class, however, you're being asked to read in a special way: you're being asked to perform *literary analysis*. To analyze something means to break it down into smaller parts and then examine how those parts work, both individually and together. Literary analysis involves examining all the parts of a novel, play, short story, or poem—elements such as character, setting, tone, and imagery—and thinking about how the author uses those elements to create certain effects.

A LITERARY ESSAY IS NOT A BOOK REVIEW

You're not being asked whether or not you liked a book or whether you'd recommend it to another reader. A literary essay also isn't like the kind of book report you wrote when you were younger, where your teacher wanted you to summarize the book's action. A high school– or college-level literary essay asks, "How does this piece of literature actually work?" "How does it do what it does?" and, "Why might the author have made the choices he or she did?"

The Seven Steps

No one is born knowing how to analyze literature; it's a skill you learn and a process you can master. As you gain more practice with this kind of thinking and writing, you'll be able to craft a method that works best for you. But until then, here are seven basic steps to writing a well-constructed literary essay:

1. Ask questions

2. Collect evidence

3. Construct a thesis

4. Develop and organize arguments

5. Write the introduction

6. Write the body paragraphs

7. Write the conclusion

1. ASK QUESTIONS

When you're assigned a literary essay in class, your teacher will often provide you with a list of writing prompts. Lucky you! Now all you have to do is choose one. Do yourself a favor and pick a topic that interests you. You'll have a much better (not to mention easier) time if you start off with something you enjoy thinking about. If you are asked to come up with a topic by yourself, though, you might start to feel a little panicked. Maybe you have too many ideas—or none at all. Don't worry. Take a deep breath and start by asking yourself these questions:

> **What struck you?** Did a particular image, line, or scene linger in your mind for a long time? If it fascinated you, chances are you can draw on it to write a fascinating essay.

What confused you? Maybe you were surprised to see a character act in a certain way, or maybe you didn't understand why the book ended the way it did. Confusing moments in a work of literature are like a loose thread in a sweater: if you pull on it, you can unravel the entire thing. Ask yourself why the author chose to write about that character or scene the way he or she did and you might tap into some important insights about the work as a whole.

Did you notice any patterns? Is there a phrase that the main character uses constantly or an image that repeats throughout the book? If you can figure out how that pattern weaves through the work and what the significance of that pattern is, you've almost got your entire essay mapped out.

Did you notice any contradictions or ironies? Great works of literature are complex; great literary essays recognize and explain those complexities. Maybe the title totally disagrees with the book's subject matter. Maybe the main character acts one way around his family and a completely different way around his friends and associates. If you can find a way to explain a work's contradictory elements, you've got the seeds of a great essay.

At this point, you don't need to know exactly what you're going to say about your topic; you just need a place to begin your exploration. You can help direct your reading and brainstorming by formulating your topic as a *question*, which you'll then try to answer in your essay. The best questions invite critical debates and discussions, not just a rehashing of the summary. Remember, you're looking for something you can *prove* or *argue* based on evidence you find in the text. Finally, remember to keep the scope of your question in mind. Is this a topic you can adequately address within the word or page limit you've been given? Conversely, is this a topic big enough to fill the required length?

GOOD QUESTIONS

"Are Romeo and Juliet's parents responsible for the deaths of their children?"

"Why doesn't Hamlet kill Claudius right away?"

"Is Lady Macbeth a villain or a victim?"

BAD QUESTIONS

"What happens to Nick Bottom in A Midsummer Night's Dream*?"*

"What do the other characters in Julius Caesar *think about Caesar?"*

"How does Iago remind me of my brother?"

2. COLLECT EVIDENCE

Once you know what question you want to answer, it's time to scour the book for things that will help you answer it. Don't worry if you don't know what you want to say yet—right now you're just collecting ideas and material and letting it all percolate. Keep track of passages, symbols, images, or scenes that deal with your topic. Eventually, you'll start making connections between these examples, and your thesis will emerge.

Here's a brief summary of the various parts that compose each and every work of literature. These are the elements that you will analyze in your essay, and that you will offer as evidence to support your arguments.

ELEMENTS OF STORY

These are the *whats* of the work—what happens, where it happens, and to whom it happens.

Plot: All of the events and actions of the work.

Character: The people who act and are acted upon in a literary work. The main character of a work is known as the *protagonist*.

Conflict: The central tension in the work. In most cases, the protagonist wants something, while opposing forces (antagonists) hinder the protagonist's progress.

Setting: When and where the work takes place. Elements of setting include location, time period, time of day, weather, social atmosphere, and economic conditions.

Narrator: The person telling the story. The narrator may straightforwardly report what happens, convey the subjective opinions and perceptions of one or more characters, or provide commentary and opinion in his or her own voice.

Themes: The main idea or message of the work—usually an abstract idea about people, society, or life in general. A work may have many themes, which may be in conflict with one another.

ELEMENTS OF STYLE

These are the *hows*—how the characters speak, how the story is constructed, and how language is used throughout the work.

Structure and organization: *How the parts of the work are assembled.* Some novels are narrated in a linear, chronological fashion, while others skip around in time. Some plays follow a traditional three- or five-act structure, while others are a series of loosely connected scenes. Some authors deliberately leave gaps in their works, leaving readers to puzzle out the missing information. A work's structure and organization can tell you a lot about the kind of message it wants to convey.

Point of view: *The perspective from which a story is told.* In *first-person point of view*, the narrator involves him- or herself in the story. ("I went to the store"; "We watched in horror as the bird slammed into the window.") A first-person narrator is usually the protagonist of the work, but not always. In *third-person point of view*, the narrator does not participate in the story. A third-person narrator may closely follow a specific character, recounting that individual character's thoughts or experiences, or it may be what we call an *omniscient* narrator. Omniscient narrators see and know all: they can witness any event in any time or place and are privy to the inner thoughts and feelings of all characters. Remember that the narrator and the author are not the same thing!

Diction: *Word choice.* Whether a character uses dry, clinical language or flowery prose with lots of exclamation points can tell you a lot about his or her attitude and personality.

Syntax: *Word order and sentence construction.* Syntax is a crucial part of establishing an author's narrative voice. Shakespeare, for example, is known for writing in iambic pentameter, intermingling prose and verse, and scrambling the usual word order of a sentence.

Tone: *The mood or feeling of the text.* Diction and syntax often contribute to the tone of a work. A novel written in short, clipped sentences that use small, simple words might feel brusque, cold, or matter-of-fact.

Imagery: *Language that appeals to the senses;* representing things that can be seen, smelled, heard, tasted, or touched.

Figurative language: *Language that is not meant to be interpreted literally.* The most common types of figurative language are *metaphors* and *similes*, which compare two unlike things in order to suggest a similarity between them —for example, *"All the world's a stage,"* or *"I'll warrant him, as gentle as a lamb."* (Metaphors say one thing is another thing; similes claim that one thing is *like* another thing.)

3. CONSTRUCT A THESIS

When you've examined all the evidence you've collected and know how you want to answer the question, it's time to write your thesis statement. A *thesis* is a claim about a work of literature that needs to be supported by evidence and arguments. The thesis statement is the heart of the literary essay, and the bulk of your essay will be spent trying to prove this claim. A good thesis will be:

Arguable. *"Julius Caesar* describes the political turmoil in Rome after the murder of Julius Caesar" isn't a thesis—it's a fact.

Provable through textual evidence. *"Hamlet* is a confusing but ultimately very well-written play" is a weak thesis because it offers the writer's personal opinion about the book. Yes, it's arguable, but it's not a claim that can be proved or supported with examples taken from the play itself.

Surprising. "Viola changes a great deal in *Twelfth Night"* is a weak thesis because it's obvious. A really strong thesis will argue for a reading of the text that is not immediately apparent.

Specific. "The relationships in *A Midsummer Night's Dream* tell us a lot about the fickle nature of romance" is almost a good thesis statement, but it's still too vague. What does the writer mean by "a lot"? How do the relationships tell us about the fickle nature of romance?

GOOD THESIS STATEMENTS

Question: In *Romeo and Juliet*, which is more powerful in shaping the lovers' story: fate or foolishness?

Thesis: "Though Shakespeare defines Romeo and Juliet as 'star-crossed lovers' and images of stars and planets appear throughout the play, a closer examination of that celestial imagery reveals that the stars are merely witnesses to the characters' foolish activities and not the causes themselves."

Question: Does Hamlet's misogyny prove his madness?

Thesis: "Hamlet's misogynistic behavior toward Gertrude and Ophelia can be seen as evidence that he really is going mad, because these scenes have little to do with his quest for justice, and yet they seem to provoke his strongest feelings. We see little evidence in the play that either Gertrude or Ophelia is guilty of any wrongdoing, yet he treats them both with paranoia and cruelty, suggesting that Hamlet has lost the ability to accurately interpret other people's motivations."

Question: How does blood function as a symbol in *Macbeth*?

Thesis: "Once Macbeth and Lady Macbeth embark on their murderous journey, blood comes to symbolize their guilt, and they begin to feel that their crimes have stained them in a way that cannot be washed clean. Blood becomes a permanent stain on the consciences of both characters, and it plagues them throughout life."

4. DEVELOP AND ORGANIZE ARGUMENTS

The reasons and examples that support your thesis will form the middle paragraphs of your essay. Since you can't really write your thesis statement until you know how you'll structure your argument, you'll probably end up working on steps 3 and 4 at the same time.

There's no single method of argumentation that will work in every context. One essay prompt might ask you to compare and contrast two characters, while another asks you to trace an image through a given work of literature. These questions require different kinds of answers and therefore different kinds of arguments. Below, we'll discuss three common kinds of essay prompts and some strategies for constructing a solid, well-argued case.

TYPES OF LITERARY ESSAYS
Compare and contrast

Compare and contrast the characters of King Lear and Gloucester in King Lear.

Chances are you've written this kind of essay before. In an academic literary context, you'll organize your arguments the same way you would in any other class. You can either go *subject by subject* or *point by point*. In the former, you'll discuss one character first and then the second. In the latter, you'll choose several traits (attitude toward life, social status, images and metaphors associated with the character) and devote a paragraph to each. You may want to use a mix of these two approaches—for example, you may want to spend a paragraph apiece broadly sketching King Lear's and Gloucester's personalities before transitioning into a paragraph or two describing a few key points of comparison. This can be a highly effective strategy if you want to make a counterintuitive argument—that, despite seeming to be totally different, the two objects being compared are actually similar in a very important way (or vice versa). Remember that your essay should reveal something fresh or unexpected about the text, so think beyond the obvious parallels and differences.

Trace

Choose an image—for example, birds, knives, or eyes—and trace that image throughout Macbeth.

Sounds pretty easy, right? All you need to do is read the play, underline every appearance of a knife in *Macbeth*, and then list them in your essay in the order they appear, right? Well, not exactly. Your teacher doesn't want a simple catalog of examples. He or she wants to see you make *connections* between those examples—that's the difference between summarizing and analyzing. In the *Macbeth* example above, think about the different contexts in which knives appear in the play and to what effect. In *Macbeth*, there are real knives and imagined knives; knives that kill and knives that simply threaten. Categorize and classify your examples to give them some order. Finally, always keep the overall effect in mind. After you choose and analyze your examples, you should come to some greater understanding about the work, as well as your chosen image, symbol, or phrase's role in developing the major themes and stylistic strategies of that work.

Debate

Does Iago in Othello *hate women?*

In this kind of essay, you're being asked to debate a moral, ethical, or aesthetic issue regarding the work. You might be asked to judge a character or group of characters (*Is Caesar responsible for his own demise?*) or the work itself (*Is* Romeo and Juliet *a feminist play?*). For this kind of essay, there are two important points to keep in mind. First, don't simply base your arguments on your personal feelings and reactions. Every literary essay expects you to read and analyze the work, so search for evidence in the text. What does Iago have to say about women in *Othello*? How does Iago treat women in *Othello*? As in any debate, you also need to make sure that you define all the necessary terms before you begin to argue your case.

What does it mean to hate a whole gender? What makes a play feminist? You should define your terms right up front, in the first paragraph after your introduction.

Second, remember that strong literary essays make contrary and surprising arguments. Try to think outside the box. In the *Othello* example above, it seems like the obvious answer would be yes, Iago hates women. But can you think of any arguments for the opposite side? Even if your final assertion is that the play depicts an angry, misogynistic man who distrusts women, acknowledging and responding to the counterargument will strengthen your overall case.

5. WRITE THE INTRODUCTION

Your introduction sets up the entire essay. It's where you present your topic and articulate the particular issues and questions you'll be addressing. It's also where you, as the writer, introduce yourself to your readers. A persuasive literary essay immediately establishes its writer as a knowledgeable, authoritative figure.

An introduction can vary in length depending on the overall length of the essay, but in a traditional five-paragraph essay it should be no longer than one paragraph. However long it is, your introduction needs to:

Provide any necessary context. Your introduction should situate the reader and let him or her know what to expect. What book are you discussing? Which characters? What topic will you be addressing?

Answer the "So what?" question. Why is this topic important, and why is your particular position on the topic noteworthy? Ideally, your introduction should pique the reader's interest by suggesting how your argument is surprising or otherwise counterintuitive. Literary essays make unexpected connections and reveal less-than-obvious truths.

Present your thesis. This usually happens at or very near the end of your introduction.

Indicate the shape of the essay to come. Your reader should finish reading your introduction with a good sense of the scope of your essay as well as the path you'll take toward proving your thesis. You don't need to spell out every step, but you do need to suggest the organizational pattern you'll be using.

Your introduction should not:

Be vague. Beware of the two killer words in literary analysis: *interesting* and *important*. Of course the work, question, or example is interesting and important—that's why you're writing about it!

Open with any grandiose assertions. Many student readers think that beginning their essays with a flamboyant statement such as "Since the dawn of time, writers have been fascinated with the topic of free will" makes them sound important and commanding. You know what? It actually sounds pretty amateurish.

Wildly praise the work. Another typical mistake student writers make is extolling the work or author. Your teacher doesn't need to be told that "Shakespeare is perhaps the greatest writer in the English language." You can mention a work's reputation in passing—by referring to *Romeo and Juliet* as "Shakespeare's enduring classic," for example—but don't make a point of bringing it up unless that reputation is key to your argument.

Go off-topic. Keep your introduction streamlined and to the point. Don't feel the need to throw in all kinds of bells and whistles in order to impress your reader—just get to the point as quickly as you can without skimping on any of the required steps.

6. WRITE THE BODY PARAGRAPHS

Once you've written your introduction, you'll take the arguments you developed in step 4 and turn them into your body paragraphs. The organization of this middle section of your essay will largely be determined by the argumentative strategy you use, but no matter how you arrange your thoughts, your body paragraphs need to do the following:

Begin with a strong topic sentence. Topic sentences are like signs on a highway: they tell the readers where they are and where they're going. A good topic sentence not only alerts readers to what issue will be discussed in the following paragraph but also gives them a sense of what argument will be made about that issue. "Jealousy plays an important role in *A Midsummer Night's Dream*" isn't a strong topic sentence because it doesn't tell us very much. "Jealousy plays out most obviously among the quartet of Athenian lovers, who find themselves in an increasingly tangled knot of misaligned desire" is a much stronger topic sentence—it not only tells us what the paragraph will discuss (jealousy) but how the paragraph will discuss the topic (by showing how jealousy creates a set of conditions that leads to the play's climactic action).

Fully and completely develop a single thought. Don't skip around in your paragraph or try to stuff in too much material. Body paragraphs are like bricks: each individual one needs to be strong and sturdy or else the entire structure will collapse. Make sure you have really proven your point before moving on to the next one.

Use transitions effectively. Good literary essay writers know that each paragraph must be clearly and strongly linked to the material around it. Think of each paragraph as a response to the one that precedes it. Use transition words and phrases such as *however, similarly, on the contrary, therefore,* and *furthermore* to indicate what kind of response you're making.

7. WRITE THE CONCLUSION

Just as you used the introduction to ground your readers in the topic before providing your thesis, you'll use the conclusion to quickly summarize the specifics learned thus far and then hint at the broader implications of your topic. A good conclusion will:

Do more than simply restate the thesis. If your thesis argued that *The Merchant of Venice* can be read as a study of religious differences, don't simply end your essay by saying, "And that is why *The Merchant of Venice* can be read as a study of religious differences." If you've constructed your arguments well, this kind of statement will just be redundant.

Synthesize the arguments, not summarize them. Similarly, don't repeat the details of your body paragraphs in your conclusion. The readers have already read your essay, and chances are it's not so long that they've forgotten all your points by now.

Revisit the "So what?" question. In your introduction, you made a case for why your topic and position were important. You should close your essay with the same sort of gesture. What do your readers know now that they didn't know before? How will that knowledge help them better appreciate or understand the work overall?

Move from the specific to the general. Your essay has most likely treated a very specific element of the work—a single character, a small set of images, or a particular passage. In your conclusion, try to show how this narrow discussion has wider implications for the work overall. If your essay on *The Tempest* focused on the character of Prospero, for example, you might want to include a bit in your conclusion about how he fits into the play's larger message about power, humanity, or the pursuit of knowledge.

Stay relevant. Your conclusion should suggest new directions of thought, but it shouldn't be treated as an opportunity to pad your essay with all the extra, interesting ideas you came up with during your brainstorming sessions but couldn't fit into the essay proper. Don't attempt to stuff in unrelated queries or too many abstract thoughts.

Avoid making overblown closing statements. A conclusion should open up your highly specific, focused discussion, but it should do so without drawing a sweeping lesson about life or human nature. Making such observations may be part of the point of reading, but it's almost always a mistake in essays, where these observations tend to sound overly dramatic or simply silly.

A+ ESSAY CHECKLIST

Congratulations! If you've followed all the steps we've outlined above, you should have a solid literary essay to show for all your efforts. What if you've got your sights set on an A+? To write the kind of superlative essay that will be rewarded with a perfect grade, keep the following rubric in mind. These are the qualities that teachers expect to see in a truly A+ essay. How does yours stack up?

- Demonstrates a thorough understanding of the book
- Presents an original, compelling argument
- Thoughtfully analyzes the text's formal elements
- Uses appropriate and insightful examples
- Structures ideas in a logical and progressive order
- Demonstrates a mastery of sentence construction, transitions, grammar, spelling, and word choice

SUGGESTED ESSAY TOPICS

1. How does the suicidal impulse that both Romeo and Juliet exhibit relate to the overall theme of young love? Does Shakespeare seem to consider a self-destructive tendency inextricably connected with love, or is it a separate issue? Why do you think so?

2. Discuss the relationships between parents and children in *Romeo and Juliet.* How do Romeo and Juliet interact with their parents? Are they rebellious, in the modern sense? How do their parents feel about them?

3. Apart from clashing with Tybalt, what role does Mercutio play in the story? Is he merely a colorful supporting character and brilliant source of comic relief, or does he serve a more serious purpose?

4. How does Shakespeare treat death in *Romeo and Juliet?* Frame your answer in terms of legal, moral, familial, and personal issues. Bearing these issues in mind, compare the deaths of Romeo and Juliet, Romeo and Mercutio, and Mercutio and Tybalt.

A+ STUDENT ESSAY

In *Romeo and Juliet*, which is more powerful, fate or the characters' own actions?

In the opening Prologue of *Romeo and Juliet*, the Chorus refers to the title characters as "star-crossed lovers," an allusion to the belief that stars and planets have the power to control events on Earth. This line leads many readers to believe that Romeo and Juliet are inescapably destined to fall in love and equally destined to have that love destroyed. However, though Shakespeare's play raises the possibility that some impersonal, supernatural force shapes Romeo and Juliet's lives, by the end of the play it becomes clear that the characters bear more of the responsibility than Fortune does.

Though the Prologue offers the first and perhaps most famous example of celestial imagery in *Romeo and Juliet*, references to the stars, sun, moon, and heavens run throughout the play, and taken as a whole that imagery seems to express a different view of human responsibility. In Act I, Romeo says that he fears "some consequence yet hanging in the stars" (I.iv.) when he and his gang approach the Capulet's ball. In his next mention of stars, however, Romeo doesn't refer to their astrological power. Rather, he uses the image of stars to describe Juliet's otherworldly beauty. Most of the subsequent celestial images in the play follow in this vein, from Romeo's love-struck comparison of Juliet to the sun to Juliet's own wish to "cut [Romeo] out in[to] little stars" (III.ii.) when he dies. Throughout the play, these astral images are more often associated with the two lovers than with divine fate, emphasizing that, as the play's action escalates, we cannot simply place the blame for the tragedy on some impersonal external force.

It's true that Romeo and Juliet have some spectac-
ularly bad luck. Tybalt picks a fatal fight with Romeo
on the latter's wedding day, causing Capulet to move
up the wedding with Paris. The crucial letter from Friar
Lawrence goes missing due to an ill-timed outbreak of
the plague. Romeo kills himself mere moments before
Juliet wakes up. It's also true that the lovers aren't solely
responsible for their difficult situation. Their friends,
their families, and their society each played a role in
creating the tragic circumstances. However, even if we
allow that fate or some other divine force caused Romeo
and Juliet to fall in love at first sight, thereby setting the
action into motion, Shakespeare makes it clear that it
was the characters' own decisions that pushed the situation to its tragic conclusion. Either Romeo or Juliet, it
is suggested, could have halted the headlong rush into
destruction at any of several points.

Romeo's propensity for rash action gets him—and
his beloved— in a lot of trouble. His impulsiveness has
made him a romantic icon in our culture, but in the play
it proves his undoing. From the very beginning, Shakespeare cautions us not to view Romeo's sudden fits of
passion too idealistically—after all, Shakespeare makes
a point to show that Romeo's love for Juliet merely dis-
placed another, earlier infatuation. Through his hasty
actions, Romeo arguably drives the play toward tragedy
more aggressively than any other character. He climbs
over Juliet's wall the night they meet and presses her
to bind herself to him. He kills Tybalt in a blind rage.
Then, thinking Juliet dead, he poisons himself. Romeo
never thinks his actions through, and his lack of foresight
makes him responsible for their dire consequences.

Though Juliet proves a strong-willed partner for
Romeo, she bears less of the blame for their joint fate
because she, at least, is wary of the speed at which they

progress. In the balcony scene, she compares their love to lightning, which flares up suddenly but can just as quickly fade into darkness. Unlike Romeo, each of Juliet's fateful choices is a logical response to a situation. She agrees to marry him because she needs evidence that he is truly committed to her. She takes the potion not out of despair, but because she believes Friar Lawrence's plan will set things to rights. Though each of her choices ends up getting her and her lover deeper into trouble, those choices are at least the result of sober, careful reflection. Only when she sees her beloved dead does she succumb to his style of rashness, killing herself out of grief.

Romeo and Juliet concludes with a strong condemnation of the characters' actions. In the closing family portrait, the Capulets and the Montagues gather around the tomb to witness the consequences of their absurd conflict. Even if you don't believe that Romeo and Juliet could have saved themselves, you must admit that their families' blind hatred caused the situation, not the gods. As the Prince notes, even "the sun, for sorrow, will not show his head" (V.iii.) on that tragic day—even the heavens are pained at the human foolishness they see below.

GLOSSARY OF LITERARY TERMS

Antagonist
The entity that acts to frustrate the goals of the protagonist. The antagonist is usually another character but may also be a non-human force.

Antihero / Antiheroine
A protagonist who is not admirable or who challenges notions of what should be considered admirable.

Character
A person, animal, or any other thing with a personality that appears in a narrative.

Climax
The moment of greatest intensity in a text or the major turning point in the plot.

Conflict
The central struggle that moves the plot forward. The conflict can be the protagonist's struggle against fate, nature, society, or another person.

First-person point of view
A literary style in which the narrator tells the story from his or her own point of view and refers to himself or herself as "I." The narrator may be an active participant in the story or just an observer.

Hero / heroine
The principal character in a literary work or narrative.

Imagery
Language that brings to mind sense-impressions, representing things that can be seen, smelled, heard, tasted, or touched.

Motif
A recurring idea, structure, contrast, or device that develops or informs the major themes of a work of literature.

Narrative
A story.

Narrator
The person (sometimes a character) who tells a story; the voice assumed by the writer. The narrator and the author of the work of literature are not the same person.

Plot
The arrangement of the events in a story, including the sequence in which they are told, the relative emphasis they are given, and the causal connections between events.

Point of View
The perspective that a narrative takes toward the events it describes.

Protagonist
The main character around whom the story revolves.

Setting
The location of a narrative in time and space. Setting creates mood or atmosphere.

Subplot
A secondary plot that is of less importance to the overall story but that may serve as a point of contrast or comparison to the main plot.

Symbol
An object, character, figure, or color that is used to represent an abstract idea or concept. Unlike an emblem, a symbol may have different meanings in different contexts.

Syntax
The way the words in a piece of writing are put together to form lines, phrases, or clauses; the basic structure of a piece of writing.

Theme
A fundamental and universal idea explored in a literary work.

STUDY GUIDE

Tone

The author's attitude toward the subject or characters of a story or poem or toward the reader.

Voice

An author's individual way of using language to reflect his or her own personality and attitudes. An author communicates voice through tone, diction, and syntax.

A NOTE ON PLAGIARISM

Plagiarism—presenting someone else's work as your own—rears its ugly head in many forms. Many students know that copying text without citing it is unacceptable. But some don't realize that even if you're not quoting directly, but instead are paraphrasing or summarizing, it is plagiarism unless you cite the source.

HERE ARE THE MOST COMMON FORMS OF PLAGIARISM:

- Using an author's phrases, sentences, or paragraphs without citing the source

- Paraphrasing an author's ideas without citing the source

- Passing off another student's work as your own

HOW DO YOU STEER CLEAR OF PLAGIARISM?

- You should always acknowledge all words and ideas that aren't your own by using quotation marks around verbatim text or citations like footnotes and end-notes to note another writer's ideas.

- For more information on how to give credit when credit is due, ask your teacher for guidance or visit www.sparknotes.com.